READING WOMEN'S MAGAZINES

BARNSLEY COLLEGE
HONEYWELL
LEARNING CENTRE

D0308268

38594

For Pieter and Sacha

Reading Women's Magazines

An Analysis of Everyday Media Use

Joke Hermes

Polity Press

Copyright © Joke Hermes 1995

The right of Joke Hermes to be identified as author of this work has been asserted in accordance with the Copyright, Designs and Patents Act 1988.

First published in 1995 by Polity Press
in association with Blackwell Publishers Ltd.

Reprinted 1997

Editorial office:
Polity Press
65 Bridge Street
Cambridge CB2 1UR, UK

Marketing and production:
Blackwell Publishers Ltd
108 Cowley Road
Oxford OX4 1JF, UK

Published in the USA by
Blackwell Publishers Inc.
238 Main Street
Cambridge, MA 02142, USA

All rights reserved. Except for the quotation of short passages for the purposes of criticism and review, no part of this publication may be reproduced, stored in a retrieval system, or transmitted, in any form or by any means, electronic, mechanical, photocopying, recording or otherwise, without the prior permission of the publisher.

Except in the United States of America, this book is sold subject to the condition that it shall not, by way of trade or otherwise, be lent, re-sold, hired out, or otherwise circulated without the publisher's prior consent in any form of binding or cover other than that in which it is published and without a similar condition including this condition being imposed on the subsequent purchaser.

ISBN 0–7456–1270–9
ISBN 0–7456–1271–7 (pbk)

A CIP catalogue record for this book is available from the British Library and the Library of Congress.

Typeset in 10 on 12pt Palatino
by Photoprint, Torquay, S. Devon
Printed in Great Britain by Hartnolls Ltd, Bodmin, Cornwall

This book is printed on acid-free paper.

Contents

Acknowledgements

I am grateful to all of those who have helped me complete this project. I should like to thank my informants (and especially my mother), who made me welcome in their homes and generously gave me their time and attention and answered my questions. Sylvia Nickel, Mina Padmini-Lachman, Linde Berntrop, Charlotte Koch, Yvonne van Arragon, Saskia van der Laken, Toine Al, Madeleine Mes and Rebecca Roos completed the thankless job of transcribing the interviews with good cheer. I am especially grateful to Carin Mulié-Velgersdijk for co-ordinating their work.

My colleagues at the Department of Communication at the University of Amsterdam I wish to thank for their critical comments and their support, particularly my supervisor, Denis McQuail, Piet Bakker, Harry Bouwman and Peter Neijens. Ute Bechdolf, Kirsten Drotner, Richard Johnson and Kim Schrøder suggested and sent me copies of articles, for which I thank them. Sandra Kemp's insightful and carefully formulated comments improved chapter 1. Many helped in turning what was originally a Ph.D. thesis into this book. I wish to thank Janice Winship, Jon Bird and my editors at Polity Press for their suggestions and their support.

I am especially indebted to Ien Ang, Ann Gray, Véronique Schutgens, Mariette van Staveren and Evelien Tonkens, who read draft versions and helped me think through the project, occasionally fed me and, most of all, helped me restore my confidence in making sense of how women's magazines are made sense of. Véronique Schutgens was also a co-researcher on the case study of how feminist magazines are read. I should like to thank her and Joppe Boodt, who helped interview male readers, for their enthusiasm and their help and for sharing their views with me.

I do not know how to thank Pieter Hilhorst and Liesbet van Zoonen, who have always been there for me, who cheered me up when I was depressed, who gave me the benefit of their sharp insight in the project, who read draft upon draft of this text, who shared the joy of seeing the project develop. I would not have been able to do it without them.

Author's Note

All translations of quotations and interviews originally in Dutch are my own.

In the interview transcripts the following conventions are used. An ellipsis of three points denotes a pause and also the editing out of a maximum of two or three words or sounds ('emph', 'ahh' and so on) that have no substantial meaning but are used to fill in time. The ellipsis is set in parentheses when more than a few words of the transcript have been left out. All editorial explanations and comments are set in square brackets.

Introduction

I have always felt strongly that the feminist struggle in general should be aimed at claiming respect. It is probably for that reason that I have never felt very comfortable with the majority of (feminist) work that has been done on women's magazines.[1] Almost all of these studies show *concern* rather than *respect* for those who read women's magazines. Concern belongs to what Joli Jensen (1990) has called the 'modernity discourse' in media criticism. Jensen shows how the media in this type of discourse are seen as a Janus-faced monster: agent of change and progress, but also the devil in disguise, agent of alienation, anomy and despair in the powerfully seductive guise of provider of entertainment and excitement. Older feminist media criticism in particular can be seen as partaking in modernity discourse, even though the media in that case are primarily an agent of oppression dressed up as popular pleasures. The worry and concern in older feminist media criticism lead to a highly unequal relationship between the feminist author and 'ordinary women'. The feminist media critic is prophet and exorcist, even while being, as many claim, an 'ordinary woman' too. Feminists using modernity discourse speak on behalf of others who are, implicitly, thought to be unable to see for themselves how bad such media texts as women's magazines are. They need to be enlightened; they need good feminist texts in order to be saved from their false consciousnesses and to live a life free of false depictions as mediated by women's magazines, of where a woman might find happiness.

I would advocate a more postmodern view, in which respect rather than concern – or, for that matter, celebration, a term often seen as the hallmark of a postmodern perspective – would have a central place.

In my view, it needs to be accepted that readers of all kinds (including we critics) enjoy texts in some contexts that we are critical of in other contexts. I would even go so far as to claim that it is more productive to respect the choices and uncritical acceptance of some readers of genres such as women's magazines than to foreground a distancing criticism or concern towards them all. If, as feminists, we aim to bring about changes in the societies in which we live, we had better understand the investments we and others have in them first. In this book, therefore, I have tried to understand how women's magazines are read while accepting the preferences of those I interviewed. Before discussing the research, let me provide a very brief overview of the debate on women's magazines in feminist media criticism.

In her classic text *The Feminine Mystique* Betty Friedan ascribed mythic power to women's magazines to keep women within their homes ([1963] 1974: 59). Gaye Tuchman, in another classic text, writes: 'The ideal woman, according to (women's) magazines, is passive and dependent. Her fate and happiness rest with a man, not with participation in the labor force' (1978: 18). According to her, young women would be unduly influenced by this and would be ill-prepared for their place in society and in the work force. Analysis of the text, and occasionally the production process (women's magazine journalism and the structure of ownership in the women's magazine market), led to these pessimistic and sometimes angry evaluations. Given that readers were supposed to be 'socialized' by magazines and made to see the world according to the magazines' priorities, there was no theoretical or other need to interview readers (see Dardigna, 1978; Ferguson, 1983; Wassenaar, 1976).

The more recent work on women's magazines, influenced by and benefiting from the new consensus on popular culture of the 1980s and its installation as an academic discipline (in its turn fuelled by the original feminist attention for the popular genres that women used), would seem more promising. Briefly summarized, post-structuralism, psychoanalysis and postmodernism led to the acknowledgement that pleasure was an important aspect of the study of popular culture in its own right (see, for example, Coward, 1984; Kaplan, 1986). Researchers began first to write about their own pleasures and pleasure in general (Vance, 1984), and then to take the small step to an interest in how others found pleasure in popular texts. Studies of popular culture included the perspective of readers more and more. Often the perspective of readers was studied in a fairly limited way. New kinds of text analysis laid bare the polysemic character of popular media texts, rather than reporting on what readers had to say. The consensus about how important the perspective and experiences of readers are, however, had changed irrevocably.

In women's magazines research too this trend was followed. Some of this research, though interesting, remained within the domain of text analysis (Blix, 1992, Röser, 1992; Steiner, 1991), but two other studies are, partially, based on the experiences of readers. *Women's Worlds: Ideology, Femininity and the Woman's Magazine* (1991) by Ros Ballaster, Margaret Beetham, Elizabeth Frazer and Sandra Hebron includes a chapter which reports on group interviews with female readers. Janice Winship's *Inside Women's Magazines* (1987) is a study of one reader, the author herself. Regretfully, the text of Ballaster et al. is preoccupied with how feminism can most effectively challenge gender difference as it is reified and fixed by women's magazines throughout their centuries long existence. It echoes the older feminist position of concern, which is combined uneasily with a more postmodern, celebratory tone that stresses the pleasure, the creativity and the criticism of readers: 'When talking about magazines, women endlessly, and delightedly, parody and mimic them, displaying their own literacy and mastery of its generic conventions' (Ballaster et al., 1991: 35). On the other hand the harmful quality of women's magazines is emphasized, and this, however implicitly, undermines the respect shown to readers for their point of view: 'Despite the clear-sighted criticism offered by a number of readers, it is not our view that the construction of femininity we find in the magazines is harmless and innocuous' (Ballaster et al., 1991: 131). How do women's magazines 'harm' readers? Do they do so more than other media or other constructions of femininity? Do harmless and innocuous constructions of femininity exist at all? These are questions the reader is left with. Consequently the only relatively comfortable reader position as regards this book is to share the authors' mixture of pleasure and guilt: 'When we began work for this book we realised that our enthusiasm stemmed from our mutual pleasure in reading women's magazines themselves, tempered by the knowledge that this pleasure is by no means pure, unambiguous or unproblematic . . . Reading women's magazines can have exactly the same effect as eating two or more bars of chocolate – the original craving was real but in the end seems to have been for the wrong thing' (Ballaster et al., 1991: 1).

I find Janice Winship's *Inside Women's Magazines* a much more inspiring text, even if the only reader whose voice is present is

Winship's. The two most important things I learned from her book are that other readers than me (such as Winship herself) may read strange combinations of magazines, and that as a feminist and a researcher or a critic one should guard against being too much of a moralist. *Inside Women's Magazines* is a study of the text of three women's magazines, Winship's personal favourites, situated historically. *Woman's Own*, *Cosmopolitan* and *Spare Rib* are all analysed for the pleasures they offer and the criticism one might have as a reader at the same time. When appropriate, I have referred to Winship's insights in the chapters to come (especially 2 and 3), so I will not give elaborate examples here. Suffice it to say that this is a book that can make one understand the pleasures of women's magazines more than any of the other texts available. Of course, there is an edge to this compliment. I do not think that Winship did justice (or tried to, for that matter) to the everyday nature of reading women's magazines for the majority of readers (a subject dealt with in this book).

Winship's book also taught me that it is very unbecoming to moralize as an author. Let me give two examples. At one point Winship discusses the at times racist position adopted by *Woman's Own* and attacks its editor, Iris Burton: 'Leaping to protect white women as if black women are a threat to them conveniently ignores what has been a much longer-term unnerving – the daily and relentless imposition of white cultural values on black people in Britain. To be fair to Iris Burton (and who am I anyway, as another white woman also deeply implicated in racist practices, to criticise another?), since she made this comment in August 1982 *Woman's Own* has made visible gestures, if not towards confronting racism, at least towards acknowledging that cultures other than white exist in Britain' (p. 95). Likewise, Winship defends *Cosmo*'s 'inclinations towards feminism' while upholding her own criticism of the magazine: 'My own view is that it is cutting off our nose to spite our face to outlaw wholesale what *Cosmo* stands for, to say nothing of manifesting the worst aspects of a political "holier than thou" moralism' (p. 115). It is probably easier to show both one's appreciation of a magazine and one's criticism of it than to do this when speaking of human beings. I felt it to be absolutely improper to be critical of the people I spoke to, or to imply that I could look into their heads and devine their innermost thoughts, wishes and convictions. I have been critical, though, for example, of the idiotic arguments and excuses some men found in order to avoid an interview. Winship's lesson for me is that it is possible to be both appreciative and critical as long as it is done in a self-reflexive vein. Given the importance self-reflexivity has for my academic practice (and for me the academic is as personal as the political), I would characterize my position as that of a postmodern feminist (see Flax, 1990; Fraser and Nicholson, 1988). Besides self-reflexivity, a postmodern feminist position for me implies, as mentioned above, respect rather than concern: appreciation that readers are producers of meaning rather than the cultural dupes of the media institutions. Appreciation too of the local and specific meanings we give to media texts and the different identities any one person may bring to bear on living our multi-faceted lives in societies saturated with media images and texts of which women's magazines are a part. This makes researching any one particular genre a challenge.

Alas, with the exception of Winship's book, existing studies of women's magazines did not convince me; they were either too concerned or too optimistic. I felt that Winship's strong view that any cultural criticism should be self-reflexive needed to be combined with research that let readers speak for themselves. At the time I started this research project this last requirement had been taken up by media and cultural studies. My work is doubtless much more a product of the direction research within this field took than of the tradition of women's magazine research. As I see it, within the field of media and cultural studies there are two approaches to popular culture (or the media) and its audiences. First of all, I was inspired by the work of Ien Ang and Janice Radway, which is certainly connected with the fact that especially reading romances, but also watching soap operas, have always been and still are favourite pastimes. Transposing what I had learned from their analyses of *Dallas* and its audience, and romances and their readers, was not totally impossible, but the process made clear what I have come to see as the inadequacy of how everyday media use had been theorized; these studies do not address everyday sense-making because they focus too much on specific texts. David Morley's and Ann Gray's work represents the other approach towards media audiences. Their studies of, respectively, television viewing and use of the video recorder in the home have also been very important to me. Although their work does not explicitly address how meaning is produced from television texts, it puts in perspective the overriding contextual nature of any kind of media use, one of the most notable contexts being that of gender power relations in the home.

What I have aimed to do in this book is to create a middle position between the combined text and audience analyses that Ang's and Radway's mid-1980s studies represent, which privilege study of a genre and the text over the everyday aspects of media use, and the work that concentrates on a media technology or form and privileges the situatedness and everydayness of media use, such as the studies of Gray and Morley, which do not address at length how the texts that are used are made meaningful. As far as I know, this is a unique position to take (in media studies, that is). I have tried to reconstruct the diffuse genre or set of genres that is called women's magazines and how they become meaningful exclusively through the perception of their readers. Text analysis would not suit such an approach, for it would always imply that readers 'miss' things in texts, such as their deeper meanings. In its place has come theorization of meaning production in everyday contexts. This has enabled me, I hope, to redress a little the power balance between researcher and researched. Obviously it is *my* interpretation of how readers interpret women's magazines. In the text numerous quotations are given, though, to allow the reader of this text to follow how I have interpreted what my informants said and, possibly, to reconstruct alternative meanings.

Women's magazines are indubitably one of the best examples of what Clifford Geertz (1983) has called a 'blurred genre'. One of my interpretative steps therefore consisted of reconstructing subgenres within this umbrella category. As in ethnographic research, I followed members' (my informants') definitions. A broad division shows three main subgenres: traditionally oriented magazines, feminist magazines and gossip magazines.

Gossip magazines (such as the British *Hello!* or *Chat*, or the Dutch *Privé* and *Story*) are usually rather tasteless. Most of them come in a low-price range, with the exception of those royalty magazines that are printed on high-quality paper, which are much more expensive.

Feminist magazines (*Spare Rib*, *Everywoman*, the German *Emma*, the Dutch *Opzij*) with a reasonably large circulation tend to be monthlies. They are not cheap, with the exception of women's papers (which use cheap printing and have volunteer editorial boards). Most of those, though, did not survive the 1980s; while they lasted, they were low-priced. Dutch examples are *Serpentine* and *Katijf*.

Traditionally oriented women's magazines are either domestic weeklies (also called 'service weeklies'), which have a strong emphasis on practical advice and come in a fairly restricted, moderate price range (the British *Woman*, *Woman's Own*, *Best*, *Bella*, *Me*, the Dutch *Margriet*, *Libelle*, *Viva*, *Flair*), or high-priced monthlies, often called 'glossies' because of the expensive paper they are printed on. Many glossies are franchised and appear in different languages, for example *Cosmopolitan*, *Elle* and *Marie Claire*.

The differences within these subgenres (domestic weeklies, glossies, gossip magazines, feminist magazines) are quite large. In terms of how readers accord meaning to them, however, this division works well. All of these subgenres can be traced to the exceptionally long history of women's magazines (see Ballaster et al., 1991; Shevelow, 1989; White, 1970), a subject that will not be discussed in this book, though the chapter about the Dutch feminist magazine *Opzij* and the chapter about reading gossip magazines open with a short description of their recent histories (chapters 4 and 5).

How readers accord meaning to the magazines they read (or browse in) has been not only the basis of dividing magazines into three main subgenres, but also the logic behind the organization of this text. The book starts with a general, theoretical chapter about meaning production and everyday life as they concern media and popular culture analysis. It concentrates on the mundaness of media use and on how reading women's magazines and watching television are often secondary activities that provide ways of filling 'empty' time, without having much meaning at all. The meanings magazines in the end appear to have for readers must be seen against this background. Chapters 2, 4 and 5 deal with how traditionally oriented, feminist and gossip magazines are read and made meaningful. Chapter 3 is a portrait of two readers, one of whom is my mother. Appendix 4 describes at length how the study was designed and what kind of methodological choices are involved in this kind of qualitative research – a type of exposé that is regrettably rare in qualitative media studies.

Since 'making meaningful' is such a central concept in this book, let me briefly explain it. By 'making meaningful' I mean the process of making sense of a text by recognizing and comprehending it and assigning it associative signification (levels of meaning production that are often referred to as denotation and connotation), as well as giving it a place in one's knowledge and views of the world. This last level of meaning production consists not only of cognitive thought processes, but also of a reader's imaginative response and the practical and/or emotional and fantasy uses to which she or he anticipates putting the text.[2] Genres, another central term, can be taken to stand for a collection of conventions, an agreed code between communicator and audience that shapes both the production process and the expectations of readers.[3]

My analysis has been pitched at the level of 'repertoires', or the ways there are of talking about women's magazines, reconstructed from interview fragments. Even though everyday talk tends to leave many things implicit, given a certain amount of interviews (and my eighty interviews were more than enough), the shape of these icebergs of shared cultural knowledge's and interpretations can be discovered. Repertoires are the cultural resources that speakers fall back on and refer to. Which repertoires are used depends on the cultural capital of an individual reader. What is quite clear, though, is that a relatively small number of repertoires would appear to suffice when we want to talk about women's magazines, even if for each woman's magazine subgenre the set of repertoires used is different. For example, when talking about traditional women's magazine genres, readers often referred to the practical value that women's magazines have, the useful tips and so on. Chapter 2 shows how the recurrent theme of practical value led to the reconstruction of the repertoire of practical learning and how the investment of readers in and through this repertoire has to do with constructing a temporary ideal self. Another example is the repertoire of emotional learning and connected knowing used for both traditional and feminist women's magazines. This, however, would be combined with such repertoires as the vanguard repertoire and the repertoire of moral duty (chapter 4) and linked to a totally different fantasy of a perfect *alter ego*. The combination of repertoires and the fantasies they revolve around offer an explanation of how women's magazines become meaningful for readers and what makes reading them worthwhile.

Although I feel I am a feminist in heart and soul, I have not taken over, I hope, the concern (or the celebration) and its implicit connotations that seem so typical of feminist studies of this particular blurred genre. I considered it necessary to subdue my own views and opinions regarding women's magazines in order that the voices of readers be heard loud and clear, albeit through my agency as an interpreter and an organizer of what all eighty of them had to say. I have often chosen to write in a personal tone and to include, where appropriate (see especially appendix 4), considerations, choices and doubts. Chapter 4 is probably the most outspoken of the chapters that are built on what readers had to say. It deals with the Dutch feminist monthly *Opzij*, but also with my – perhaps slightly naïve – shock at realizing how emotive the label 'feminism' is, even for readers of a magazine that on its cover calls itself 'feminist monthly'. An earlier version of this chapter appeared as an article. Reactions were diverse: many recognized themselves in it, or in the specific repertoires it describes; others, however, criticized it for attacking the magazine and its implicit moralism. No amount of reflexivity can help in such a situation. I suppose that, being brought up in modernist social research and feminist traditions, it has become part of me to want to take stands. I suspect that it is even the case that any kind of feminism has to have a certain measure of moralism. I hope the measure, in this book, is not too large and sufficiently tempered by the willingness of the text to take a look at itself.

Given all this talk of reflexivity and openness, I had better also say something about my feelings towards women's magazines. They are not my favourite popular genre (those are romances and women detectives), but I like some parts of them, especially the recipes and, in small doses, gossip items and fashion spreads. As a teenager I read every letter in the Dutch young women's magazine *Viva*, alongside the novels of Sartre and de Beauvoir (in that order, I am afraid), but that seems a long time ago. When I think about women's magazines, I am mostly struck by their polysemic content, which ranges from being very traditionally 'feminine' to being outspoken, emancipated and even feminist. Part of me can understand why they continue to inspire concern and criticism in feminist observers. Women's magazines' emphasis on 'woman' and 'femininity', however liberated parts of them have become, remains unsettling, given that they are still overwhelmingly heterosexual in orientation and predominantly white in colour. Would I then be happier with women's magazines that were more or less the same but included lesbians, males of different persuasions, models, interviewees and columnists in all sorts of colours? That is difficult to say. When I remarked that she had not expressed a desire to see more black models, one of my informants who enjoyed glossy magazines said, 'That's a kind of double-edged sword. In a sense, I do. But then, it's a bit like complaining about the lack of black people in the conservative party. On the one hand there's a bunch of racists who need to have that racism taken out of them. On the other hand I don't want to see more black Tories because of the politics' (Terry Atkinson).

1

Everyday Media Use

The small but steady stream of publications about women's magazines has, until recently, hardly ever taken the perspective or the
experiences of the reader into account (Dardigna, 1978; Ferguson,
1983; Illouz, 1991; Wassenaar, 1976; White, 1970; Winship, 1991). It
seems highly probable, therefore, that we know more about the
concerns and the views of researchers than we do about actual
practices of women's magazine use and the experiences of other
readers, who, after all, make up the majority of women's magazine
users. In this book everyday use of women's magazines, as reported
on by readers, takes centre stage. Since I am interested in their
accounts of how women's magazines have meaning for them, there is
no analysis of the women's magazine text. Text analysis assumes that
texts offer a limited range of meanings that cannot but be taken up by
readers. My perspective is that texts acquire meaning only in the
interaction between readers and texts and that analysis of the text on
its own is never enough to reconstruct these meanings.

I could, of course, have combined text and reception analysis, as
other studies of women's magazines have done (Ballaster et al., 1991;
Winship, 1987). Again, there is a strong argument against proceeding
thus. Text analysis is, in fact, the academic's reading of women's
magazines. Although the criticism ensuing from text analysis can
certainly be very valuable, the academic voice is the authorial voice
and its account is bound to be far more powerful than any other
account of everyday reading. To focus on both text and readers can
easily drown out the accounts of readers, and thereby eliminate the
added value of seeing women's magazines through their eyes.

Moreover, the readers' perspectives, though not easily made manageable for academic use, are fascinating in their own right.

To find out how women's magazines become meaningful in everyday life and what 'meaning' can be taken to be in everyday contexts, I chose to employ an ethnographic perspective and to hold lengthy interviews with readers. An integral element in such a project is the fact that the researcher is a participant rather than an outsider or an observer (see Hammersley and Atkinson, 1983: 17–19). Throughout this book I aim to show my personal involvement in the research. Given the inherently unequal positions of interviewer and interviewed, I cannot claim this text is a series of dialogues or a polylogue – a goal interpretive ethnography should aim for, according to some of its practitioners (see Marcus and Fischer, 1986). It is the product, though, of some eighty conversational interviews that took the form of dialogues. To elicit information from my informants and to redress the balance of knowledge (who gets to know more about whom), in the interviews there were many personal 'digressions' in which I told my informants about myself or gave my opinion, though seldom on the subject of women's magazines, because I wanted to avoid any suggestion that my views were the 'correct' way of looking at women's magazines. That would have been absolutely at odds with my request for information and my explanation that I would use readers' categories and views rather than my own to structure the research. I decided not to make these digressions part of the book, though they would make fascinating research material for a project on field relations and conducting interviews (such as Kauffman, 1992). In keeping with the spirit of ethnography, however, I have employed a personal style of writing.

The goal of the eighty lengthy interviews with women and men was to reconstruct how women's magazines become meaningful. The interviews were a success in terms of social interaction. Although interviewing is tiring work, I enjoyed it. I was made most welcome by very diverse people, a majority of whom appreciated women's magazines and read them regularly. Informants were talkative enough – but they did not have much to say about women's magazines. Interpreting the interviews presented serious problems. Reception studies of other popular genres had led me to expect that faithful women's magazine readers (and there were some among my informants) would have no trouble in recounting narratives or arguments from articles they had enjoyed or found interesting. Although some readers ponder what they have read and remember specific articles to some extent, most readers did not. Many could not give specific examples, and usually references were vague. Quite often informants would hunt for a copy of a magazine if they wanted to say something about it. Generally speaking, although many readers have generic knowledge of women's magazines, the practice of reading women's magazines apparently does not call for reflection or involvement of a readily communicable kind.

The interviews were long: on average one and a half hours of interview was taped. Before and after the interview I explained the research and invited comments. The transcribed tapes fill a few thousand pages. I could simply have extracted all that was said about women's magazines, but that would have meant using only 2 or 3 per cent of the material (which is still, given the amount of material gathered, a reasonable amount of text). That would, in itself not be a bad method, but it would need contextualization to avoid suggesting that women's magazines are meaningful for readers to a much higher exent than they actually are, and thereby giving a blatantly false picture of women's magazine reading. To have taken the tiny bits of interview text that directly addressed women's magazines and women's magazine use would not have done justice to the impression that slowly built up during the research period: women's magazines are qualitatively different from other genres (which were talked about with much more enthusiasm by the same informants); and it could also well be the case that popular media research has not done justice to the everyday character of the majority of media use.

In this chapter I reveal the theoretical framework I developed to make sense of how readers make sense of the magazines they read, paying attention to the contextual and everyday nature of this particular kind of meaning production. I shall briefly discuss the recent research on popular culture that shaped my expectations and ideas, to clarify why I was so disappointed in the interview material, before turning to theories of everyday life and everyday meaning production. The chapter closes with a sketch of the theoretical toolbox I will, by then, have prepared, in which the notion of 'interpretive repertoire' has a central place.

Popular culture research and the fallacy of meaningfulness

My decision to interview readers was motivated by what has come to be known as 'the move towards the reader' in popular media research. Dissatisfied with a modernist privileging of the text as the place where meaning is produced and with 'grand narratives' (Lyotard, 1979) and politically inspired by the wish to 'strike back at the empire' to show that Thatcherism, Reaganism and the New Right had not brainwashed the consumers of popular culture, popular culture research turned from texts to specific groups of readers who were pictured as subversive and resistant to dominant meanings. Although not labelled as such from the start, this new orientation has come to be called 'postmodern', even though in most popular culture research one does not find postmodernism of the most radical kind (see, for example, Ross, 1988). While a radical postmodern view would dictate that all meaning is locally produced, independent of the text or grand theory, popular culture research usually recognizes some relation to the media text. It steers a middle course between text-based and text-independent interpretations of how media use is meaningful. In fact, much popular culture research is still genre-based, and as a result meaning production is seen as being held together or incited by texts that share a certain set of literary rules of form and content, rather than by how they are used.

Janice Radway's pioneering study on romance reading (1984) may serve as an example of the 'New Audience Research' that gave a central place to the reader. Through lengthy interviews with readers she reconstructed the 'ideal' and the 'failed' romance to establish what it is women like in romance novels and what it is that makes them read them over and over again. She also asked her informants when and how they read romances. She found that for the women she interviewed reading was a qualitatively different activity from for instance, housework, because it was the only activity they did for, and time they spent on, themselves. Romance reading, writes Radway, is a 'declaration of independence', a minor rebellion against the position accorded these readers by dominant patriarchal discourse: the position of the ever available and nurturing housewife and mother. Their rebellion is ultimately turned into submission to patriarchal discourse, however, because of their very reading. Reading romances also means investing energy in the imaginary (and wishful) reconstruction of masculinity, for readers interpret romances as stories about male transformation: from hard and insensitive machos to loving and caring human beings. *Reading the Romance* is a well-founded and clever book in which textual and interview examples abound. Even though the 'pleasurableness' of romance reading (Ang, 1988) is not addressed but is traded against a view that believes feminist political struggle is more important than patriarchy (fans of the genre, feminists or not, might want to dispute the point), the book shows that researching popular media use can be highly productive.

I would have liked nothing better than to follow in Radway's footsteps, or in those of Angela McRobbie (1978; 1991). Her analysis of teenagers reading the girls' magazine *Jackie* is another argument in favour of researching popular women's media through interviews. How could my women's magazine readers have so much less to say than Radway's romance readers or McRobbie's *Jackie* readers, when Radway and McRobbie, I gather, employed much the same interview strategy? In what textual and practical respects are women's magazines (or is reading women's magazines) so different from either romances or girls' magazines? Of course, women's magazines come in diverse subgenres, and even single subgenres or single titles are fragmented and circular texts (the same topics return every few issues, years or couple of years). More pertinent is the observation that women's magazines do not create audiences that develop strong *narrative* interests or *cult followings*. As a rule women's magazines do not have fans, whereas girls' and young women's magazines inspire such interest and following (see Frazer, 1987; Lewis, 1987). The most important difference between women's magazines and other popular genres (with the possible exception of the outlier subgenre of gossip magazines) seems to be that women's magazines are read with far less concentration and much more detachment than other popular genres. That is what I have come to believe after interviewing readers about all kinds of women's magazines, from traditional and glossy to gossip and feminist.

McRobbie's and Radway's studies are exemplary for work done on specific media audiences and subcultures. In general, research on popular culture aims to reconstruct pleasure and meaning production and focuses on isolated bodies of text (Ang, 1985: prime-time soap *Dallas*; McRobbie, 1978, 1991: girls' magazine *Jackie*; Schrøder, 1988: prime-time soap *Dynasty*) or on interviews with readers who, on average, are more knowledgeable than other viewers or readers (Livingstone, 1990, found viewers through advertisements who could recall soap opera plots; Radway, 1984, interviewed an existing group of self-identified romance readers). The certainly unintended consequence of these condensations – isolating specific texts from everyday media use and taking the knowledgeable reader for an average reader – is that popular culture is given the status of high culture. It is made into a discrete text that offers a unique and possibly liberating perspective on the world. Paul Willis's work with Simon Jones, Joyce Canaan and Geoff Hurd on the symbolic activity of young people in everyday culture (1990) explicitly starts from the point of view that there is no difference between high and popular culture with regard to processes of meaning production. Although laudable in its intention to reassert the value of low-valued popular culture, there are dire consequences to such an approach: general, everyday media use is identified with attentive and meaningful reading of specific texts, and that is precisely what it is not.

Media use is not always meaningful. From time to time it is virtually meaningless or at least a secondary activity. David Morley's work on television (1986) makes the point very clearly. His analysis shows, on the one hand, how gendered power relations within the family are reconstructed through different styles of interaction around the television; on the other hand the family portraits in *Family Television* make clear that television is not always meaningful as text. One of Morley's respondents had a habit of turning the television on in the early morning: 'Sometimes I intend to look at it,' she said, '. . . but . . . at the end of it I've seen everything but I've heard nothing' (1986: 56). Magazines may be opened or leafed through, television sets may be on, but that is hardly an indication that they are 'read' consciously, seriously or with animation. How women's magazines are read and how television is watched appear to be inextricably tied in to everyday routines. Both television and women's magazines have become such standard parts of our lives that their status is almost unquestioned. Television, the newer medium, might occasionally lead viewers to find explicit legitimation for viewing; women's magazines are almost too familiar to be noticed.

My disappointment in the interviews I held with women's magazine readers can be seen to have a positive side. It alerted me to several dangers. As a researcher, without intending to be, one is drawn to 'fans',[1] to knowledgeable readers and viewers who easily express themselves. Can one take fans to be representative of ordinary viewers? A tricky question. John Fiske sees fandom as a heightened form of popular culture and fans as 'excessive readers' who differ from 'ordinary readers' in degree rather than in kind (1992: 46). I disagree with Fiske and with Lisa Lewis, editor of *The Adoring Audience*, a collection on fan culture and popular media that starts from the assumption that academia is still caught in its 'historical propensity to treat media audiences as passive and controlled' (1992: 1). Media and cultural studies, by now accepted disciplines or interdisciplinary approaches, have trained themselves to conceptualize the reader as active and to treat media audiences as such. In fact, current research and theorizing appear overburdened by their attention to fans[2] and to the reading and watching experiences that people are enthusiastic about, to the detriment of theorizing the mundaneness of everyday media use. This leads to what I would call the fallacy of meaningfulness, by which I mean the unwarranted assumption that all use of popular media is significant. Although readers may recognize the codes of a given text and accord it limited associative meaning, they do not always accord it generalized significance, that is, a distinct and nameable place in their world-views and fantasies.

As academics we are in the business of meaning production and interpretation, while the majority of media users are not: much media use is routine and insignificant, it has no distinct, generalizable meaning. Of course, viewers and readers love texts that offer spellbinding escape, a learning experience, suspense, moral outrage or good melodrama. But watching television or reading magazines may also have the reassuring character of a much repeated, well-known activity that does not ask us to concentrate or to think. There is pleasure in saying; 'Reading those tips, you are reminded of all sorts of things that you knew but had kind of forgotten', as an older, female informant remarked, but it is a very different pleasure from the pleasures and meanings that have, up till now, been described in academic popular culture research.

The fallacy of meaningfulness leads popular culture researchers to privilege knowledgeable viewers and to use only their most expressive utterances. We prefer our analyses to be economic and evocative, our quotations to be to the point and edited into readable English and logical arguments. The fallacy of meaningfulness leads me to expect lay theories and surprising views of women's magazines from my informants, or at least examples and knowledgeable references. But those were extremely scarce. Ordinary viewers are not lay theoreticians, as has been observed by others (Lindlof and Meyer, 1987: 4). If one wants to understand reading women's magazines, or watching television for that matter, it should not be assumed that the media text is always important or that readers' views have the status of lay theory. On the contrary, readers may have little to say or may express contradictory views and use conflicting discourses (see Morley, 1986), as was the case with my interviewees.

To understand and theorize everyday media use a more sophistic-ated view of meaning production is required than one that does not recognize different levels of psychological investment or emotional commitment (see Henriques et al., 1984: 238) and reflection. Popular culture research has not set itself such a task. Since I was confronted with the fact that women's magazine readers described an important part – though not all – of their use of women's magazines as almost meaningless, I set myself the task of finding theoretical tools to understand and explain how media use at times is meaningless – or has a more or less 'hidden' meaning – and at times is meaningful. I will focus here on the work of the French structuralist philosopher and researcher de Certeau, on social phenomenological insights in everyday meaning production and on social psychological views of how everyday meaning production can be traced.

Theorizing everyday meaning production

Everyday meaninglessness?

De Certeau's views of everyday life (1988) were introduced in popular culture research by, among others, John Fiske (1990). Fiske used de Certeau's view of everyday practices as resisting dominant knowledge and dominant codes to show how the enjoyment of, for example, quiz shows may be a statement of resistance[3] rather than a form of incorporation in dominant capitalist or patriarchal norms. According to de Certeau, everyday practices are made up of ways of resisting dominant knowledge – which includes prescribed ways of reading a text. Non-dominant knowledges, he believes, are fleeting and transient: 'Writing accumulates, stocks up, resists time by the establishment of a place and multiplies its production through the expansionism of reproduction. Reading takes no measures against the erosion of time (one forgets oneself *and* also forgets), it does not keep what it acquires, or it does so poorly, and each of the places through which it passes is a repetition of the lost paradise' (1988: 174). In *The Practice of Everyday Life* (1988) Michel de Certeau suggests not only that reading subverts institutional power/knowledge in the Foucauldian sense (of which academic knowledge is a part), but that reading, defined as the imprint or formative influence of a text upon a reader, is unresearchable. Texts, according to de Certeau, do not have the power to impose meanings. The pleasures and meanings of reading are transient and short-lived. Thus, supposedly, the only thing that can be researched or described is the practice of reading. And, more than that, the only thing popular culture researchers following de Certeau can do, if the meanings and doings of ordinary, everyday life can only be understood by doing them, is research their own experiences. The drawbacks of such a self-reflexive approach are put thus by John Frow: 'in the absence of realized texts which can be subject to determinate analysis – in the absence of a definite and graspable object – the analyst will inevitably reconstruct such an object. [The result of which] is a politically fraught substitution of the voice of a middle-class intellectual for that of the users of popular culture' (1991; 60).

I feel no wish to celebrate reading women's magazines as an as yet undiscovered liberating practice of resistance and neither do I want to research my own reading experiences or claim privileged insight in a *vox populi* that cannot be heard except by the empathic and critical researcher (see Morris, 1988). While I admire de Certeau's inspired description of the deep inequality of social relations and the repercussion of such a state of affairs on meaning production – that is, that there are forms of meaning production that are of an order other than academic, official meaning production – I disagree that everyday reading as such is virtually unresearchable. There is a 'realized text' that can be researched. Interview transcripts do not offer much, but they show fragments that appear to relate to a structure of meaning. The challenge is to understand both why much women's magazine use hardly seems to have meaning (or significance in terms of anticipated pleasures, fantasies and uses to which the text might be put) and how the largely hidden meanings, which one also sees glimpses of, are structured. Moreover, while interpreting interview transcripts may be a laborious and convoluted process, involving a good deal of hand-wringing over countless meaningless 'you knows', it also seems a more respectful course of action than simply abandoning the project of understanding media use through the recollections and reports of readers. I will use de Certeau's analysis, however, to contextualize my search for the structures of meaning underpinning women's magazine use and to understand the apparent superficiality and meaninglessness of my interviews and the character of everyday media use.

To describe or recollect in substantive detail what reading women's magazines means or has meant is difficult. I can hardly explain what it was I liked so much about *Viva* when I regularly read that magazine some ten years ago (to invoke my own experience, despite Frow's argument). In a de Certeauian framework this loss of meaningfulness would be explained by reference to the difference between tactics (ways of making do, *arts de faire*) and strategies. Strategies are used by total institutions, such as armies, cities and supermarket chains, to create and delimit their own place, a 'proper'. Tactics are the weaponry of the powerless. Tactics are calculated actions determined by the absence of a proper locus that tend to insert themselves in the spaces created for the maintenance of power (de Certeau 1984: 36–7). Reading, according to de Certeau, is a tactic and therefore dependent upon the structures and spaces created by strategies. It does not have a 'space' of its own. Everyday reading is pleasurable because it is done in your own time, when there are no obligations, no boss to tell you what to do. Your own time, by definition, is time stolen from the system, spent outside its grasp, outside the strategies that fence off places and set rules. You do not need to memorize everyday reading or even to remember it, you do it simply to enjoy yourself and, therefore, over time you forget.

De Certeau is a romantic about everyday life in its more 'practical' sense. He has chosen to overlook most people's everyday duties: having to prepare your family's meals seven days a week; going to work every day; raiding the shops to find bargains in order to stretch a limited budget; or desperately trying not to get bored out of your mind spending your entire day on home-making and looking after children in a suburb. Exactly what readers invest in reading in terms of fantasy, identity or diversion (the nomadic and ungraspable side to reading of which de Certeau says:'one forgets oneself *and* also forgets') is intrinsically part of such daily constraints and obligations. Reading may be, like poaching, strolling, cooking or dwelling, 'wandering through an imposed system' (1988: 169), the system of the text, analogous to the constructed order of a city or supermarket. It is also taking a little time off for oneself; using the 'natural' breaks in a day of looking after a child or simply filling empty time, which makes it a part of everyday obligations. In so far as it is an escape, it is an activity in line with, rather than opposed to, the overarching structure of people's daily lives (Radway, 1988: 366). While you remember the structure and that there were things you had to do, you forget what you did in the empty time, the minutes of pleasure or of boredom spent doing nothing of consequence.

Reading women's magazines, even if it is not important in itself, may still have its place or its importance in the structure of everyday routines, and thus lose its meaning while not disappearing entirely from readers' memories. One of the men I interviewed, Paul Mortier, works on a drilling rig (on a seven days on, seven days off rota). When he is at home, he reads the women's magazines his wife buys: 'in the morning, when I get up, I usually make myself comfortable, have coffee and a fag and then I might get a *Libelle* and browse a bit. [If you had a morning newspaper, do you think you'd still read

Libelle?] I don't know. I might. There are dead moments in a day, just before dinner, like now, when you get a magazine.' Many women told me they started to read women's magazines after they had children. Modern-day child care imposes rigorous schedules that do not seem to allow for any activity that cannot be immediately broken off, to be taken up again later: 'I hardly read romances any more . . . I do more knitting now than reading. Because the moment you've settled nicely, he'll wake up, of course. You learn fast enough not to look forward to an hour's reading. And a romance is really difficult to put down. And you can't do that, can you? Because I have to read a romance, he would have to be absolutely quiet?' (Joan Becker). Women with school-going children seemed to have less demanding schemes. Still, a good deal of waiting is involved: waiting for children to come home from school, waiting in doctors' surgeries. Women with jobs outside the home, part-time and full-time, give other reasons for reading women's magazines. They are 'light' matter that can be taken to bed for a quick read. Women's magazines will not keep you up for half a night, though an exciting novel might.

Reading women's magazines is often described by informants as a secondary activity requiring little concentration or involvement: 'Sometimes I read magazines when I'm watching television. Not when I'm watching *Derrick* [a police series] but when I watch *Achter het Nieuws* [a current affairs programme] or something else, and it's boring, then I'll read' (Elizabeth Veenstra). Undoubtedly, women's magazines are occasionally read with full concentration and fascination, but from the interviews I have concluded that it is more usual for women's magazine reading to be a low-priority means of spending leisure time or unoccupied minutes. To understand reading women's magazines one has to understand everyday life: its particular routines and hierarchies of activities.

De Certeau's rendering of everyday life, though thought provoking, is rather sombre: pleasure cannot be found in things we are forced to do; only when we escape our obligations, when we can wander, are we free to have pleasure. Even if pleasure itself does not last, could not the context or memory of experiencing pleasure last? And cannot such contexts have the structure of routines? The woman who said; 'I love to read all those tips. Reading those tips, you are reminded of all sorts of things that you knew but had kind of forgotten', may forget what she reads, but she does not forget to read. People read women's magazines because it suits their everyday routines. Such everyday routines may revolve around working inside or outside the home, studying and doing odd jobs, 'being a pensioner' or 'doing nothing' (see Canaan, 1991). In discourse, for de Certeau, there are only the polemological space and the utopian. I would say that much is lost between a space in which 'the strong always win and words always deceive' (1988: 16) and 'a site that is impregnable, because it is a nowhere' (1988: 17). Such a dichotomy does not do justice to the variety of ways in which people describe their everyday lives and life histories, how they adapt, what they are proud of or what they have to laugh about.

De Certeau does not offer a framework for understanding everyday talk when it is used to negotiate the meaning of everyday activity. According to *The Practice of Everyday Life*, language belongs to the powerful, words always deceive. Should I then understand the superficiality of my interview transcripts and the meaninglessness surrounding women's magazine reading as intentional or unintentional obfuscation? Because the subordinated would not want to reflect on their everyday lives and help collect academic knowledge that may be used against them? I do not think so. I was given some information and, more importantly, I received a warm and sincere welcome from informants. Rather, it is the case that readers are not in the habit of reflecting on everyday routines or of preserving memories of what made reading pleasurable. Still, in the interviews some memories cropped up and were savoured. At the end of the interview many said they had greatly enjoyed talking about reading women's magazines and about their lives, which surprised them because they had never given women's magazine reading much thought. This is exactly the issue adressed by social phenomenology. From a phenomenological perspective the apparent meaninglessness of much media use can be explained in terms of routines rather than resistance. It is to phenomenology I now turn.

Everyday meaning and implicit understandings

Phenomenology respects that everyday talk does not pose rigorous standards on reflection or logical felicity. It has championed the cause of everyday reasoning, which has so often, though subtly, been denigrated as non-scientific knowledge. Phenomenology set itself the task of elucidating the relation between experience and knowledge; between a practical and a theoretical attitude; between common sense and reason. Important to my argument is Schutz's work on everyday meaning. Schutz would definitely think modest expectations were befitting to an interviewer interested in everyday practices. He argued that in everyday life we expect things to continue largely as they are and that we expect to be able to repeat particular solutions. We make sense of the world around us by routinely applying types or categories to order our experiences. In the words of Mary Rogers:

> Any process of type construction or reconstruction is 'broken off' when the individual has constituted sufficient knowledge for mastering the situation and anticipated similar situations. The break-off point, however, is not a commitment to closure. It is a turn toward the taken-for-grantedness that presupposes idealized, implicit expectations in the form of 'and so forth and so on' and 'again and again'. The first idealization is that my world exhibits a stability that indefinitely validates my determinations and guarantees the fundamental familiarity of my experiences; the latter more basic idealization is that I can repeat my succesful actions as long as the former idealization remains tenable. These idealized expectations undergird all common-sense thinking and typification. (1983: 41)

Lived experience thus consists of interpreted realities. Everyday reasoning is governed by what phenomenologists call the *epoche* of the natural attitude, in which doubt in the existence of the social world is suspended, as are doubts that the world might not be what it appears (Natanson 1986: 66; Schutz, 1962: 229). Meaning, in this context, is the relationship established between the self and its experiences. Phenomenology stresses the situatedness and time-relatedness of 'meaning'. (Meaning) is 'the result of my explication of past lived experiences which are grasped reflectively from an actual now and from an actually valid reference scheme' (Schutz and Luckmann, 1974: 16). The meaningfulness of any practice will change over time. Thus, one's experiences make up one's life-world, which is always already there, an inhabited world, a pre-existing cultural, historical and social order. Although Schutz held the view that meaning production is an inherently reflective process, it is not always consciously so.

> Meaning . . . is not a quality inherent in certain experiences emerging within our stream of consciousness but the result of an interpretation of a passed experience looked at from the present Now with a reflective attitude. As long as I live *in* my acts, directed toward the objects of these acts, the acts do not have any meaning. They become meaningful if I grasp them as well-circumscribed

experiences of the past and, therefore, in retrospection. Only experiences which can be recollected beyond their actuality and which can be questioned about their constitution are, therefore, subjectively meaningful. (Schutz, 1962: 210)

Thus, everyday sense-making is based on routines that are opened up only if new situations arise. Experiences become meaningful only in looking back upon them. Everyday reading practices follow the same path, they are part of everyday routines; as such they are not often reflected upon and therefore do not have conscious meanings. This explains why it is truly difficult for readers to enlarge upon why and how they read.

Schutz's definitions of 'language' – a 'treasure house of ready-made pre-constituted types and characteristics' (1970: 96), – and 'know-ledge' may add further to an understanding of everyday meaning production. Knowledge

has to be conceived in the broadest possible sense; not as the result of ratiocination nor in the sense of clarified and distinct knowledge, nor clear perceptions of truth. The term rather includes all kinds of beliefs: from the unfounded, blind belief to the well-founded conviction, from the assumption of mere chance or likelihood to the confidence of empirical certainty. Thus, knowledge may refer to the possible, conceivable, imaginable, to what is feasible or practicable, workable or achievable, accessible or obtainable, what can be hoped for and what has to be dreaded. (Schutz in Natanson, 1986: 31)

It would be overly credulous to expect too much from informants. Schutz would typify them as 'men on the street, living, in a manner of speaking, naïvely in their own and their in-group's intrinsic rele-vances' (1970: 241). No matter that most of them are women.

I find phenomenology's understanding of everyday life perspicacious, but a critical note needs to be added to its characterization of everyday meaning production. Phenomenology is rather rigid in its conceptualization of the natural attitude: women and men in the street, supposedly, are successful in keeping all doubts and critical reflection at bay. Desire for change or simply doubts about the social order or the world as it is today appear to have the status of an anomaly. Another point of criticism is Schutz's focus on the working 'man' and his 'acts' as the basis of the meaningful structure of the social world. I should think that for men and for women fantasy and imagination are also important sources of a meaningful structuring of the social world. While Radway's analysis of how her romance readers balance social and imagined worlds to concoct liveable surroundings may be lacking with regard to a precise analysis of their actual household arrangements and their relations to their flesh-and-blood husbands (Curran, 1990: 154), it makes a point about the importance in everyday life of the desire for change.

Likewise, Birte Bech Jørgensen[4] criticises Schutz's exclusive emphasis on the taken-for-grantedness of everyday life. In her research on female youth employment she found that such a perspective did not suit her material: 'Modern everyday life is created as doubleness on the one hand of continuity, of trust and certainty, made possible by the norms, rules and routines of everyday life. And, on the other hand, change and a more or less frightening and joyful urge for autonomy' (1990: 22).

Hermann Bausinger (1984) has formulated some very helpful proposals for media research, which he bases on social-phenomenological theorizing of everyday life. According to Bausinger, media consumption functions as a mark of confirmation. An undelivered newspaper is missed not because of its content but because it disrupts the structure of everyday life. Despite its seeming irrationality, everyday life consists of ritualized structures of perceptions and expectations that should be read not in terms of a 'mystique of immediacy', but rather in terms of the capacity of such structures to naturalize and stabilize. As an example Bausinger introduces Mr Meier and the weekend sport coverage.

Mr Meier makes a series of conscious, tactical decisions in order to maximize his pleasure in following events in the football league. He does not listen to the radio, but waits for the late evening sports programme on television so that he is able to see the goals without knowing the score in advance. His tactical decisions are interfered with because of such mundane things as the weather, irritation over his son sleeping late and his wife coming down for a glass of water when he thought she had gone to bed. Bausinger uses this example to make several related points about media consumption. Meaningful study of media use has to take the 'media ensemble' into consideration. As recipients we integrate the content of different media: radio, television, newspapers, magazines. His other points are that the media are seldom used completely or with full concentration. On the contrary, the media are an integral part of the way everyday life is conducted. Thus, media use is never an isolated, individual process, but a collective process. And, finally, media communication cannot be separated from direct personal communication (1984: 349–50).

A phenomenological account of everyday reading and meaning production provides an explanation, at least partly, for the 'relative meaninglessness' of everyday media use, while it does not close off the road to further inquiry. Like de Certeau's interpretation of everyday practices, phenomenology stresses the situatedness of reading, even if sometimes the emphasis on routines can be too heavy, to the detriment of understanding change, as is argued by, for instance, Jørgensen. A phenomenological understanding of everyday practices strengthens the cultural studies view that an analysis of reading women's magazines would have to be twofold. On the one hand the practice of reading and how it has acquired unquestioned space in women's and men's lives need to be researched. On the other hand the implicit understandings of reading, the ideas and categories people vaguely refer to in everyday conversation (and in lengthy conversational interviews, of course), have to be made explicit. Only by putting the reading of women's magazines in a wider perspective, by denaturalizing the activity of reading this particular genre and comparing it with reading other genres and with other references to interpretive frameworks, will it be possible to understand reading women's magazines at all.

How women's magazines are made meaningful

Media and cultural studies theory in general, such as exemplified in the work of David Morley (1980, 1986), would stress that a rough framework for the study of everyday media use would see readers as active, meaning-producing agents. The possible meanings they may give texts will be delimited by the contexts in which they are used and, to some extent, by the texts themselves. Texts may be said to have 'preferred meanings' that invite a reader to read them in line with dominant meaning systems (Hall, 1980). However, this invitation need not be taken up. Readers may negotiate with texts or even read them against the grain. This depends largely on a reader's place in the social formation and on the range of knowledges and experiences a reader has had access to.

Inspired by the cultural studies framework and by the theoretical approaches discussed above, I used two different strategies to analyse how women's magazines are used and interpreted and thus become meaningful. I have sought to show the specific and contextual nature of women's magazine use and interpretation by focusing on specific life histories. This particularizing move demonstrates how media use and interpretation exist by grace of unruly and unpredictable, but in retrospect understandable and interesting,

choices and activities of readers. At the same time the cultural
knowledge readers use and have access to needed to be charted. To
do so I analysed my interviews using a concept developed by two
social psychologists, which they have named 'interpretive repertoire'.
Interpretive repertoires are defined by Jonathan Potter and Margaret
Wetherell as 'recurrently used systems of terms used for characterizing and evaluating actions, events and other phenomena' (1987: 149).

Potter and Wetherell see these systems of terms as adding up to a
structural explanation of the different cultural resources that may be
used to talk about, explain and legitimate reading women's magazines. They hold a functional perspective that highlights people's
need to communicate adequately: if one kind of explanation or way of
telling a story does not work, other repertoires or other styles to
which a speaker has access will be used. Repertoire analysis, though
grounded in post-structuralist theory, differs from other forms of
discourse analysis in that the social subject is theorized not just as an
intersection of discursive structurings but as an active and creative
language user. For readers repertoires have the form of 'cash and
carry' knowledge: repertoires are available knowledge that readers
will refer to in everyday talk. Because they are used, repertoires
change over time.

Although repertoire analysis is typically a micro-sociological
approach, it can be contended that it is also a tool that helps to lay
bare what underlying structures of meaning look like and thus to
explain how culture as a whole is organized. Bearing directly on this
question, Karin Knorr-Cetina (1981) has argued that what is
commonly called the macro-structure is a summary representation
actively constructed and pursued within micro-situations. Thus, the
macro-structure

> is seen to reside within . . . micro-episodes where it results from
> the structuring practices of agents. The outcome of these practices
> are representations which thrive upon an alleged correspondence
> to that which they represent, but which at the same time can be
> seen as highly situated constructions which involve several layers
> of interpretation and selection . . . Agents routinely transform
> situated micro-events into summary representations by relying on
> practices through which they convince themselves of having
> achieved appropriate representation. (Knorr-Cetina, 1981: 34).

This complex process of representation, the result of which is
'culture', can usefully be pictured as a series of repertoires. Following

the authors discussed above, I define 'culture' as a system of beliefs, values and ideas about the world that meaningfully organize a way of life in a process of negotiation and struggle between those with different positions in the social formation and with different social and cultural power resources.

Repertoire analysis is not a prescriptive or rigorous method. It simply consists of going back and forth through the text, summarizing interview transcripts according to different criteria, for as long as it takes to organize the bits and pieces in meaningful structures. One looks for statements or manners of speech that recur in different interviews. Once such key elements have been found, it is a matter of trying to fit them together. My understanding of these sets of recurrent statements has led to the formulation of different repertoires. Most of the repertoires I found (or, rather, that I reconstructed) centre around anxieties, vague fears and the solutions that women's magazines offer, which usually were not taken up directly but were used for imaginary or fantasy reconstructions of what one might do or how a threatening or frightening situation, if it arose, could be coped with. Women's magazines of all kinds address what readers perceive as sensitive areas that they have less control over than they would like to have. Thus, like other media, women's magazines are used indirectly in identity building and maintenance, which is an important part of attaching generalized, evaluative significance to texts. It must be repeated, though, that the fantasy and affective investments of readers in women's magazines are expressed and defined much less than in the case of other popular media. Even within the blurred umbrella genre of women's magazines, there were important differences in the extent to which the magazines inspired such investments, whereas gossip magazines were a source of much fantasy activity, domestic weeklies and glossies were far less obviously a source of such investments.

Although repertoire analysis in itself is no guarantee against not being trapped in what I have called the fallacy of meaningfulness, there seems less chance of that when repertoire analysis is used not only to reconstruct the meanings women's magazines have, but also to detect recurring themes in descriptions of how women's magazines are used. (From these it became clear that women's magazines are read in short periods of 'in-between' time and that they are valued because they are easy to put down.) A second 'guarantee' is located in how informants were sought (different kinds of 'ordinary' readers were interviewed, rather than fans or exceptionally knowledgeable readers), which is discussed at length in appendix 4. In chapter 2, the repertoires readers employ to interpret their own practices of use and to describe how they read the magazines are considered in relation to each other. Although I show that women's magazines, like other popular genres, contribute to identity construction, this is set against the background of how readers talk about what makes women's magazines primarily attractive to them: they are easy to put down. The portraits of two readers (in chapter 3) make it even clearer that women's magazine use is part of and dependent on everyday routines and habits. When they break down, readers lose interest in women's magazines.

2

Easily Put Down: How Women and Men Read Women's Magazines

My interviews made clear that for a reader it is not all that easy to explain what it is exactly that makes reading women's magazines worthwhile. Not only are women's magazines among the most taken for granted media, available public discourse (often elitist and reflecting high cultural values) concentrates on why one should not read women's magazines. Thus, for the two non-readers I also interviewed, it clearly was not very difficult to explain why they had never (or hardly ever) read women's magazines. Reading women's magazines simply was 'not done' because it signified lack of discernment. Lies Machielse, one of the two non-readers, had a brief stint of reading women's magazines when her children were small: 'When my children were born, I thought, I have to knit. You owe it to your children to knit them things. So I took those magazines. Children tie you to the home, you cannot study, you're not in the mood, you get those women's magazines, although it was looked down on. You couldn't have a *Libelle* on your table. And I thought, now I have sunk to *Libelle*.' Margot Klein comes from a highly cultured socialist family. They did not have women's magazines. It was simply 'unthinkable' that they would be brought into the house. For her it still feels perfectly natural not to spend money on them. The wife of one of my male respondents briefly joined the interview and said, implying that this was self-evident, 'My parents were intellectuals, so we didn't have those magazines' (Caroline Smit, partner of Peter Smit).

The women's magazine readers I talked to offered another kind of example that illustrates the self-evidently low status of women's magazines. Some had husbands who heavily criticized them for buying trash: 'The other day I wanted to buy *Weekend*. I saw it in the shop and I really wanted to buy it. But my husband was waiting outside and I didn't dare take it because I always get such a load of comment' (Tina Poorter). Some felt criticized by non-readers who commented on what the readers thought was a significant fact or story by saying, 'Have you been reading *Viva*?' (Linda Zijlstra), making it clear that information from such a source could not possibly qualify as valid. Or non-readers would say (not always to censure, but at times, perhaps misguidedly, to comfort by appealing to a reader's good sense), 'You shouldn't believe all that you read.' (One of my male informants, Paul Mortier, says this in reply to his mother's stories about what she has read in gossip magazines). Readers agreed that non-readers do not seem to grasp what makes women's magazines interesting – just as those who read gossip magazines would agree with non-readers that you cannot believe all that you read (and will hurry to say so), but would differ with them as to how interesting stories can be that are not wholly true. (Reading gossip magazines is discussed extensively in chapter 5).

The women readers I spoke to seemed not to mind all the criticism too much. They were used to it and chose to live with it, rather than fight it. Some of them occasionally showed resentment, but most simply took it in their stride. Remarks by Linda Zijlstra and Elizabeth Veenstra were the proverbial exceptions to the rule that readers do not reflect either on reading magazines or on the contempt that they then suffer. I interviewed Linda Zijlstra together with her friend Karen de Wit. Karen complained of comments she gets about reading *Viva* (a magazine for younger women). Elizabeth Veenstra was more amazed that people feel they can judge others on what they like to read.

Karen: Well, it has happened to me that I said I read *Viva* and then it turns out to be *not done*! That it is absolutely ridiculous. I find that very strange. [She is amazed and indignant.] And now they've also started about *Cosmo*!

Linda: I think men are afraid of them. Because someone opened her mouth against her boyfriend because of an article in *Viva*. And they don't have [articles like that] so much now, but there used to be a lot about sexuality in *Viva*.

I do wonder what right people have to judge others . . . Why would you look down on someone who reads *Libelle* or romances?

BARNSLEY COLLEGE
HONEYWELL
LEARNING CENTRE

. . . Reading magazines: there's nothing in them, is there [slightly mimicking her critics], so you're not supposed to read them. (Elizabeth Veenstra).

From the available quotations on women's magazines and women's magazine reading in the interviews, this chapter attempts to reconstruct through which repertoires women's magazines become meaningful for readers. As was explained in chapter 1, a repertoire analysis starts with the interview material itself and tries to find recurrent themes and issues. These themes and issues are understood to be references to underlying meaning systems, which are called 'repertoires'. In this chapter I will concentrate on fragments that relate to the traditional women's magazine genres (domestic weeklies, glossies such as *Cosmopolitan* and *Elle*) and work from a description of recurrent themes and issues in the interviews towards the two highly descriptive repertoires (the easily put down repertoire and the repertoire of relaxation) that dominate all talk about women's magazines, and from there to the two main repertoires (the repertoire of connected knowing and the repertoire of practical knowledge) that structure women's magazines' meaningfulness. (When quotations indicated that gossip magazines or other magazines were used in the same way as domestic weeklies and glossies are used, they have been incorporated.) The first part of the chapter, in which the repertoires are reconstructed, concentrates on the interviews with women. The second section asks whether men use the same repertoires to talk about women's magazines as women. This question is answered with quotations from interviews with the men, held by me and by a co-researcher, Joppe Boodt. In this chapter fragments from interviews with thirty women and fifteen men (including the two non-readers quoted above) are used.

How do women's magazines become meaningful for female readers?

'Easily put down' and 'relaxation': two descriptive repertoires

Typical recurrent phrases and themes in the interviews were value for money, reading for relaxation, learning, picking things up, more advertisements than text, giving the shopping pages a look, recognizing yourself, being easy to put down, 'I love to read', 'I cry over sad stories', emancipation. All these were used in describing the

activity of reading women's magazines. Most of them were considered self-evident explanations of women's magazine reading.
Contradictions between, for example, learning and relaxing were
hardly ever addressed, or only in a very vague manner. The special
merit of repertoire analysis is that it recognizes that speakers will refer
to different repertoires during a single conversation or interview.
Since it is interested in the diversity of repertoires speakers use and
not in any one speaker's attitude, interview fragments are all
recorded individually and added to statements from other interviews.
The more variable a respondent's discourse is, the more a discourse
or repertoire analyst can lay bear underlying cultural sources of
meaning.[1] To summarize: a single reader will use different repertoires. Although, as this chapter will show, specific repertoires tend
to be used for specific magazine subgenres, that does not absolutely
exhaust the uses to which a reader may put such a repertoire. Some of
the repertoires in this chapter may quite possibly be used for other
popular media or other social phenomena. I found no instances of
readers being particularly fond of a single repertoire. Occasionally
repertoires are used for traditional and glossy women's magazines
that are more often used for, say, gossip magazines. This chapter will
provide some examples.

As was pointed out briefly in chapter 1, the characteristic of
women's magazine reading that is referred to markedly often (and the
first repertoire I wish to discuss) is that women's magazines are so
'putdownable'. Reading women's magazines is the ultimate 'in-
between' activity. It fills empty time, it does not require much
attention. Women with young children and women who had raised
children stressed this point more than most, but others would look to
women's magazines for a nice quick read too. Some examples:

> When the children were small, in the afternoon, oh [that used to be]
> nice! I had a subscription then. I'd come in and I'd sit down with my
> magazine, just for a quick read. You cannot let [reading] monopo-
> lize you. [Women's magazines], you can pick up and put down
> again. (Christine Kenter's mother, who came and sat in the room
> during the interview)

> When I go home, I'll put the shopping away and sit with a cup of
> tea and a magazine and glance through it, or at night, in bed. (. . .)
> Especially when [children] are smaller [you read women's maga-
> zines]. Obviously when they're having naps and things. And
> you've got nothing to do. You can't work because they're sleeping

upstairs. I mean, I never read a [magazine] before I had her. I wouldn't sit down to pick up a magazine and read it. (Rebecca Priest, who runs a flower-shop and has a young child)

When you're having a cup of coffee, you get a mag; you can throw it down again whenever you like. If you were to really start reading a book, you'd be reading the whole evening, if it was captivating. (Mrs Dobbel, housewife and mother of two children)

[I read them] when I have time off. In the afternoons between four and six . . . if there's nothing on television that I find interesting. And in the evening, but that is always half-hours, you know; magazines are easiest, you can put them down. Like, I'll read that tomorrow. Or a subject might be very interesting and you'll think, I'll just finish this bit. It's all so short anyway. (Jeanne Rousset, mother of two teenagers)

I love to read Konsalik novels [best-selling thrillers], that is something completely different, of course. I really love them. But usually I don't have time for them because when you start reading them, you have to keep your thoughts together, or you'll miss part of the narrative. And that is what I like about these magazines. You need to use your brain with some of the articles, but you don't have to really concentrate. (. . .) I can't read during the day, but in the evening when [the children] are in bed, then, or when I'm in my bed, wonderful, blissful. (Pam Gradanus, police officer and mother of two young children)

I like short pieces. (. . .) I like reading, I read a book occasionally. (. . .) I hardly ever [sit and read at a stretch]. It's usually in between, for a short while. During the day I don't do that [read a book]. [It is impossible with the busy goings-on in her household.] It catches your attention too much. And with these, it'll take two or three minutes, or how long would [a magazine article] take? And in between you can do other things, listen or I don't know what. You can't do that with a book. (Elizabeth Veenstra, who takes care of three young children)

My husband gets it when he buys the newspaper. He knows what I like and I glance through it, have a cup of tea. (. . .) I do read a book, but I don't love picking books up and putting them down. (Mrs Parry, retired factory worker, mother of three grown-up daughters)

Look, when you read a magazine like *Opzij* [a Dutch feminist journal similar to *Spare Rib* and *Ms*], it feels like you really have to read, while browsing in *Viva* [young women's magazine], you'll read every now and then, you know. With *Opzij*, you don't feel like having a quick, cosy look over a cup of tea. (Linda Zijlstra)

I have a child. Reading the newspaper with him around is really the limit; and *Margriet* and *Libelle* [domestic weeklies], because they are so easy to read. It isn't like: Ha! I'll read *Libelle* thoroughly. (Lauren Terberg, who lives with a young child)

I don't read during the day. It's at night-time, when I go to bed . . . And it is only magazines that I read. (. . .) Just have trouble sleeping, which everybody does, and that is what started me reading in bed . . . to put me to sleep. (Mary Croston)

Women's magazines constitute a genre that does not make demands: they can easily be picked up and put down again. Since, as readers, we know magazines will not capture us totally or carry us off, they are quite safe to read. Hard-working academic Terry Atkinson said, 'I don't allow myself to read novels for relaxation. But I don't feel too guilty reading a mag. They don't take up much time.' Many of the others indicated that they liked to read books and preferred them to women's magazines. Part of this may be to do with status: books have a higher social value than magazines. Part of it seems a very accurate description: they do not have the peace and quiet to sit down with a book. Women's magazines, I would argue, are typically second-choice reading matter that adapts to a noisy background, to other obligations. They are read more for their adaptability than for their content. Their status can be compared to that of the radio, which many women like to have on while they work in the house, as was put forward by the interviewees of Dorothy Hobson (1978, 1980), or that of the television, which some of the soap opera viewers of Seiter et al. (1989) had on during the day. Not only can women's magazine reading be made to adapt to the rhythms of housework, it accords well with any kind of work in which one has short breaks. Pam Gradanus (police officer) and Carla Willems (security guard) read magazines during work breaks. Rebecca Priest reads women's magazines at home and when it is quiet in her flower-shop.

The pickupable quality of women's magazines also makes them eminently suited to fight the dangers of boredom and obligatory sports viewing. In virtually all the households I visited there were television sets. When the set does not offer anything captivating, readers will take a magazine to browse through and watch television at the same time. Of course, since many live with others, they are not always in charge of what is watched. David Morley's interviews with London families (1986) make this abundantly clear. One woman said of her husband, 'If I put soap opera on, he will read' (Morley, 1986: 97). Going by what my respondents said, sport was more of a problem than soap opera in their households. Magazine reading suggested itself as the most companionable solution. Only if there were other programmes the women particularly wanted to watch would the second set many households had be used.

> For the most part, we put on sports on the television. [Do you like watching that?] No, I get my bundle of magazines and I'll read. (Dot Groeniers)

> I have the TV on when I am reading a magazine]. (. . .) You take a quick look, like this, especially if it is something that doesn't interest me – I don't watch. I read a book. (Solema Tillie)

> If there's nothing on television, I just pick up a magazine or a bit of knitting. (Mrs Parry)

> Sometimes I read women's magazines when I'm watching television. Not when I'm watching *Derrick* [a police series], but when I watch *Achter het Nieuws* [a current affairs programme] or something else, and it's boring, then I'll read. (Elizabeth Veenstra)

> [Do you watch television regularly?] Well, it's on fairly often, but I'll have a *Libelle* in my lap . . . It's just for the noise, I think. And every now and then, you'll watch for a while. (Lauren Terberg)

> There is a lot of soccer on right now [European Football Championship], so I'll get my *Privé* [gossip magazine]. (Tina Poorter)

From these descriptions of how they used women's magazines sprang ready explanations of why they read women's magazines: for relaxation. When I asked Mrs Dobbel (who reads domestic weeklies and gossip magazines) what makes magazines interesting, she said, referring, I think, especially to gossip magazines, 'Relaxation. (. . .) Doesn't really matter what is in them. You forget as soon as you've read it.' Elizabeth Veenstra said, 'They are entertaining.' Jeanne Rousset also gave relaxation as the reason when I asked her why she read women's magazines. Terry Atkinson was the only one to enlarge: 'Sometimes I have magazine mania and I just go out and spend ten or twelve pounds on magazines . . . those magazines will be lying around somewhere in the house . . . And then, one night the next week, when I've really had it rough at college, I'll be lying in the bath for an hour, reading that magazine [*Elle*] and I don't want to be too bothered about politics at that moment. It's a bit like watching an Agatha Christie film, or something. It is relaxation, really.' Clearly, 'relaxation' is a stop word. It is highly ideologically loaded. It appears to be as much a description as a defensive means to mark private territory. Like taste, it is someone's personal business.[2] Given that women's magazines are a low-valued genre, such a line of defence might be felt to be necessary. It underlines that speakers wish to make clear that women's magazines have little significance for them. Since I was interested in how women's magazines become mean- ingful, I decided to try to delve beneath the explanations that they are 'easy to put down' and that they are 'relaxing' – though I think they are highly valid descriptions of the use value of women's magazines – and concentrated on the other recurrent themes in the interviews (such as learning, emancipation) to see whether there were underly- ing structures of meaning.

I found that the majority of these other recurrent phrases and themes point to the existence of two other interpretative repertoires, which I have named the repertoire of practical knowledge and the repertoire of emotional learning and connected knowing. These two repertoires are not always clearly separate from one another. The repertoire of practical knowledge is about 'giving the shopping pages a look' (such a lamp could make the bedroom look nice) and 'picking things up' (handy tips and recipes). The repertoire of connected knowing is about 'learning' (you could fall ill, lose a child: better prepare in case that happens) and 'recognizing yourself in stories and articles'. Obviously, in some cases a respondent will say she 'picked something up from a magazine' while the 'something' is more in line with the emotional learning other respondents have described. Although the actual phrase used suggests the repertoire of practical knowledge, I have taken such a quotation to belong to the connected knowing repertoire.

The repertoire of practical knowledge

Most of the examples that were given under the heading of 'tips' and 'picking things up' work towards legitimation of women's magazines as a professional journal for the housewife and home-maker. Recipes, dress patterns, tips for removing stains from clothing or for opening a pot with a tight lid are all suggested as handy and worthwhile. They are only so if cooking, dress-making and cleaning are one's (everyday) responsibility. Fairly often book and film reviews were mentioned in terms of 'practical knowledge' too. *Viva* and *Cosmopolitan* in particular, have several pages with reviews and ideas for cultural outings. This kind of tip works towards another kind of legitimation of women's magazine reading: mentioning the reviews says that the speaker is a cultured person who actively builds on to the knowledge that she regards as the ground for such an identity.

Because the repertoire of practical knowledge stresses the practical use of magazines (as exemplified by the judgement of whether magazines were 'good value for money', that is, whether they provided useful information), it is also a way to legitimate spending money on them. The expenditure will benefit the whole household. The rhetorical character of this line of defence was underlined from time to time by what I observed: such as the shop-bought blouse and skirt of a respondent who claimed that women's magazines were so useful because of the dress patterns, which she, as a person who made all her own clothes, especially appreciated. The non-specific quality of the quotations suggests that it is often the idea of finding a nice recipe or a good knitting pattern that makes women's magazines attractive, rather than using the patterns and the recipes, going to that particular film or reading that book, and preparing the meal or knitting the sweater.

> I like that about *Margriet* and *Libelle*, the recipes. Recently they had 'Sweet Margriet'. I skipped that one – I don't have a sweet tooth. But when they have other little things, I do cut out a lot of recipes and I do save them. [Do you have a special place to keep them?] No, I'll find them again, sometime or other. (Pam Gradanus)

> Tips in *Story* and *Privé* [gossip magazines] aren't frightening [which the medical pages in other magazines for Tina Poorter are] and I do read those. If you have dandruff, [they tell you] what to do about it. Or, for example, the weird spots I have on my feet. Your GP says it's nothing and you've tried everything and nothing helped. And then a week later they print answers from other readers, like, 'My husband had the same thing, you should use those drops.' Those I cut out. When I think, that's useful. Or for your face, spots and things. (Tina Poorter)

Sometimes they have things about how you can make a face mask very cheaply, with egg-yolk and lemon and honey. I like to do that. Or if you don't have any shampoo, you can wash your hair with egg and lemon, it's just like shampoo. I never did that, but I did try the mask with egg and you feel your face tighten. Or how you can remove stains from clothing, or a diet to loose weight. Not that I need it [she doesn't], but I do read it. Maybe later it'll come in handy. You can always try it. (Solema Tillie)

I particularly like *Best* because it is a nice chatty little [magazine], if you know what I mean. It gives recipes which I use sometimes. It also gives a free pattern, dress-making pattern and knitting pattern, which you can pull out. And they also give little interesting tips on household things, you know. (. . .) In *Me* there's also a page, I think, 'Know about Health', and things like that. It's surprising what you pick up, really, and what you know about this and that. (. . .) [About *Bella*] I find little tips on your health, you know, and things like that interesting. (Mrs Parry)

I cut out a lot of things that I find useful, everything that has to do with sewing and gardening, plants and medical advice that I find important. Nowadays I ask my husband to make a photocopy. You can't cut up a magazine that has to go to someone else. (. . .) [Where do you keep all those cuttings and photocopies; it must be a mountain!] It is. Well, I put all of it in a box and when it gets old, I put it in a plastic bag and put that in the attic. (. . .) It may be that I never do anything at all with it, but it would be a waste to throw it all away. (Marie Stemerdink)

[I like] *Avant Garde*. It features a lot of fashion, a lot about travelling, hotels, restaurants, top quality ones . . . I especially like to keep informed about the travelling; I like to travel. I collect information about restaurants. To go back to them and to pass on to others . . . although that is difficult sometimes, as someone else's taste could be different from your own. (Jeanne Rousset)

You read about that kind of thing [how to deal with your fear of dentists, how to handle the situation when you need a complete overhaul of your teeth] in the magazines, you pick things up about that. (Ina Dammers)

I find the book reviews [in *Cosmopolitan*] very useful. (Pauline van de Voort)

Although fragmented, the tips constitute a particular body of knowledge that has value from a perspective that recognizes that being a housewife is a (part-time) profession, not just the only alternative for those who lack career ambitions. The book, film and restaurant reviews, mentioned less often, have a comparable function. Through reading them readers constitute themselves not only as consumers of culture, but also as cultured people, and it may help them to feel that they are taking care of their family, partner or themselves culturally as well as materially and emotionally, simply that they are enriching both their cultural knowledge and their status as cultured people. Jeanne Rousset, who collects restaurant and hotel reviews, likes to accompany her husband on business trips as well as to plan family vacations. In both cases she feels it is her duty (and her pleasure) to do so in the best way she knows.

The repertoire of practical knowledge does more than simply legitimate reading and buying women's magazines in terms of their practical use. It also furnishes readers with a temporary fantasy of an ideal self. Depending upon one's background and upon context, one may fantasize oneself into someone who is up to date regarding new products, who knows a whole litany of small remedies, who knows where to go and what to read, where to stay, someone who can handle medical specialists, who is clever with her hands. (Elizabeth Veenstra, Mrs Parry and Valerie van Eijck all felt it was very rewarding to make things with your hands and that those who are clever with their hands are generally admired for that.) The ideal self that the repertoire of practical knowledge helps one to fantasize, is pragmatic and solution-oriented, and a person who can take decisions and is an emancipated and rational consumer; but above all she is a person who is in control. Whatever may happen, she has trained herself to come up with solutions for virtually anything. Such a fantasy very much contradicts the stereotype of the silly, narcissistic housewife or of the trivial, unimportant and boring activities connected with home-making that many women feel they are up against. To feed such a fantasy is a weapon in this battle; it can make you feel stronger and less vulnerable.

It is important to note that the repertoire of practical knowledge is used to accord meaning to widely different magazines: cheaper and more expensive domestic weeklies, a young women's magazine that leans towards feminist ideas (*Viva*) and a glossy (*Avant Garde*). *Prima*, *Cosmopolitan* and *Good Housekeeping* were also mentioned, though not by name. Moreover, the use of the repertoire of practical knowledge is not restricted to women's magazine reading. Janice Radway (1984) found it in her interviews with romance readers. She calls it the 'reading for instruction' explanation, but, contrary to my belief that this is important for readers, considers it no more than a secondary justification for reading romances (1984: 107). One of my respondents, Nathalie Brooks, felt 'picking something up' was one of several pleasurable aspects to romance reading. Since she was in a position to check the information given in one particular romance novel, and it proved accurate, romances for her are a valuable source of information; they have practical value in the same way as women's magazines may do: 'They pick up different things, you know, whether it is medical or something . . . you always pick up something. (. . .) One time a story took me to the West Indies [where she lived as a child]. It was about a journey from Antigua to St Kitts to St Bartholomew, right to the Virgin Islands. [And] they went ashore in St Kitts and I wanted to know where they were going, where they passed; and different roads were right and things were right. They do their research pretty well.'

Texts do not directly have meaning. The various repertoires readers use make texts meaningful. Repertoires are rhetorical tools. The arguments readers put forward do not necessarily reflect what they do with the magazines, but rather what they may wish to do with them or what they have fantasies of doing. These fantasies are not always expressed directly. Nor are readers in the habit of reflecting on why they continue reading particular magazines. Readers will say: 'maybe later it'll come in handy' (Solema Tillie), 'when I think, that's useful' (Tina Poorter), 'interesting tips' (Mrs Parry), 'things that I find useful' (Marie Stemerdink), 'I like to keep informed' (Jeanne Rousset).

Of course, patterns and recipes are occasionally used, though not as much as is suggested in some of the fragments (as will be argued and illustrated at some length under the heading 'Empowerment and criticism'). Helen Carson, a retired child-care officer, who bought magazines for the knitting patterns and had knitted consistently for years and years (her knitting was boasted about by Terry Atkinson, who introduced me to her), was an exception. The repertoires feed fantasies much more than they help develop real skills. In the case of the repertoire of practical knowledge the fantasy is of a very rational and practical self. In fact, the whole repertoire can be seen as the rational explanation of 'why someone would read women's magazines'. They are useful, they are not expensive; one may pick up handy information. The repertoire of emotional learning and connected knowing, discussed below, is its emotional and sentimental counterpart. As will become clear, reading women's magazines may involve fantasizing oneself as a perfect person along very different lines.

The repertoire of emotional learning and connected knowing

The focal points of this repertoire are human emotions and how to deal with them. Different forms of insecurity are voiced through reading and thinking about feature stories and problem pages in the magazines. In some cases the magazines are primarily used to learn about other people's emotions and problems, in other cases readers are more interested in learning about their own feelings, anxieties and wishes.

> I am not the kind of person who reads all the columns in women's magazines, but when there are short pieces about people who have had certain problems . . . how such a problem can be solved, how you can give it a twist, solve it, I like to read that. Maybe it'll happen to me, and I'll have an idea of what to do about it. (. . .)
> They have very good tips about how [medical] tests are done and about people who have had them. Real life examples. And I think, well, you'd better give this some thought, because you can become a victim too, it can happen to you, you'd better be prepared. (Carla Willems, who reads *Cosmopolitan*, among other magazines, and works as a security officer at an airport)

> *Tineke*:   There is one thing in *Libelle* [domestic weekly] that I do read. I'm not bowled over by it, but it is written kind of well. I won't ring my friends and tell them about it, or my husband, but . . . It's about a woman who has lost her husband and she writes about how she goes on. (. . .) Every week. And I do go for that. Maybe it is a bit overdone . . . but, shit, she has her good weeks and her bad days . . .
> *Carla*   Isn't it called 'Farewell'? She never had a chance to say goodbye. One day he left for work and he never came back.
> *Tineke*:   Yes, and she has two children. And I think, imagine that happening to you. I can imagine waking up wet with sweat and thinking, no, he's not here. (Fragment from group interview about *Cosmopolitan*)

Sometimes they talk about a man who is divorced and if you are his second wife, how you experience that, that kind of thing, what happens then. And sometimes you recognize things, it makes you think, yeah, I recognize that. (Felicia Landman)

My favourites are fashion and problem pages. I always read them and the personal stories. What I don't like are . . . horoscopes . . . and features and what they write about sex. I've seen all that before . . . like: what else can we come up with? . . . [Do you talk about it with friends?] Yeah, but that would be about the personal things. People talk about what has happened to them and you'll say, 'Wait till you hear this' or 'I recognize myself in that', and I'll talk about that with a friend . . . Things that touch me.

[In the second interview] You read about those problems and their answers and you do learn from that. What really frightened me was this article in *Viva* about chlamydia [a venereal disease], and you think, I'd better remember that. (Karen de Wit)

It's like you read something in a magazine and you think about it. Whether you agree or not. Or maybe you'll think, I would never do it like that. It's the same thing if you look at other people and think, I'd do it like that or I wouldn't. It influences how you do things. I really pay a lot of attention to children at the moment. There were a lot of people around us who had children a year older than [her son] is. Well, one let him cry, the other picked him up at the first sound she heard and another did it the way you would. You observe and you choose. It's the same thing [in magazines] when they pose a question and print fifty answers. You decide whether you like their way of doing things or whether it's stupid. (Joan Becker, who has a young child)

It's not that these stories make me do things differently. I am realist enough to see that it depends on a whole lot of things whether something happens in a specific way . . . But it sort of gives a feeling of how it could be . . . I like to read about how people deal with things. My baby never died, but I can imagine what it must be like now and I can imagine how people around me will react, the sort of difficulties to expect. How to cope with it, where to go for help. (Lauren Terberg)

I like to read things like 'Mother and Daughter'. That is a column in *Libelle*. I like to know how others get on with their children. I think that is important. Couple in therapy, because of a divorce or illness. I read that kind of thing. Especially about illness. And they also give a doctor's opinion and questions from people. I would not write myself , but I can imagine that when you are feeling down, you want advice. I like to read the answers they give, you can learn from that. Maybe later you will be able to use it . . . or help people near you. (Marie Stemerdink)

What I like about the therapeutical articles [in *Cosmopolitan*] is that they give lots of examples. So and so has been through such and such an experience after which follows the life story of the lady in question. Things really looked bad, this woman has a hard time with her problem, but then she realized this or that, went to see a therapist or talked about it with her boyfriend or a woman friend or someone, and then they describe her solution to show you that she is really happy now. So it is really about how you can make yourself change. They're nice stories. They lift the spirits. (May Han)

You do pick things up from the magazines. I never really read the medical page, because they use such difficult words, but when they have something on menstruation, or a little pain here or there, I read that. It soothes me, it makes me think, oh, I don't have to worry over that . . . If you think, something is wrong and you read about it, you think, no, it's quite normal. (. . .) And sometimes they have things about psychic problems and that kind of thing happens with people you know or, like, in my work I see that kind of thing happen. (. . .) I work in surveillance. I work in the street, come into people's homes, and you have to deal with that kind of thing. (. . .) No one teaches you, tells you how to handle that. But you do pick those things up from a magazine. (Pam Gradanus, police officer)

I love the problem pages, I really do . . . It's the answers. I always think, if somebody wants to ask you a question like that . . . and I sort of knew what they, the editors, put in . . . I might be able to tell them what they said . . . because it does give you a better outlook. (Mary Croston)

I really like [the regular columns]. (. . .) I have two children myself and often you can recognize things. (Mrs Dobbel).

Just Seventeen had lots of problems and wonderful problems, you know. You're sure the people are making it up, but you want a view on it . . . you learn a lot from other people's problems, I think, and the advice they give. (Mona Brooks)

Reading about other people's experiences ratifies your own. To recognize that other people have the same problems raising their children makes us feel better about what we have achieved ourselves. Stories related by others in the magazines may help give meaning to problems and experiences that could not be analysed before. The repertoire that brings together the quotations above explains women's magazine reading as a quest for understanding. Field Belenky et al. (1986), in a study on epistemological development in women, characterize the difference between 'understanding' and 'knowledge' as follows:

> By *understanding* we mean something akin to the German word *kennen*, the French *connaître*, the Spanish *conocer*, or the Greek *gnosis* (. . .) implying personal acquaintance with an object (usually but not always a person). Understanding involves intimacy and equality between self and object, while *knowledge* (*wissen*, *savoir*, *saber*) implies separation from the object and mastery over it. Understanding . . . entails acceptance. It precludes evaluation, because evaluation puts the object at a distance, places the self above it, and quantifies a response to the object that should remain qualitative. (pp. 100–101)

They introduce the concept of 'connected knowers', who, according to them,

> develop procedures for gaining access to other people's knowledge. At the heart of these procedures is the capacity for empathy. Since [they hold the view that] knowledge comes from experience, the only way they can hope to understand another person's ideas is to try to share the experience that has led the person to form the idea. (p. 113)

It will be clear that connected knowing is not highly self-reflexive. Experience and intuition are valued over (pure) reason. It is exactly this form of knowing that is illustrated by the above quotations. It is evident that the speakers value hearing about how others cope. The kind of solution they are interested in, when they read about other people's problems, is views rather than rules or procedures. Women's magazines are regarded as a stock of visions rather than as an absolute authority. Although both the repertoire of practical knowledge and the repertoire of connected knowing and emotional learning are about gaining a form of control over one's life, control is fantasized in vastly different ways. Moreover, the situations and potential problems one would like to have control over are very different.

Basically, the repertoire of connected knowing addresses crisis situations, which involve aspects of one's personality that are different from those required when simply maintaining daily routine by, for example, deciding what to prepare for dinner. The repertoire of connected knowing is one way of trying to come to terms with what in the end are the highly shaky pillars we build our lives on: the expectation that a love relationship will continue, that loved ones will be healthy and will, preferably, outlive us, that we ourselves will be healthy, that our careers will not be wrecked, that our children will grow up to be responsible adults and not drug users, cheats or prostitutes. Respondents refer to (emotional) learning as a means of becoming less insecure, less frightened by all that may destroy the safe and comfortable routine of their lives, their relationships, their confidence that they are doing 'the right thing'. They try to imagine what they would do or how they would feel if that happened to them.

The ideal self as conjured up by the quotations grouped under the heading of the repertoire of connected knowing and emotional learning is very different from the fantasy self as conjured up by the repertoire of practical knowledge. This fantasy self is prepared in case something befalls us or those close to us; it is at peace with the imperfections of humankind, as well as our own. Our personal worries, mistakes and faults are erased in a comparative understanding. The fantasy is also of being a 'wise woman'. Marie Stemerdink talked of being able to 'help people near you'. Pam Gradanus said, 'They have things about psychic problems . . . No one teaches you . . . how to handle that.' Mary Croston felt the problem pages gave her a 'better outlook' and that she might be able to tell someone who asked her a question about something she'd read what the editors said. Understanding does not preclude some playfulness. May Han, for example, had much fun with the quizzes in *Cosmopolitan* and other upmarket women's magazines, but also felt she learned from them.

Neither the non-worrying ideal woman, who is at peace with her own imperfections, nor the wise woman is necessarily a mother or a motherly person. Women who do not have children or wish to have them and women who live without a partner share in these fantasies just as much as those who live with children, as is illustrated by my informants. The women's magazine text does not need to apply directly to one's personal circumstances to be of interest. Mary Croston hopes that she will be able to help other people when they ask her for advice. May Han likes to read uplifting stories about how other women cope: with men, careers and so on. Both use the repertoire of connected knowing to feel stronger.

Of course, the repertoire of connected knowing may also help to boost professional confidence. Pam Gradanus stated (see above) that articles in the domestic weeklies dealing with psychic disorders inform her about how to cope with such situations in her work as a policewoman as well as in her private life. Later on in the interview she mentioned that she also reads a popular, general audience weekly, for diversion and to learn from it, in the same way as she reads women's magazines:

> What I also read, from time to time, is *Panorama* [a popular, general audience weekly]. They have good articles. Lots of background stuff. Like, one of their reporters had been in a jail for a couple of days. I like to read that kind of background article . . . things that have to do with your profession. They had this analysis, recently, about that guy in Rotterdam who stabbed all those women. *Panorama* had a background article on him. I like to read that. What kind of person is he? Why did he do it? 'Cause in the end, he doesn't know himself. But why do they do it? (Pam Gradanus)

Boundary areas between the repertoires

As has been mentioned above, the repertoires are analytical constructs. The boundaries between them, on the level of everyday talk, are not always easy to recognize. Readers mix repertoires, just as everyday speakers will mix metaphors or come up with new ones. Two overlapping boundary areas are important in relation to the repertoire of connected knowing, one of which is with the repertoire of melodrama (which will be discussed more extensively in chapter 5).

The repertoire of melodrama recognizes the tragic quality of life much more strongly and in a much more sentimental and emotional vein than the repertoire of connected knowing. Instead of seeking reassurance, calmness or wisdom, the repertoire of melodrama almost relishes wrongdoing, injustice and misfortune. It recognizes that nothing much can be done about it. The same kind of sad story that at other times serves as an example of what one may learn from women's magazines and how they help you to prepare for the vagaries of life serves as an example of life's unfairness, of the agony measured out to those who least deserve it, which could just as easily have been you. Although the repertoire of melodrama was used more often to talk about gossip magazines, in the quotations below it is used instead of the repertoire of connected knowing to talk about domestic weeklies. The repertoire of connected knowing portrays the reader as impressed but collected; the repertoire of melodrama portrays the reader as overcome. The margin between being impressed and learning, and having a good cry, is a small one. Note the similarity of what Elizabeth Veenstra says to what Lauren Terberg said in one of the examples quoted above ('My baby never died, but I can imagine what it must be like now').

What I really find awful . . . I cried my eyes out . . . they had a story about a small child who was incurably ill and who died . . . That is so awful. I can really imagine [that happening]. (Elizabeth Veenstra)

[Can you remember a nice story you read recently?] Well, an impressive story, of a family whose little boy had some kind of illness, and he had had a blood transfusion and it turned out that he had been infected with AIDS – a little child, a boy of ten years old, and he died of it. She told the whole story: child in the hospital, child out of the hospital, how she told him about it, how the outside world reacted. That was very impressive. (Ina Dammers)

Lauren Terberg mentioned that she 'reads the Christmas specials, you know, with those awfully pitiful enclosures'. Others moved seamlessly from women's magazines to genres they enjoyed far more when they used the repertoire of melodrama. Solema Tillie especially liked the cheapest kind of romance novel, the ones that resemble exercise books: 'I prefer when it is about a mother and child. I really like that. And they are so pitiful that tears well up in your eyes . . . You read them to give you something to do, but sometimes they are really instructive.' Dot Groeniers was, as she herself put it, 'addicted' to a particular kind of film that she had to cry over. She gave an example involving a tragic love affair. Other examples concerning women's magazine melodrama, the tragic quality of life and 'enjoying other people's misery', as one informant called it, will be found in chapter 5, which discusses the repertoires through which reading gossip magazines is made meaningful.

The other overlapping repertoire boundary that is relevant here is the one between the repertoire of connected knowing and the repertoire of practical knowledge. Ina Dammers's account of how she talked to her new dentist about her fears regarding all the treatment required – she had not been to a dentist in twenty years – may serve as an example: 'I was afraid of the dentist . . . then we had this new dentist, who explained what needed to be done, and it [the reconstruction of her teeth] wasn't too bad . . . I wouldn't just say, 'Oh dear, oh dear', I'd talk about it. And that is the kind of thing you learn from women's magazines. (. . .) For I like to be a bit certain; I really hate being uncertain.' Ina Dammers talks about learning from women's magazines to alley her anxiety through understanding her fears, and about her ideal of being a pragmatic, rational consumer (or, in this case, a dentist's patient) who is in control.

Empowerment and criticism

Both the repertoire of practical knowledge and the repertoire of connected knowing may help readers to gain (an imaginary and temporary) sense of identity and confidence, of being in control or feeling at peace with life, that lasts while they are reading and dissipates quickly when the magazine is put aside. At least, that is my explanation for the fact that I found remnants of these forms of empowerment in the interviews, but also criticism and disappointment. Of course, readers do pick up practical tips, ready-made solutions for everyday problems, and they may feel prepared for all sorts of relational and emotional disasters. But, judging by the interviews, this is not the most important goal they served. However paradoxical this may sound, the pleasure of reading and the effectiveness of women's magazines seem situated at a level that is relatively far removed from everyday life. The recipes and patterns, for example, that were often mentioned were just as often not very good or could never be found again when they were needed. Marie Stemerdink and Pam Gradanus were the only two who emphasized that they collected recipes. Marie Stemerdink kept old recipes in plastic bags in the attic because it would be a shame to throw them out. Pam Gradanus thought she *might* be able to find them again (my emphasis). Joan Becker had collected pull-out booklets with tips and patterns that she threw out after a couple of years. Valerie van Eijck had endlessly kept magazines and thrown them out in a fit of clearing up. Mary Croston has no problems in hanging on to interesting recipes; she puts them in an old cookery book. The gardening tips are another matter, however: 'Oh, yes! Cooking tips. I cut some of them out sometimes. I've got an old cookery book and if I see tips in [the magazines], I cut them out and keep them all together right there. Mind you, I do that with some of the gardening tips sometimes. When I go to look for them, I can't find them! [She laughs.]' Mrs Parry simply likes reading tips and she does not cut them out; she is amazed sometimes at how much she knows when she comes across a tip she has seen before. Karen de Wit had tried a *Viva* cake recipe, which came out of the oven like a brick. She is not going to try *Viva* recipes again, no matter how interesting they may look. Rebecca Priest also enjoys the tips: 'I like the ones that give you ideas, information, cookery, recipes . . . practical magazines that come up with ideas. [I'll] tear them out and put them somewhere and try them. (. . .) And with some of them you get a free pattern. [Do you ever use them?] Once [she laughs], but it was drastic, didn't look at all like in the picture.' Tina Poorter still plans 'to make a book with those tips'.

These remarks relativize women's magazines' practical use. They make clear that the tips, the recipes and the patterns in themselves hardly constitute the value of women's magazines for readers. It is only through a repertoire that allows readers to fantasize about being well-organized, perfect women who keep the tips they collect in handy files, who can find the right recipe or tip whenever they want to, that the magazines become meaningful and worthwhile. Janice Winship stresses the fictional quality of the pleasure ('mental chocolate') women take in women's magazines. She relates her argument in particular to the advertisements: 'Women's magazines offer . . . imaginative story lines in which women achieve the successes and satisfactions everyday life cannot be depended upon to deliver' (1987: 53).

Mary Croston's fond memories of crocheting intricate little table-mats and the like still make her look for patterns in the magazines, even though she cannot crochet them any more. She savours the memory over the pain reading must also bring: 'If there are any crocheting patterns in, I like to have a look at those. (. . .) Sometimes I take the patterns out. It depends. Some things are beyond me. (. . .) These little lace mats that you crochet with cotton, they are beyond me now, with my eyes. (. . .) I make so many mistakes and I have to keep unpicking it, you know. It's no fun doing it any more.'

As regards the repertoire of connected knowing, the chances are that when a child dies or becomes very ill, or when a relationship goes wrong, the magazines will not be much help. In chapter 3 I quote an example of how a divorce ruined everyday existence and the reassurances built into everyday routine to such an extent that what had been read in women's magazines paled into insignificance. Women's magazines are simply too much part of and predicated on those routines. Some readers were also sceptical about the capacity of women's magazines to emancipate readers – to help them, for example, to talk back to overbearing specialists and to be more in control of their own health and health care: 'Those specialists in the magazines are always so nice and friendly and understanding. Well, I never met those in a hospital. "You can ask me anything." "Don't let them fob you off." That's nonsense. You don't stand a chance. They can always browbeat you. I have a ready tongue, but it has happened to me too' (Elizabeth Veenstra).

In general, it seems to be true that the medical advice, which so many described as reassuring and interesting, inspires both positive and negative comments. Some of my informants were very critical of the flood of medical advice that is printed. Annie Duindam felt it was useful to compare your experiences with those of others, after you have been through something. But to read these things in advance, would serve only to make you eternally anxious. 'You'd be thinking every day, I may have breast cancer tomorrow. You wouldn't have a life.' Mrs Dobbel also thinks reading medical pages makes sense only when you see something about an illness you have had. Tina Poorter was even more explicit: 'I have had it with those medical pieces, I was at my GP's every day! When I read about it, I thought I had it too. The children were small and you'll catch anything and you're easily depressed . . . In the end my GP said, "What have you been reading again? Don't read that rubbish." (. . .) And then you think, dammit, why do they print all that!?'

It will be clear that the repertoire of connected knowing does not help us to feel in control, once the possible dangers become too real. Margot Klein, who is not a women's magazine reader, was struck by all the information that is printed on breast cancer in the newspapers alone, which supposedly could be made sense of by using the repertoire of connected knowing. Her husband died of cancer and she herself has had treatment for breast cancer. She is very critical: 'You get so overfed with information. Even when you only read the newspapers. This can influence [having cancer] or your personality structure, the kind of life you have had, anything else you can think of . . . You start to feel that it is being blamed on you: you didn't live a healthy life, it's your own fault that you have this. (. . .) It drives me completely nuts, and that can't have been their intention, can it?'

Women's magazines may empower readers temporarily at precisely those moments when they are read by helping them to build fantasies of ideal selves that may or may not correspond to real life, or to one another, and give readers the feeling they will be able to cope. The things you learn and pick up may feel like a store of knowledge and thus give a certain authority. Temporarily the fantasies inspired by reading strengthen particular identities. One should speak of 'moments of empowerment', then, rather than of empowerment *tout court*. Empowerment suggests one-way reinforcement and a prolonged effect, whereas there seems to be a continuing dialogue between readers and magazines. Readers are often disappointed with particular titles. Some reflect sarcastically on the genre as a whole, such as Elizabeth Veenstra, who quite likes reading women's magazines: 'If you had to do all those things they write about [cook, knit, sew and the rest], you wouldn't have time to do anything else any more.' It is not surprising, therefore, that subscriptions are cancelled or changed regularly. Readers will turn to other genres and other media. All reading pleasure, be it of the edifying kind or not, is temporary. 'I used to buy *Flair* every week. I don't do that any more. At times it revolts you. I've noticed I don't read the magazines from cover to cover any more. I don't relish them any more. I think that has changed. I only realize that now [that I am talking to you] . . . It's the same with reading romances. There are periods and for two weeks you read one a day and then you think pfff, and you feel silly and ridiculous for doing that, and God, don't I have anything better to do?' (Lauren Terberg).

How women's magazines become meaningful for male readers

Men are not generally noted for their capacity to listen or for their powers of understanding. Stereotypical males are 'doers' rather than 'listeners'. The repertoire of connected knowing would seem to be particularly far removed from the male experience of the world, to overstate the case slightly. The repertoire of practical knowledge too would not seem to suit men, in the form described above. Since they are still not doing half or even a quarter of household chores and do not, in overwhelming numbers, take care of children, despite over twenty years of women's struggle (Driehuis and Meeus, 1986; Hochschild, 1989), they would probably not find fantasies of being a perfect home-maker highly appealing. Going by stereotypes, it is hard to fathom why men read women's magazines at all. But they do, as will become clear from the quotations cited below. The stereotypical male, who would never own up to reading women's magazines, is not wholly a figure of popular imagination, though. Many women readers had vivid examples. The following is from a group interview with British students in Amsterdam:

Mona Brooks: And they want their wives to buy them and then they read them.

Natacha Cuellar: Definitely, definitely, I remember *Jackie* at school – boys definitely read it, of course they do. (. . .) I honestly don't think men are lying [when they say they don't read women's magazines] . . . I think they have a false image of themselves. They think themselves more macho than they really are. They do it without realizing it.

The most loathsome aspect of women's magazines from a male point of view seems to be the problem page. At the end of the first interview I had with Linda Zijlstra I challenged her to find out how the men she socialized with thought about women's magazines. Indignant, she reported on her finds in the second interview. She had asked male friends what a male version of a women's magazine such as *Woman's Own* – a *Man's Own*, so to speak – would have to look like to appeal to them.

I talked about men's magazines [a male version of women's magazines] with some guys I know, and [they said] 'Would I have to read about other people's problems!?' So I said, 'well, no problem page, fine. What would you want to be in such a magazine?' And I said, 'A horoscope?' Guys usually like horoscopes, a good short story, a page with new products that you can buy; recipes were OK, if they were easy, microwave. And I thought, how disgustingly this confirms sex-role patterns. I simply named a few categories of articles, but they wouldn't hear of having a problem page, they thought that was really [too much]. (Linda Zijlstra)

But men who value women's magazines in their own right and are willing to own up to that do exist, even if it is rather difficult to find them. Most of the men Joppe Boodt and I spoke to read the magazines their partners buy, but some buy their own. 'There was a time I bought them for Kitty, pretending I was not buying these for myself but for my girlfriend . . . while actually I liked to read them very much' (Ard Pennings). Karel Messing exchanges magazines with his mother and sister and occasionally buys *Viva* or *Flair* (magazines for young women) when they have feature articles he feels he will be interested in, such as interviews with famous actors or actresses, 'or an interview with a Russian soldier' (which took place during the fall of the Soviet Union). Frank Stevens treats himself to expensive glossy magazines.

In the interviews with the men too women's magazines were valued for providing instant, short reads.

> [Do you like reading short stories?] I do, before I go to sleep . . . That's where I usually read [the women's magazines] . . . in bed. That's where they are. Caroline reads them in the morning and I read a few snippets at night. A couple of problems every day. By then I'm fast asleep, so I take my time with *Viva*. Or, when I've finished the newspaper, I'll look for something else to read and that could be *Viva*.
>
> [Later on in the interview] I wouldn't read *Opzij* [a Dutch feminist magazine]. I don't particularly like long articles. [An article about] four women professors, I seem to remember, but I never finished it. Although sometimes they have quizzes, quizzes and tests, and I do love those . . . about women–men relations . . . men and children, the new fatherhood. (Peter Smit)

> That's how I read a magazine [leafing through a copy], like this. This kind of thing takes me much too long [points to a feature article] and I won't read it, or it would have to be very interesting, but that hardly ever happens. Usually . . . those medical things, are short pieces, I like to read those, like about German measles, because we have a little daughter of our own now. (Paul Mortier)

> I like to read them in the evening, when the others have gone to bed. (Tom Vonk)

> The problem page is a bit like a video clip. Short bits, you read it and you're done. A whole article, I wouldn't read that. (Yao Hua Han)

> I read them quite a lot because I work at a [sports centre], they have this collection and when you have an hour off, then you read quite a lot. (Charles Vlaming)

> I think it does depend on the environment you live in. I mean, when there are children, you spend more time at home. My wife'll

buy one of those mags; she goes to the supermarket and comes back with *Libelle*. I am watching television, doing nothing, that thing is lying there. I've finished the newspaper, I'll read that mag. And every now and then there's something interesting in them' . . . [Leo is a physiotherapist in a group practice; at his workplace there is a collection of magazines for the waiting-room]. If it is very interesting, a longer article, or a special issue, I'll take it home for the weekend. (. . .) Usually what happens is that a patient cancels an appointment or they are having [machine] treatment for ten minutes and I am in the coffee room for ten minutes on my own. I have to kill time. It's too short to read professional journals, so I try to relax a bit and I'll start reading that *Margriet*, or whatever is lying on top. (Leo de Jong)

Men, even more than women, read magazines because they are available. They are in the house, next to the bed, and they provide short and easy reads. Note, though, that what in the women's description of reading was called the 'easily put down' theme, for most of the men has to do not only with other obligations they have, but also with the limited extent (compared with the women) to which they find the content of women's magazines interesting. For them women's magazines are easy to put down too, but both in the literal and in the metaphorical sense of the expression. They take it far less for granted that there will be interesting articles in the magazines.

Given that men, on average, work outside the home more than women, and, also on average, spend more hours per week working outside the home (women tend to have part-time jobs far more than men), it is not really surprising that the men reported that they read at work and for their work – like Carla Willems or Rebecca Priest, who reads when it is quiet in her shop, or like Pam Gradanus, who occasionally uses what she reads in women's magazines for her work as a police officer.

> Like those fashion pictures, they are trendsetters. They set a trend for the next season, and if I have to do a commercial, I have to go along with that. (Menno Bottenburg, film producer)

> I put copies in the classroom for children who are bored. (Frank Stevens, teacher)

> Garden design used to be my profession, so the interest stays. (. . .) Every now and then they have something about English gardens, cottages, that is very beautiful. (Lodewijk van Straten)

I always read the medical page. But that is professional interest. People come with questions. They often describe obscure ailments, an unknown syndrome or a difficult illness that occurs in 1 in 300,000, but people come and ask whether they have it (. . .) especially with joints. Or if there's something new for rheumatism. (Leo de Jong, physiotherapist)

The cult of women's appearance is kind of funny for guys to read about. (. . .) Gives you different thoughts. As women, you need half a day to look passable and it costs you half your salary as well. I tend to look at [articles about] it, because it occupies me too, as a visual artist. (. . .) I paint mainly. And there is a parallel between an attractive kind of painting and an attractive woman's face. It is a kind of palette, painting of the face. (Yao Hua Han)

When I had just started working [as a nurse for mentally deficient children], you know, I read a lot about parents who had a mentally deficient child . . . that kind of thing. [To have an idea of what they experienced?] For my own education; you will carry it with you towards the parents when they come. (Charles Vlaming)

How men use the repertoires

In the interviews with men one occasionally catches a glimpse of the repertoire of practical knowledge and the repertoire of connected knowing. Tom Vonk is interested in the recipes, which he makes photocopies of. (His family subscribes to a magazine collection, and the magazines they read have to be returned at the end of every week in exchange for a new set.) Paul Mortier reads the medical page if the subjects are relevant in relation to the health of their little daughter. Leo de Jong felt: 'With those cooking columns, you get to know other products. It keeps you informed.' The more extensive articles made him 'pick things up'. Menno Bottenburg said, 'An article about cancer of the cervix is interesting to me too', when asked whether he felt closed out of the community of intended readers.

When I have time, I read the recipes and the ingredients and I think, oh, I'll make that one – not that I ever do . . . but I do like to read them. And what I also like is to read about emotional problems, about relationships and so on, and what they say in the magazines. In [this month's] *Avenue* [Dutch glossy magazine] they have something about relationships and sexuality, or so it says on the cover. I read that kind of thing. [Do you read about that kind of thing in a domestic weekly like *Margriet* too?] I'm always interested in reading about the problems women have with men. [Funny that you say, 'problems women have with men'.] Well, if they had gents' magazines about the problems gentlemen have among themselves, I might read that too. But I don't know such magazines. (Frank Stevens)

I really prefer *Viva* [to *Cosmopolitan*, which his sister passes on to him] . . . like the help page, and that kind of problem, they make that really . . . interesting. (. . .) And *Flair* has articles that interest me, about plastic surgery, going out and fashion. (. . .) I must say, *Viva* has things about relationships and how to handle problems, that have enlightened me. I do think I have learned something from reading [women's magazines]. I look at problems in a different light, or situations, or relationships, or how to manage a certain kind of problem; you start to see these things in a new light, and that is discussed on the help page. (. . .) *Margriet* and *Libelle* deal with such things much more comprehensively. Like how to live with a partner who is ill . . . and they'll have a two- or three-page article. And that can move me, how people have managed to go on after a stroke, or how they have handled not being able to have children, or that they really would like to have them and how such a process works. Or someone who has lost her husband. (Karel Messing)

When they discuss one issue and they have different people talking about it, their opinion, or what kind of problem they have, they discuss it more extensively. There isn't one answer. But those problem pages have answers that really irritate me. I think . . . it ain't that simple, folks. There are no stupid questions, I'll think, there are only stupid answers. You do learn from it. (. . .) When they have something about someone who is very surly, or autistic children, just to give an example. (. . .) When you meet such a child and they turn away or don't react at all, you think, that's a sweetie. And you think, I'll get going, ciao. But when you know that child is autistic and you know what that means, you don't react that way. (. . .) You do, occasionally, read about things that have happened to you too, because they always have such general problems. And you think, that happened to me too, see what their answer is. You get that in interviews too and people give their own solutions. (Lodewijk van Straten)

Obviously, men also use the repertoires of practical knowledge and of connected knowing. They partly use them in exactly the same way as the women do, but at times there is a difference. Women may occasionally make fun of their pleasure in the problem page and talk about reading it with a gleam in their eyes, but our interviews suggest that men tend to be more critical or even dismissive. They give their words an ironic or satirical twist that goes much further than the – also self-reflexive – fun the women make of reading – and in a way enjoying – other people's problems. The men identify far less often with what others write or talk about in interviews. They tend to show distance rather than connectedness, as much about their own reading as about the content of the magazines, as will become clear in the next section.

Apologetic reading: ironizing women's magazines

Apparently the difference between being moved and being amused is not all that big. It seems to lie in whether or not problems are (also) taken seriously. Tom Vonk is a typical borderline case. I found his appreciation of the letters to the editor slightly disturbing. At first it seemed as if he read women's magazines through the repertoire of connected knowing. A closer look revealed that he finds the letters to the editor touching because they are always slightly awkward. He does not like them because he can identify with their writers or relate to them on the same level, he positions himself as an observer. Likewise, when he says he learns from some of the articles, he means the articles help him to understand his wife better, rather than himself.

Joke: What do you like about the letters from readers?
Tom I think they represent real life. Someone recounts experiences from his [*sic*] life. What I really like about them is that it is not professional but, often, *a little awkward*. It is touching . . . funny too, when someone tries to make something funny out of a tiny thing. (. . .) It has real emotion.
Joke: What is so exciting about 'real life'?
Tom: I am enormously interested in people and in meeting people and in what keeps them busy and what makes them go on this earth . . . And I do think that sometimes you start to understand about people. How they deal with different things, what moved them in a specific situation. That is the kind of thing you cull from [readers' letters] more easily than from [one of those professional columns]. With them I think, you have been observing that on purpose.
Joke: Do you feel you understand more about yourself by reading those letters?

Tom: Sometimes . . . it may happen that I understand things better in
my relationship with my wife. That I understand better how *she*
has reacted to certain things. [My italic]

Tom Vonk's answers reflect a form of male conceit. He does not seem
to feel he either needs or would like to learn more about himself, even
though he is interested in knowing more about other people. His
answers reminded me more of the professional column writers he
scorns than of the readers whose letters he likes to read. He does not
seem to identify with them at all. He observes them and enjoys their
slightly clumsy efforts.

Interviews with other men give the same impression of distance, of
'this cannot touch my core, my personality; this is not who I am'. The
interview with Peter Smit provides a good example of the difference
between what his wife, Caroline, who briefly sat down with us
during the interview, and he pick up from women's magazines. Peter
has been making fun of the problem page.

Joke: You tend to take a rather distanced attitude towards [letters
people write to magazines]?
Peter: I would never write a letter myself. (. . .) But maybe men,
well, sometimes men write letters . . .
Joke: Every once in a while they do, don't they?
Peter: Well, I don't feel any affinity to them. It's not like, here is
someone who speaks on my behalf too.
Joke: Funny, I do have that, sometimes.
Caroline: I have that too. I think . . . that I recognize something. Not all
of it, but you do get things out of it . . . That is the way I read
them too.
Peter: Maybe that is because it is usually women who write . . .
because those men who write, they write about 'Aren't I
modern and emancipated?' You read that with a . . . [We all
laugh.]

Peter Smit makes clear that men writing to women's magazines (or at
least the kind of letter that is printed, as he points out later) can be an
object of ridicule. But he does not pick up my point that he feels no
connection at all with what the women write. Below he makes fun of
the letters teenagers and young women write, after having explained
why he occasionally likes to read women's magazines.

I think [some women's magazines] are kind of nice; it varies, really.
Some articles have my full attention and other things I pass by, like

fashion . . . I am not interested in that. (. . .) What I do find interesting is short stories and those pages with film and book and record reviews, which keep you in touch, and interviews about a certain kind of subject: relationships, mothers and daughters and, I don't know, how people lose their boyfriends and those kinds of questions of life and then four or five people relating their story. [He gives more examples and then makes a joke about his favourite page.] There is one page about how to get rid of spots and I am especially in favour of broken relationships and 'What do I do?' [Laughter] 'My boyfriend hasn't made love to me for five years, what do I do?' (. . .) Sometimes you laugh because of the ignorance of people, a kind of gloating, and sometimes it is nice to read because you think, what would I answer?

In this quotation almost all the themes and repertoires discussed in this chapter are mixed together. He implies that he 'learns' from more or less serious articles on relationships. He likes to read short bits and pieces. He relates what he reads to his work (he is a psychologist, and in that capacity also acts as an adviser to people). He finds women's magazines practically useful: to keep him up to date about what one should read, listen to, go to. However, neither he nor Tom Vonk or any of the other men seem to share all that much in the particular fantasies that resound in the interviews with the women.

Karel Messing seems to be an exception in that he, like the women, talks about how reading women's magazines has changed him: 'I do think I have learned something from reading [women's magazines]. I look at problems in a different light, or situations, or relationships, or to how manage a certain kind of problem.' He shares in the fantasy of building a new, better self, more attuned to other people's needs; he might well experience feelings of authority as well as identity, tied up with understanding other people. The other men too indicate that they at times learn from women's magazines. It does not seem to touch them, however. If reading does touch upon fantasies of ideal selves, on imagined forms of identity and authority, it seems to be routed through their professional selves: being a psychologist or the head of a school. Although they appear to be talking about emotional learning, they do not appear to use the repertoire of connected knowing. They do not read or learn for their own, personal sakes. Peter at times thinks, what would I answer? Tom Vonk's reply focuses on being amused.

Their slightly wry tone also implies an apologetic stance – which, in a way, is warranted by the situation, but may also point to a more general difference between how women and men talk about reading.

The men were, of course, well aware that they are not women's magazines' intended audience. To be interviewed about a genre that is not produced for you could make anyone feel slightly uncomfortable. Irony and sarcasm are means to keep things at a distance. Irony detaches the speaker from what she or he is speaking about. Irony enables a male speaker to say, at the same time, I am a reader of a rather dreadful genre and I cannot be identified with it. I therefore interpret the way Tom Vonk, Peter Smit and Leo de Jong use the repertoires in a slightly different way than I interpreted the women's investment in the repertoires. Partly, they share in the fantasy of the well-informed rational consumer (the repertoire of practical knowledge), though their imaginary construct is of a consumer of culture (books, new albums, films and cooking, not of household tips). In as far as they are interested in reading and learning about people's emotions, it is to feed a fantasy of 'a wise man' with a strong sense of self, who oversees and consequently literally looks down on the problems of others. The 'wise woman' ideal self, in contrast to the 'wise man', shares, compares and recognizes. She tries to learn about her own feelings and her own personality through the stories of others. The 'wise woman' fantasy does not involve a hierarchical difference as the fantasy of being a 'wise man' does.

I am not suggesting that men and women read women's magazines in highly different ways. On the contrary, I have shown that the same repertoires surface in the interviews with the men. In some of the interviews (not, for instance, in the interview with Karel Messing) it seemed to me that the repertoire of emotional learning and connected knowing was given a slight twist. Possibly this was the result of a sense of uneasiness on the part of the interviewed men. It certainly seems influenced by the fact that Tom Vonk and Peter Smit in particular had recourse to highly suitable professional identities to legitimate their interest in other people's personal stories. Various authors have shown that for men professional identities are often much stronger than personal identities (Segal, 1990; Seidler, 1991; Tolson, 1978).

Two things are important to note. The men I interviewed used the repertoire of practical knowledge more than the women to mould themselves into well-informed consumers of culture. Like, among others, some of the women in the *Cosmopolitan* group interviews, they underscored that they were cultured persons rather than persons interested in taking up a position that would come close to the stereotype of the housewife. My material suggests that creating a (temporary) position of the cultured consumer is not a highly gendered form of identity work. Like the repertoire of practical knowledge, the repertoire of connected knowing does not need to feed into highly gendered fantasies and positions, however unconsciously taken up. Both women and men may choose to present or fantasize about themselves as professional connected knowers. Pam Gradanus, for one, explicitly took up both: she felt she learned from the magazines about mental illness, for example, and that she would benefit from this if something happened to someone she knew or if she came across it in her work as a police officer.

The other point is that if two interviewers can find ironic detachment and even outright derision (see below) in interviews with men who did identify with the idea of occasionally reading or browsing through women's magazines, it seems more than likely that women readers will receive a great deal more unfavourable comment from all those men who would never identify themselves as 'occasional women's magazine readers'. As we found out, there are many of those. Below is a quotation taken from the interview with Menno Bottenburg. His mild derision seems to cross over from making fun of women's magazines into camp, which will be discussed more extensively in chapter 5. It was used more for gossip magazines than for 'regular' women's magazines, either domestic weeklies or glossy monthlies.

> For me [women's magazines] have little value. (. . .) And I don't think they have all that much value for women either. If I think of how those magazines are read at my parents', it is browsing. Newest fashions. And a story [in *Cosmopolitan*] about some men having an orgasm in two minutes and others in ten; those girls couldn't care less as long as it goes OK . . . But for me that is enough to make me die laughing. (. . .) As a kid, I read those magazines [domestic weeklies] at the home of a friend, the problem page and those stupid problems: 'Now that I am on a diet, my breasts are starting to sag.' That kind of things stays with you when you are a teenager, that appeals to you. (Menno Bottenburg)

It needs to be stressed again that derision is not the prerogative of men. Women can be just as harsh in their contempt, even if they are less often so. If anything, men seem to be more naïve than women about the impact of their critical remarks and about the cultural status of women's magazines. Lodewijk van Straten, for example, had asked colleagues whether they read women's magazines and was astonished by their reaction that reading women's magazines, especially for men, was 'not done': 'It seems to be taboo for men to say that they read women's magazines.' Yao Hua Han, like so many, used the interview to reflect on women's magazines. Throughout the interview he leafed through the magazines that he buys and reads out of what he (like Frank Stevens) calls 'visual interest'. His almost surprised conclusion – while speaking he realized he also likes women's magazines for some aspects of their content – may serve as a suitable final quotation to characterize how men read women's magazines.

> They have just about written everything there is to say about [problems, relationships, emotions] and they keep having to come up with new problems, of course. I didn't read this article . . . but that is interesting. Not just about one person but about everybody, that you can do something with yourself [interpret your own feelings rather than have an expert interpret them for you. I mind those] mini bibles at the end. (. . .) I do like that category of feature in general, and it is typical of women's magazines. That kind of story, you won't find in any other kind of magazine . . . It is unique to women's magazines. Human interest in the private sphere. I don't know any other kind of magazine that has those kinds of things. If it was on television . . . it would be psychology for beginners. (Yao Hua Han)

The gendered significance of women's magazines

The repertoires offer readers a means by which to fantasize about perfect selves: the perfect listener, the perfect cook, the up-to-date consumer or cultured person, the calm, confident realist. These fantasies are not to be found at the surface of how reading women's magazines is talked about. The surface often consists of denial and standoffishness or remoteness. Readers will say women's magazines are not all that important to them, or that if there were no women's magazines, they would probably find something else to read. The reconstruction of reading in this chapter is not meant to deny the truth or sincerity of what readers said. Rather, it may be gathered from their sparse comments on the subject that they gave substantial arguments for reading women's magazines, rather than descriptions of how and why they read them (because they are easy to put down and because they are available), that women's magazines also become meaningful through brief moments in which the combination of magazines and repertoires provides unique forms of affirmation, reassurance and dreams of perfection.

In so far as it is possible to generalize on the basis of such a small sample, it would seem to be that men use the repertoires that make women's magazines meaningful in slightly different ways from women. Of course, what male and female readers say about how they read women's magazines (the only way we can have knowledge of how they make sense of them) is influenced by cultural norms regarding what is suitable for women and for men to do and to say. The men tended to be more ironic about reading women's magazines; they made fun of them more often. The women were more serious in their evaluation of the magazines. Is it the case, then, that women and men have different fantasy and identity investments in the magazines?

If gender difference is not foregrounded (or at least not reified), it is possible to analyse the repertoires as divided along fault-lines of taste and professionalism. The repertoire of practical knowledge, which feeds a fantasy of being a well-informed consumer, can be used to mould oneself into a critical consumer of culture (who values magazines for their reviews) or into a consumer of home-related products. Note that both consumers are also producers: the cultural consumer creates 'good taste' or simply 'culture', the home-maker consumer different kinds of produce, such as food, sweaters, tablecloths. Both men and women take up both varieties of the repertoire of practical knowledge, though, admittedly, women talk more about home-making than men do.

The repertoire of connected knowing is likewise divided into two dominant fantasies. Both fantasies are about control (a sense of authority as well as identity) through understanding other people's emotions. One version, however, is directed towards family relationships and oneself, while the other version has to do with professional understanding. (Being a housewife and home-maker is not recognized as a profession or as a skill for which you need particular training. You cannot earn a salary by taking care of a home and a family.) In both cases anxiety (what do I do if such and such happens?) is laid to rest by imagining different scenarios of how one might cope. While, given the dominant image of women as home-makers and providers of emotional care, one would be inclined to think that men would take up the 'professional' version of this repertoire and women the 'personal' version, this is not wholly true. It is the case that women and men generally identify with different versions of the repertoires. But the interview material also shows that men use women's genres and sometimes take up positions and fantasies that are thought to be 'female', whether or not they report on this ironically, and women sometimes read a 'female' genre along 'male' lines, out of professional interest. Some of the women quoted gave examples of the way in which forms of connected knowing and emotional learning were beneficial to how they did their jobs.

Theoretically, it can be concluded that everyday media use becomes meaningful in a process consisting of different facets. On the one hand women's magazines are valued because they fit in easily with everyday duties and obligations, whose execution they do not threaten because they are easy to put down. On the other hand women's magazines need to provide a minimum of diversion and attractive information to make them interesting enough to pick up (though not so riveting that they would be difficult to put down). Such a minimum of diversion and entertainment has to fit into what a reader will recognize as relevant and worthwhile, which she or he does by relating it to the repertoires at her or his disposal. From the perspective of readers women's magazines need to relate to aspects of their identity. They do so by providing material that may help readers imagine 'perfect selves', by building a sense of control or authority or by making them feel 'prepared in case something happens'. As a genre, women's magazines are multi-piece invitations to invest in temporary and imaginary identities. Occasionally a single piece is picked up and used to imagine a perfect self or control over the forces threatening the equilibrium or future of everyday life as it is. This investment on the part of the reader sustains and reproduces a minimum interest in the genre and she or he will continue to use it. It is also possible that a minimum interest is not sustained, the invitations offered are not tempting enough or no longer relate to a reader's daily routines and a reader will find other ways to have a short break from other duties, to fill empty time or to relax. She or he, for the time being, will stop being a reader.

The two main tenets, then, of a theory of everyday media use are, first, that content is less important than whether or not a genre is accommodating, whether or not it can be fitted into everyday obligations; secondly, content has, in some sense, to be relevant to the fantasies, anxieties and preoccupation's of readers (or viewers, in the case of other genres). Relevancy (and thus meaningfulness) is discursively structured and related to social and cultural norms and values. Discursive structures or repertoires can be reconstructed by combining connected fragments from different interviews. Repertoire analysis will reveal on the one hand how a genre or medium is predominantly used (by isolating the most important themes in readers' or viewers' descriptions) and on the other how a genre's significance (or meaningfulness) for readers is structured. By identifying different repertoires (on the basis of interview fragments), it becomes clear how readers feel that the text addresses them, what they fantasize or think about in relation to it and to what extent the text engages or even absorbs them (a useful indication for this may be a comparison of the enthusiasm and talkativeness of readers throughout the interview with how they talk about the genre that is studied in particular).

Women's magazines are a genre that is well suited to being used during short breaks. Using them is relatively easy to defend because they are full of practical information. The attraction of the genre, however, lies in its addressing of any of a wide range of 'selves', for example, your 'practical self', or your 'worried partner or parent self', or your 'cultured person self', which are given form through the different repertoires a reader uses. As a rule readers are not deeply impressed by what the magazines offer, but sometimes a story or a report hits the mark, and that, apparently, is enough to make them return to the magazines, albeit, sometimes, after lengthy periods of non-reading.

3

Portrait of Two Readers

Few books are as impressive to read and reread as Carolyn Steedman's *Landscape for a Good Woman* (1986), in which she describes her own youth and her mother's youth as a connected tale of working-class girlhood in the fifties and twenties in England. Hers is an outstanding piece of feminist, autobiographically inspired work that reconstructs history from concrete, down-to-earth daily experience. I had not read Steedman's book or other feminist studies of women's autobiography (see, for example, Gagnier, 1991; Heilbrun, 1989; Okely, 1986) when I decided to interview my mother. But reading Steedman's powerful text made me aware that the two interviews with my mother, together with my own recollections of her life as a young woman, provided me with a unique perspective on reading women's magazines in a specific, historical context.

When I approached her, my mother and I had not been close for some years. My parents' divorce wrecked family relationships and even casual contact was still problematic. My motive for contacting her was simply to find out which magazines we had had at home. Our rows of previous years had more or less been laid to rest, and I thought I might take the chance and turn my annual visit into an interview. The resulting interview was extremely fruitful. It was a success in research and technical terms in that she provided me with a lucid account of how and why she read women's magazines. Personally, it has made us closer than we were.

The portrait I wrote is not as detailed as Steedman's, nor have I followed her in trying to explain my mother's outlook on life psychoanalytically. I want to make a much simpler point – based on and in dialogue with lengthy interview fragments – about women's magazine reading as part of, and predicated on, one's everyday routines. In chapter 2 I showed how women's magazines are valued most of all because they are easy to put down; reading them is a routine activity that has its often subordinate place among other routine activities. As regards their content, two repertoires, the repertoire of practical knowledge and the repertoire of connected knowing, were used by readers. Both repertoires incorporate fantasies of perfection and control, over highly practical matters and over potential dramas that might permanently upset the safety of one's routines and lifestyle, such as the death of a child, divorce or terminal illness. The first repertoire consists of 'recipe' knowledge, the other centres around understanding as a way of knowing. Knowing about other people's experiences can give us a feeling of being prepared, of being inoculated. In this sense women's magazines are, potentially, empowering, even if they do not always do so, *pace* the criticisms that readers also have, ranging from disappointment with particular recipes to disappointment with the genre at large. My mother's story in a way is an extreme example. It shows that when everyday routines break down – in her case as the result of a divorce – the magazines are no help at all. On the contrary, they may be an active reminder of our failure to keep our life or marriage running smoothly. Women's magazines may be effective in giving us the feeling that reading about disasters and imagining how to reduce them to manageable proportions can ward off dangers. Real life is much harder to control.

In general, this chapter's focus on two individual readers is meant to show that the repertoires structure how women's magazines become meaningful, but that that does not mean women's magazines are always meaningful or have significance. In its search for the structure of cultural meaning production and because of its attention to interview fragments rather than readers, repertoire analysis tends to make the continually shifting and changing character of readers' attachments to magazines invisible, as well as the readers themselves, who are reduced to a few brief quotations in the publication about the research. Only when one has some knowledge of readers' daily lives and personal history can it become clear that women's magazines are not always or continuously meaningful. Interest in them may lapse for all sorts of reasons, for short or long periods of time. On a more abstract level, portraying readers shows that on the one hand the daily routines of which magazine reading is a part neither require reflection on the genre nor allow for it; on the other hand portraying readers brings into focus the temporality of women's magazine reading (over periods of years, or even decades) as well as the fact that readers over time form fairly fixed notions of what magazines are like, what their qualities are or should be. Ethnographic portraits of readers make clear how readers' notions about magazines are reproduced and voiced when readers are asked to reflect on how they read and use them and how they did so in the past.

The portrait of my mother as a reader and as a young woman is followed by some excerpts from interviews with Joan Becker. Joan and I met in 1987 at a group interview on romance reading arranged by students. Because I liked her candour, her enthusiasm and her direct approach to whatever was discussed, I called her to ask if she also read women's magazines and whether I could come to interview her, which I did in January 1989. A little less than a year later I interviewed her again. I know far less about Joan than I know about my mother. From what she has told me I can see that her life story differs from my mother's in major respects, but there are also important similarities that I will use to argue another point that would be difficult to make on the basis of repertoire analysis alone: that the women's movement and feminism challenged and changed women's search for self-esteem, which changed not only the content of women's magazines, but also women's relation to them. My mother's feelings about feminism have changed enormously over the years, from ambivalence (end of the sixties and early seventies) to sympathy (now). Her feelings about women's magazines changed as markedly (though certainly not in direct relation to her more positive feelings about feminism), as the lengthy quotations in this chapter bear out. Joan is not so much ambivalent as slightly defensive when talking about feminism and the women's movement. In a more direct manner than my mother she recognizes that feminist ideology and women's magazines have been pitted as each others opponents; she feels this does not apply to contemporary (late 1980s) quality domestic weeklies, such as the Dutch magazines *Margriet* and *Libelle*, which both she and my mother occasionally read. In this chapter I refer to my mother as such and also as Valerie van Eijck, the pseudonym under which she was quoted in chapter 2.

Portrait of my mother as a magazine reader

My mother was born in 1933 in Indonesia, then a Dutch colony, as the youngest of three children. My mother's family had a long history of working in the 'Dutch Indies', and some of my great-great-grandmothers were Indonesian. My grandfather was a chemical engineer who worked for Shell, then called the Royal Dutch Petrol Company. Just before the Second World War started, they came back to the Netherlands on leave and had to stay. When Rotterdam was bombed by the Germans, they fled, to return later. On the retirement of my grandfather they moved to a quiet village, where my mother took courses in shorthand and commercial correspondence in several languages. My grandfather strongly believed in women being able to earn their own living and he forced her (as well as her older sister) to have professional training, even though she would have preferred to study art history. My mother's brother studied law. From her stories she emerges as a wayward but creative child: she could barely be kept in check by the housekeeper who was employed from her birth onwards because my grandmother was too bedridden and ill to take care of her. I used to think I must have seemed a dull and well-behaved child to my mother, whose antics sounded like heroics to me, even though she also said that she felt very lonely. Both her sister and brother are much older.

She started working at Philips as a secretary (or what would now be called a management assistant), met my father, married him, stopped working and had two children in three years. I remember her playing tennis with a couple of woman friends and I remember we used to make jokes with the children in the street about all the sherry our mothers drank. A couple of years later we moved to a bigger house. My mother had started working again. I had thought this was just because she was increasingly bored by being at home, but another likely reason was that our new house needed to be financed. The new house signalled a shift in interests and activities. While earlier my mother made many clothes for herself and for my sister and me (a dubious pleasure for us: we wanted jeans, which my mother considered unsuitable), she stopped doing that and turned to gardening more than she had before. We had only been living in the new house for a few years when my parents' marriage broke up, landing both of them in considerable financial difficulties and finally in much smaller new houses. I moved out to live on my own. In the early eighties my mother remarried and a few years later she stopped working.

I can remember that we had either *Margriet* or *Libelle*, and I read their comic sections. Later I collected the serials, which I would not read untill I had all the instalments. For some time we also had a magazine with sewing patterns. In the following quotation my mother talks about the magazines we had. My questions and interjections have been edited out of this quotation (and the ones below) wherever they were irrelevant to the narrative.

At home we used to have *Eva* and when I married I had *Eva* for a while because it was so beautifully done and had high-quality printing, beautiful pictures, and the knitting patterns were very good. The recipes were also good. For the rest it wasn't very different from other magazines. [*Eva* has long ceased to exist.] I then changed to *Libelle*, I think, and I made a very conscious choice: not *Margriet*, because *Margriet* was printed so coarsely; those photos had two or three shadows, and when you had a photo of a film actress, she was there two or three times. And film actresses were very important in those days. There were always a few pages in the women's magazines about film stars and I really loved that. It was fairy-tale like, very far away. *Libelle* I had longest, I think, because it was beautiful and nicely done and it was years before I stopped getting it, because they had old-maidish patterns and they had become boring. When I bought a *Margriet* for a change, it looked much better than I remembered. They had nice patterns, so I stopped my *Libelle* subscription. I really felt *Libelle* was in a transitional period in the early seventies. They had a different kind of article; medical articles were suddenly fashionable and that was interesting on the one hand, but on the other hand you didn't really want to read that. Because those were the 'holy of holies', you didn't talk about those things. So I stopped *Libelle*, because I didn't like it any more.

And then there were all sorts of personal troubles, which made it financially not such a good idea to [buy magazines] and then, when I came to live in this house, a few years ago, I bought *Margriet* a few times again. My memory of *Libelle*, that it was boring, really stuck. I didn't read it for a long time. Maybe it is quite nice now, I don't know. But *Margriet* really suits me. Stories with zest. Articles about young women, wo have all sorts of interesting professions. They had a series about women who work in advertising and in broadcasting, who sit behind the camera and make fashion pictures, who have their own agencies. That is all so new, I read it with tremendous pleasure. And they are twenty-five, thirty years old. It is really nice to read about how they cope. And, of course, they have the standard stories that I always read: what to do with a splitting headache. That is familiar. And *Margriet* has a page with stories by Hankie Bauer about her three daughters and that is so nice, the way she handles that. The same feeling of powerlessness at times: oh, goodness, what to do, this or that? And she answers at a guess and sometimes it's OK and at other times it is absolutely wrong and I can so well imagine what happens. That is how I read *Margriet*. It has become a really nice magazine to read.

[Wasn't it like that earlier?] No. Well, you used to have those stories about film stars and actors and that was nice, but it was also very patronizing: how you should run your household, when it was time for spring cleaning and all sorts of things, that you had to air all your clothes – you could find all that in *Libelle*. And in winter, or in the autumn, there was fruit to be preserved. The way you used to have to run a household. Maybe they still have those things, but I don't look at it now. I do notice that it isn't on the first page any more (First interview, 26 January 1989)

As an interview that first one was a success; as a renewed introduction to my mother, it was quite a shock. She had changed so much. Her hair was no longer permed, she wore trousers with a large blouse over them and low-heeled sensible shoes. During the divorce years she started looking different from the way she had looked as a younger woman (fancy dresses, make-up, smart shoes), but it was part of a slow process of ageing and feeling disappointed. Another surprise was that she had taken up studying philosophy (and painting: less of a surprise because it is so typical of a middle-aged woman) after she stopped working a couple of years into her second marriage. She also told me that she had started reading the feminist monthly *Opzij* and was more cynical and to the point about the unequal position of women than I had ever known her to be.

It seems to me there are two aspects to my mother's life story that are important to understanding the role of women's magazines in a woman's life. First, as I shall illustrate below, an individual life has its highly different stages or life cycles, which are not necessarily punctuated by a divorce, but may be marked by children growing up and leaving home, changes in relationships, changes in one's interests and ideas.[1] Different life cycles come with different needs, pleasures and problems and with different preferences as regards women's magazines (if they are of interest at all). Secondly, there is the challenge or threat of feminism (depending on one's perspective), of either recognizing the social inequality between women and men or refusing to do so. For women of my mother's generation that is not the same issue as it is for women of my generation, among whom it makes a considerable difference whether or not feminism or, for example, women's studies were part of one's (extended) education.

For many women feminism is still a highly important area of tension, which has repercussions on one's enjoyment and/or criticism of women's magazines.

Stages in a woman's life

Broadly speaking, there seem to be four major stages in my mother's life story, two of which (the second and third) will be focused on to show how the role of women's magazines may change in a reader's life. The first stage is her youth, schooling and professional training and the years before her first marriage when she worked. In the second stage she got married and gave up her job – something that was unquestioned and taken for granted – and had two children. This stage ends after roughly twelve years of marriage when she started working again and her marriage disintegrated, opening into a third, in-between stage of the last years of the marriage, the divorce, trying to cope on a low income and finally a few years of living on her own. She did not feel brought up for and nor did she like independence, though she demanded a settlement rather than alimony; the status of 'divorced woman' was not one she cared for. The fourth stage, advanced middle age, begins with her second marriage, which did not have an easy start. She stopped working and started what as far as I can see, was a rewarding process of self-development and internal growth through philosophy courses, painting and a reading club with new friends; it parallels her change in appearance and lets her feel more at ease with herself. The fourth stage extends to the present and I will touch upon it only briefly.

A young mother in the early sixties

I can give no full picture of my mother's life, nor is it possible to make a full reconstuction of when my mother read which titles and how they were part of her everyday life. Therefore I have chosen to let her tell her story by compiling interview fragments in which she makes connections between the magazines she read and her memories of her everyday life, of being a young mother, and of sexuality and marital relations. Then I will give what might be called a 'running commentary'. Neither of our texts is meant to be a 'true' rendering of the past. As Steedman says, 'the point doesn't lie there, back in the past, back in the lost time at which they happened; the only point lies in interpretation' (1986: 5). The past is used and reused to give meaning to a life, daily routines and small diversions included. Memories and interpretations of the past may poison what was once pleasurable because the object as remembered is tainted with pain and loss of status, dignity or self-esteem. Over time memories can also fade and interpretations can change, making room for new usage of, in this case, women's magazines.

Valerie: I saved up enormous piles. Occasionally I lent them to friends, but at a cleaning spree they would go to the Red Cross, who had special mail boxes for depositing them in.

Joke: Did people exchange them, pass them on, or share subscriptions?

Valerie: I am quite sure that everybody had their own subscription.

Joke: Amazing. Why?

Valerie: Well, you didn't share such things then. It wasn't done to borrow sugar or something.

Joke: Was it good middle-class rules – one had money enough to have one's own subscription?

Valerie: No, it was more a women's code for running your household properly. (. . .) What I remember is that you were not supposed to live above your means. If you had a magazine you paid for it yourself, you didn't borrow. (. . .) That would have been lazy and taking advantage. If you can't pay for it, you don't do it. Same thing with clothes.

Joke: Taking over old clothes wasn't done?

Valerie: Within a family that was done, of course, but it was a sport among women to turn old clothes into something tremendously beautiful. And the women's magazines played a big part in that. How to lengthen skirts, or to make new collars, or cuffs, and look what we can do with grandma's old dress, see how nice little Lisa looks! They ran that kind of story and you took it dead seriously because you had those clothes. I remade grandma's clothes for the two of you; that wasn't poverty, that was what you did. And there was a lot of competition, one did far better than another. My neighbour across the street, I won't mention names, she was terrific at it, but then, she was a needlework teacher. While the neighbour two houses down the street, a cosy, snug kind of person, she was very bad at it, as everybody said. But I don't believe she always had money problems because she couldn't make something new from something old. Her children usually wore new clothes. Well, that was more than scandalous. (First interview)

Having children is very special, it fulfils you at first and there is a lot of work to do. For the child you are everything. They are totally dependent on you. For the first time in my life someone was absolutely dependent on me. It did mean the end of comradeship, of doing things together in your marriage. You used to go to parties and have a drink and there was no reason at all to go home. But with children that changes. You aren't at ease. Your husband says, 'Well, there is a babysitter.' But it doesn't work like that. You want to go home. And you want attention and to talk about things, but the man works and that is another life. Instead of attention and someone who listens to what you say, there is only a sexual relationship. (Second interview, 19 December 1989)

While you are wholly taken up with your children, and sex is not a solution for the attention you need, you lose sight of your husband. Sex becomes so important. They had a saying back then: there isn't a handful but a land full of beautiful women. And it really hurt how everyone [befriended couples who lived in the same street and colleagues of my father and their wives] flirted. I don't think they slept with one another, but they did in their thoughts and that is just as bad. The things they talked about, intimate things that you had told your husband . . . I really minded that flirting. I tried to find clues in women's magazines to how things should go. And every once in a while they had something about it. Then it said that the woman had to make herself beautiful when the man came home and make sure that the children were sweet and cheerful and she had to listen with interest to his stories. And sometimes that happened. (First interview)

The first children's day-care centres started in those days, where children could go so that their mothers could start jobs again. People in the street where we lived thought that they were disgraceful. That women would stoop to bring their children to such centres . . . women's destination was motherhood. The highest thing that could happen to a woman, to throw that away! Women felt they had to defend the role that had been forced upon them. Everyone was the best mother that had ever existed. My neighbour with a son and a daughter, she was Exemplary Mother Number One. She was so marvellous with them, and she said herself that motherhood was so marvellous, beautiful, sublime. (. . .) I loved having children, but that it was my vocation in life, well, I never thought that. I loved having them and I felt a little guilty that I just liked it, that it wasn't a calling. No, I didn't have a calling as a mother. [I don't think anyone . . .] I am sure of that. No one does. It's one of the sick jokes of the church, who foisted on women that motherhood is the most beautiful thing that can happen to a woman. Maria worship . . . And men boasting about making their wives pregnant. I really thought that disgusting. What are we: sows, cows? I really minded that, I thought it was insulting. Well, in that atmosphere, children's day-care centres were introduced. And I thought, what a good idea. Maybe they'll have girls who are trained to take care of children. And I mentioned that one time we were all having coffee at someone's house, and the whole bunch turned against me, because that was scandalous, you didn't do that. A woman who failed as a mother wasn't fit to be called a woman. (. . .) And I do think that made me very suspicious of other women. Women can be so hard to one another . . . I didn't see any unity at all among women, on the contrary I saw them fighting each other and scoring off each other and playing the good mother. Oh, how I hated that. And those approving looks of the men – a woman picking up her baby was so touching – I could have hit them, or pulled the rug from underneath them. I had the most awful thoughts. (First interview)

Running commentary

From the first quotation, in the section before this one, it is clear that as a young married woman my mother was an avid magazine reader, a habit she took with her from her parents' home. She recalls the look and feel of magazines and clearly enjoyed them. From the quotations above it is evident that she thought having children was wonderful, though she felt confused by the competition for men among the young couples she and my father mixed with, through his work and in the street where we lived.

I have some very early memories of my mother going out to play tennis with friends. A few years later when I was around ten years old, that had changed. She must have been bored when first I and then my sister started going to school. She appeared to feel continually tired. Still later, we started talking to one another. My mother was glad that we were growing up and, as she said, were turning into people she could talk to. Having started working again, she was tired in a new way, more irritable. The marriage to my father must have been a heavy burden for both of them by then. We moved and their social life, which was no longer very active, dwindled further. The magazine we still took at that time must have given countless ideas for cheerful family picnics, for how to cook a special dinner for guests – things that did not happen, apart from occasional and, from what I remember, strained family visits.

My mother does not talk much any more of her marriage to my father. But I believe that she compared her marriage with the marriage of her parents, or rather, her idyllic rendering of that marriage: Grandma listening to Grandpa, who sounds like a true *homo universalis*. Maybe he was. The fact is that my mother came to know her mother very late in my grandmother's life, when she had children herself. My grandmother was one of the few people to whom my mother confided her troubled feelings about marriage. She remembers bringing up that 'men seemed to be creatures from another planet' (letter with second interview). Grandma counselled her to be discreet. Since my mother did not have many friend as a young woman – other young women were the competition, is how she puts it – and did not have much trust in the openness or discretion of her neighbours, she must have been lonely, certainly when the outings with her tennis friends stopped.

My mother's anecdotes and recollections are stories of two worlds: on the one hand a safe and rewarding world taking care of her household and of two small children; on the other hand an unsafe, at times threatening, generally uninspiring world that I would be tempted to call an outside world, were it not for the fact that her relationship with my father, in retrospect, was part of that unsafe outside world peopled by couples in their street whom my parents knew and by colleagues of my father and their wives. For my mother magazines helped mediate the codes of the unsafe outside world (especially in relation to the women in her street) while providing an intimate pleasure that was clearly inside world (daydreaming about the world of the stars and the royal family). Collecting recipes in two formidable scrapbooks and stacking packs of magazines in the attic (for future use in theory, but in practice until a large-scale cleaning), reinforced the 'good housewife' identity. My mother's interpretation of what makes someone a good housewife echoes 1950s post-war European reconstruction ideology as promoted by television pro-grammes for women and by magazines (see Leman, 1987; White, 1970). In her study of magazine content White mentions 'make do and mend', using old clothes to make new and thrift as good housewifely qualities in the post-war years, and she sees them as typical of the immediate post-war period, 1946–1951 (1970: 123–137). Evidently the changes of the mid-sixties were slow to permeate the quiet suburb where we lived. For my mother, as a reader, the magazines provided tips on how to hold her own in the street competition for being the best mother, for example when making children's clothes; at times they hinted at solutions for marital trouble.

One of the things about my mother that I slowly started to understand as a child was that her background was very different from that of my father, who comes from what, I suppose, was a straightforward lower-middle-class Dutch family. My mother's Indonesian past was highly exotic: I remember occasionally eating *rijsttafel* (a traditional meal dating from the colonial period) with my mother's family, the Malayan words they used for umbrellas and cucumbers, my grandparents' housekeeper, my grandfather's chauffeur, who had taught my mother to drive a car. I looked up to her. She was cultured, witty, sarcastic at times. Later, when she was tired and increasingly despondent, she was still a class above us. I never saw that she was also a highly conventional woman who was in the habit of burying her insecurities deep inside. When she told me her story in the interviews, I felt I had to do a complete volte-face. She had never been the strong, exotic woman I had made her out to be. She was also insecure at times and at a loss about what to do with her marriage, her life. I have since accepted that she was very naïve in some ways, ill-prepared for a marriage with the difficult person my father is and ill at ease with a set of codes of womanly behaviour that must have felt alien to her. Women's magazines were a practical help with cooking and dress-making (things she very much enjoyed doing); they gave advice about what to do with headaches and being tired, but their solutions for her headaches can hardly have helped since they were very much a symptom of her problem.

The divorce and the rupture of everyday routine

During the interviews my mother was not inclined to discuss the period of my parents' marital problems. When I asked her about reading magazines at the time of the divorce, she did not remember much and preferred to talk around the subject. The cassette recorder, but I suppose also her sense of propriety, made her prefer not to talk about such things in highly personal terms. In the first interview she just says, 'And then there were all sorts of personal troubles, which made it financially not such a good idea' to buy magazines. In passing she alludes to her disappointment in the magazines; they did not offer much advice on how to save a marriage or how to deal with sex, except by making yourself attractive. In the second interview she jumped from her criticism of the flirting going on at social occasions to her responsibility for her family and how little help the magazines offered. 'And I think that is why I ended the whole thing. *Libelle* or *Margriet* I don't remember. I couldn't dredge up any more information.'

The period spanning the divorce, the years on her own and the start of her second marriage were years in which she neither read magazines nor seems to have felt a desire to do so.

> I landed in a weird circle. Divorce, being on my own, getting married again, high expectations, things going a little less well, and then not as badly as I thought. It needed a lot of time to settle down . . . and then I found the philosophy course and that opened things up. You could talk about everything, while no one was very personal. It wasn't like a psychiatric session. You talked about yourself as if dealing with a case you knew about. And that made it much easier to talk about it, you kept your distance. (. . .) I was at that school for some three years. (Second interview)

Instead of reading magazines, she turned to philosophy and meditation, to subjects and forms beyond the scope of magazines, even though the form of introspection is slightly similar. To offer your situaton as if it were a case you know about or to compare your own experiences with those of the women quoted in women's magazines is not all that dissimilar. Women friends – no longer competitors – became more important too as partners for intimate talk as well as philosophical reflection on life, relationships, and the social position of women.

While writing this chapter, I telephoned her to ask her again how she remembered the magazines in the period just before the divorce. (We have become much more friendly with one another.) She said that at that time she did not feel 'connected' to the magazines.

> By the end of the seventies they still held up this image of the glorious task of the housewife who was there for her husband. And I felt that that didn't fit me any more. In 1986 I started buying copies of *Margriet* again and it was totally different. Back then they certainly didn't offer any help. They wrote about divorce in stories and the moral usually was that the woman had botched things up, 'she that mischief hatches, mischief catches'. They didn't have any of the difficult questions of life. While now occasionally there are

articles about alcoholism, a letter from someone with a child who takes drugs. The holiness has gone. And if you want help, you need to read [the feminist magazine] *Opzij*, it's on a higher level. For most of the magazines are still taken up with home-making niceties: plants and decoration. I would like them to do more about women who work in health care, for instance. It is always talked about so condescendingly and is such difficult and important work. (Telephone conversation, 20 August 1992)

It is surely a sign of how much she had come to loathe the magazine image of successful womanhood from the fifties and early sixties, that she continued to read it into the text of the late seventies. The magazine *Margriet*, for example, was given an award for promoting the emancipation of women among broader sectors of the population in 1978, in the same period that my mother said it was still very conservative about divorce. Maybe she hardly read the last volumes we received. I remember her as being very tired, irritable and immensely disappointed. Clearly she did not expect much from anything, least of all from magazines. The happy families, the triumphs over adversity must have been like salt in her wounds. Moreover, she had decided early on to skip articles about women's rights and feminism (she felt they were interesting but scary, as the next quotation shows) and 'medical stories' were far too sensitive and sacred a topic to sit easily with her. Whatever sense of women's strength the magazines may have conveyed to readers at that time, it was not picked up by my mother. She felt that women's magazines did not have a place in her life. They did not present a meaningful world for a woman in a crisis situation.

Advanced middle age and the rediscovery of self

When she takes up reading women's magazines again, it is after an enormous transition. She looks – she is – a different woman. The second marriage has settled down, while she has become much more her own person, much less dependent upon a husband. Women friends have become more important and so have her own activities. Reading a selection of magazines, newspaper reviews and feminist novels and books mirrors her new-found sense of ease with herself. 'I am amazed at the changes in my reading as compared with the first interview. Then I read *Margriet*, and occasionally [the gossip magazines] *Story* and *Privé* at the hairdresser. I still read *Margriet* and *Vorsten* [Sovereigns], because of Beatrix, and *Opzij* and *Nouveau*

[Dutch glossy in the *Good Housekeeping* league]. Is it reading *Opzij* or is it simply age that makes your outlook more independent?' (letter with second interview). She also sometimes buys English interior decorating magazines, such as 'House and Gardens (. . .) They are horribly expensive, of course, but if there is something that interests me . . . Because I am thinking of having a tiny bathroom upstairs. Well, they have sumptuous bathrooms with flower-pattern tiles and the like, and I think, I'll buy it anyhow. Just to have a look I tell myself, maybe they'll have an idea that I can copy in miniature' (first interview). She is very interested in what young women nowadays do, the opportunities they have and make for themselves, and is slightly bitter about the myths and unquestioned rules that she grew up with. Summing up what women's magazines mean to her now, she said:

> I look forward to the new issue of *Opzij*. I have had a subscription for a little while. I recognize a lot in it that confirms me in how I feel. Things that I have thought, or felt, are printed there, just like that. Even now, when I am talking about it, I sometimes grow cold: damn, those women say all these things just like that. I don't think I expect all that much from *Margriet*, and *Nouveau* is beautiful to browse through. But I really look to what *Opzij* writes. And what I have also started looking at is book reviews in the newspaper. What I do find irritating is that women reviewers can really run women's books into the ground. [She gives an example.] And what does that reviewer say? 'If anyone feels a need for this kind of twaddle, she should buy this booklet.' Then I feel like accosting that woman and saying 'Don't be such a nerd. Let people read it and tell your comrades that it is twaddle!' (Second interview)

Middle age for my mother has been and is a period of renewed vigour. Carolyn Heilbrun, writing a Kate Fansler detective novel under the pseudonym Amanda Cross, expounds an intriguing view of advanced middle age as an extremely important period of spiritual development for women (Cross, 1984, and see Greer, 1990). Middle age may set free those women who choose to recognize the opportunity of being free of a whole set of highly restricting conventions as to how a woman should look, dress, act and think. One of the main characters in Cross's novel *Sweet Death, Kind Death* is said to have thought of middle age 'as a time quite different from the earlier years, cut off from the ghosts of the past. One might recall those ghosts; most people . . . recall them too often. But they need no longer haunt one. You have the sense . . . of life able to begin again, if one will but let it' (1984: 15). My mother's radical change of style – her decision to stop visiting a hairdresser every Saturday to have her hair waved, to wear clothes for comfort rather than to be pretty – signals someone who has laid to rest at least some of her ghosts. She pursues interests that were dormant and enjoys not having a job any more. Women's magazines have become meaningful in a very different way from when my sister and I were small. She still reads medical advice (and even the lengthier articles these days) but most of all she likes reading about how others cope with a world (children and jobs) that she feels liberated from and that they appear to enjoy in a more open and shared way than she ever did.

In the fierce manner I remember from the time I was very young she pleads the case for women being able to choose their own styles, which are comfortable and not imposing to wear:

> I do think there are a lot of women like me who don't really know who they are. And then, when I think of the fashion industry and cosmetics, it is all controlled by men. Women ought to fight to get the fashion industry on their side to make fashion for women. Because those men only produce seductive clothes, while women like beautiful but wearable fashion. And it is the same thing with cosmetics. I get more and more irritated by all their disgusting waffle about fancy brands and packaging. From the angle of animal rights and animal testing too. I stopped buying that stuff a long time ago. I buy cosmetics that haven't been tested on animals. Very good. But when you see what is on offer . . . Like in the Bijenkorf [renowned Dutch department store], you see women drawn like magnets to those glamorous stands. That really ought to change. (Second interview)

Feminism (and introducing Joan Becker)

I feel it is a shame that my mother never read *The Feminine Mystique* (Friedan, [1963] 1974) or any of a number of feminist texts that were written in the sixties about women who were wasting their intelligence, their education and their capacities and stayed at home to look after the children and to keep house. These texts were written for her and about her. She was becoming increasingly bored with her life when we went to primary school, which we vaguely noticed. She was not offered enough to keep her mind occupied or to challenge her. I always interpreted her going back to work again as an emancipatory move, as a way to explore new horizons, even though it was symptomatic that she did not take up her old profession again but did part-time administrative work on a much lower level. She did not have the strength to break the mould of her life. Why was it so difficult for her to do so? When I asked her about MVM (Men Women Society), one of the first feminist organizations in the Netherlands (the name was later regretted by a great number of members, the vast majority of whom were women), and the huge research projects of the domestic weekly *Margriet*, 'God in the Netherlands' and later 'Sex in the Netherlands' at the end of the sixties and in the early seventies, she said:

> Yes, I do remember. I can even see those covers and I was really scared. I didn't buy them. I turned that down. Why, I don't really know. But I know they did that and I didn't have *Margriet* then, nor *Libelle* [the competing and very similar domestic weekly], I don't think . . . I watched [News shows] with a great deal of interest and curiosity, really: what are they up to? That man–woman thing was wonderful, of course, but the woman part was absolutely nailed shut, everything was fixed to one pattern. I couldn't imagine what could come out of it . . . Women live in such coils, to live the lives they live. As a woman, as a housewife and a mother, that was one role, but maybe they were three roles. And apart from that there was something with woman friends, who would occasionally talk about what kept them occupied and what they thought about. It was always in disguised terms because the competition was enormous. Which is something that always amazed me, I always thought, marriage is marriage and that's it, but that is just the start of it. All that competition between women who don't enjoy the marriages they have any more and who try for other men. I watched it with wide-open eyes. And even if you had a rotten time at home, for the outside world everything was always fine. You had to keep doors closed. There were always those who were trying to get in. And then this man–woman thing started and I had no idea where that would lead. We had a woman minister then, Marga Klompé, and I really admired her. I really thought it was terrific what that woman did. But it was absolutely impossible to put her in a man–woman relationship or in a family situation with a husband, woman and children. She was a different kind of woman.
>
> (. . .) I remember those articles about MVM, but I didn't read all of them. I wasn't really interested. I didn't think about that. I remember those articles and thinking at the back of my mind, this is pioneer work, to pry women loose from their set ways. But Dolle

Mina [feminist action group], that had nothing to do with me'. [But you started working not long after that, didn't you?] Well, that was all according to a set pattern, part-time, because 'my life was at home' and I had a job on the side too: 'That's nice, she has a small job.' I really tried to get into it, but I never made it. My age was a factor, but also, to enter the labour market as a married woman – well, why? When I started I felt really strongly that a woman should be in the home. What was I doing there? No, that wasn't very encouraging. (First interview)

There seems to have been a knot of reasons for my mother not to have become interested in feminism until relatively late in life. One thread in the knot was surely the force of convention. She felt strongly about not failing in the eyes of others (which for her is a general social code). Another thread, I suppose, was her relative isolation: she had no real close friends that I remember, nor was she all that close to her family, who, moreover, are rather conservative people. Since she felt that a marriage was a woman's responsibility, a failing marriage was her cross to bear and not something to make public or to cry out against. Other women were either competitors (rather than people in comparable situations), from whom it was best to hide her troubles, or high-minded liberated persons who preached the feminist gospel a little too forcefully. 'You looked at it, you knew it was happening, but to integrate [feminism or women's emancipation] in your life . . . My life was difficult enough. I didn't feel at all like being talked to didactically by women who had shaken loose from all that. Maybe there was some jealousy too' (second interview).

As a feminist I very much take my mother's story to heart: emancipation cannot be forced on others, it is something one discovers for oneself – as my mother ended up doing. I was also amazed by how long it took her to register that domestic weeklies such as *Margriet* and *Libelle* were changing their outlook: instead of being paternalistic and slightly condemning towards women who did not feel lke being housewives and for whom marriage was not akin to a holy institution, they took a much broader and more therapeutic approach, advising women to talk about their problems and, if necessary, to end a relationship. The memories of feminism in the media she refers to in the quotation above are of a later date than the changes I signalled in my question, at which time she still subscribed to *Libelle* or *Margriet*. It would seem to show that one's own codes and norms and routine expectations are much more important than the literal text of the magazines and also that in looking back highly personal timetables are constructed. In my mother's case, her misery over not being able to save her marriage seems to have made her fall back on patterns of knowledge dating back to the 1950s: the magazines would condemn a woman like her just as much as the *communis opinio* among the neighbours in the street that we had left behind for a relatively isolated house would.

Joan Becker: emancipation versus the force of convention

From the perspective of the magazines it seems clear enough that the reputation a magazine has can be much stronger than its actual content, and that feminism, where magazines' reputations are concerned, is an important fault-line. That is one of the conclusions I drew from the interviews with Joan Becker. To present her story here is to complete the 'moral tale' my mother's story has become. Whereas my mother was caught in prescriptive ideologies of femininity and motherhood from which she never felt able to break free, women like Joan Becker, born in the early sixties, face a choice rather than a destiny when they think of having children. Joan's story makes plain that although she made a conscious choice to have a child and to concentrate on being a mother for a while, it was not roses all the way – quite the contrary. Like my mother's story, hers is a tale of feeling caught by what being a woman and being a mother is supposed to be like. The inclusion of Joan in this chapter was prompted not only by the belief that her story and my mother's story strengthen each other, but also by the fact that she was one of my favourite respondents: enthusiastic, open-minded and sincere, as well as curious. In the quotations below Joan gives a very lucid account of how she negotiates a position of her own, steering clear of feminism and also of highly traditional ideas about being a woman.

The first interview with Joan Becker started off with her fierce attack on *Viva*, a young women's magazine, which she felt has a paternalistic feminist style. Her attack led to further discussion of feminism and emancipation.

> I hate *Viva*. Because they [*Viva* women] are [supposed to be the only real] modern working women. I am very much in favour of emancipation, but I want to decide for myself to what extent I am emancipated. They push you in a certain direction. Like, if you're working and you have a child, you have to put it in a day-care centre and fend for yourself. And sexually too you have to stand up for your rights. I don't know, but I think I can make up my own

mind, I don't want others to tell me. So I really hate *Viva*, and I don't read it. Maybe it is too feminist, though maybe it isn't. I feel pushed in a corner. *Margriet* and *Libelle* are also in favour of emancipation, but they aim at different groups. In *Libelle* they have articles about a working woman with a responsible job. And then there is an article about a housewife who does this and that, and I don't feel pushed in a corner. (. . .)

Maybe I am more old-fashioned at heart than I appear to be. Maybe I am. Although I was independent, and I am proud of that. I miss that a little. On the other hand I do like to be cuddled from time to time. And you can't have it all ways. To leave it to the guy. Maybe it sounds silly, but maybe part of me is old-fashioned. (. . .)

I don't really like the women's movement. I don't think those figures in the women's movement are representative of the whole group. (. . .) I can remember a few years back that all women had to go on strike. I had been working then for six years or so and I was taking a walk during my break. Well, I'm the prototypical working person. And there were all these girls on Dam square who had just left school, those alternative types with health sandals who were telling me what to do and what not to do. And I thought, get lost! (. . .) I wouldn't want to be among them. I don't think they are really women . . . I am in favour of equal rights and emancipation but they want women to be the boss. Although they have done good things, like providing shelters for battered women, so you don't have to put up with a man hitting you, and there are helpline phone numbers. (. . .) [Feminists] look down on things. I think that if someone wants to be a housewife, she has a right to do so. As long as you can make your own choices. That is the main thing. Some women want to work and have a problem because of the lack of day-care centres. And some women want to quit when they have small children.

Later on in the interview I introduced favourite television programmes as a topic, which provided another means by which to reflect on feminism and emancipation. Joan talks about the television series *Cagney and Lacey*, which features two women police officers in New York, one of whom has a family and children, while the other lives on her own.

There is a contradiction in that series, Chris is a certain type of [career] woman and Mary Beth, [who is much more of a] housewife, I like her a lot too. It keeps me occupied these days, now that one is full of contradictions. I expected to have no trouble at all in letting my job go. Well, I've found it harder than I thought, because . . . not because I look down on being a housewife, but others do look down on it. I had a friend visiting who asked me, 'Won't you become terribly dull?' (. . .) And I don't think so, because I am doing something worthwhile. It's just that it doesn't make money, that's the difference. And a lot of people don't understand that you like busying yourself with a child all day. Well, that was my choice. I don't want to say that I am 100 per cent happy to have a child. I am 80 per cent happy and 20 per cent of me thinks, damn, I can't sleep late again, or I don't even have an hour for myself. And that is really contradictory. You make a conscious choice and you feel guilty for not being a full 100 per cent happy. (First interview, 17 January 1989)

Joan comes from a working-class family, trained as a secretary and is still proud of what she achieved in her line of work, having started out with only limited training, 'doing her bit' as she puts it, for the emancipation of women with little schooling. When I met her for the first time in 1987, she was a 27-year-old married romance enthusiast, and read romances in the bus on her way to work and in all the spare time she had. She and her husband were planning to have a child and for her to give up her job. When we met again for the first interview about women's magazines (January 1989), her son had just been born and she appeared to be rather tired, far less enthusiastic and maybe slightly depressed. Her duty as a mother seemed a burden to her. She did not want to read romances any more because they were so difficult to put down and she would hate herself if she did not give her full attention and care to the child. The second interview (December 1989) was more lively. She and her family had moved from the flat where she used to live to a house with a small garden that felt much more comfortable. The flat had been too small for the heavy furniture they had, which now was in more agreeable, less claustrophobic proportions to the house. Since the first interview she had taken up a part-time job again at the company where she used to work. It made her feel slightly less dependent, more in command of her life and more cheerful, because she was not tied hands and feet to her child.

Joan describes herself as an inquisitive person who is interested in people around her, as someone who has a good intuition for other people's sorrows and problems and is a good listener. She is a fighter. Her favourite romance heroines are zesty women who talk back. Joan herself is not shy of a good chat and occasionally an argument, for instance about her relationship with her partner. She is fiercely loyal to the company she worked (and works) for and to her 'old boss' for giving her a chance. The job was an important learning experience. It made her outgrow her family, she said, in tastes and table manners. Her career and the self-edification it gave rise to illustrate that class position in the Netherlands is not as prominent a determinant of a woman's life as it once was. Joan has moved away from her parents' social class. In fact, her social status is on a par with my mother's, despite their different working class and professional middle-class origins. Indeed, the Becker's house rather resembles the house my parents lived in until I was twelve years old.

As a girl Joan read a girls' magazine and occasionally the comics that came in the women's magazines. When she started living on her own, she subscribed to the domestic weekly *Libelle*. Because they had a tighter budget when she left her job and she had become slightly bored with the magazine, she stopped her subscription in favour of *Ouders van Nu* (Parents Today), a parenting magazine, the subscription to which had also been stopped by the time of the second interview (December 1989). At her mother's Joan reads the gossip magazines her mother subscribes to. She likes to make fun of them and in a self-conscious way enjoys them. From time to time she buys single copies of the domestic weeklies when she fancies the subjects they write about, or the knitting patterns or the recipes.

Joan's views on feminism and women's emancipation, compared with my mother's account of the sixties, show how much rhetoric on women's role in society has changed. Joan stressed that she felt she was an emancipated person, which she illustrated by pointing out that she had worked and made a career of sorts over a respectable number of years. Emancipation as a concept for her meant having a choice. Criticism, however implicit, of her choices in life, she related to feminist paternalistic views on the one hand and on the other to a class-related discourse, whereby a person's worth is measured by the amount of money she or he makes. As a housewife and mother one does not make money, and is therefore looked down upon. In women's magazines one will not find arguments that relate directly to class position (even if the styling, tone and subjects of specific titles do reflect class difference). But the reformulation of feminist topics into emancipation, where emancipation means 'having a choice', appears to exemplify 1980s and 1990s women's magazine rhetoric.

Treading very carefully, together with other news media, women's magazines have introduced women's emancipation to a wide audience in a highly practical and pragmatic manner, which as a rule does not do justice to the complexities and tragic choices involved in the power struggle between the sexes that feminism has addressed.

Janice Winship has pointed out that *Woman's Own* in the seventies took up issues of women's work and pay, as well as, among other things, rape. However, the solutions offered in the rape article, for example, are highly individual survival strategies. Winship concludes: 'The magazine's cautiousness around feminism – not wanting to upset too many apple carts too quickly for readers – leads at worst to a misrepresentation of the women's movement, at best to an enthusiasm about what women can achieve' (1987: 93). Social conditions are not considered a fit subject for women's magazines, nor are stories or articles that could be considered depressing. As a result women's magazines treat heavy issues, such as post-natal depression, sexual incompatability, divorce, only sketchily and in so optimistic a manner that they become quite divorced from reality. There might be a 'triumph over tragedy' story that could make one despair even more, or the occasional letter on the medical advice page which probably would not offer much more than advice to 'talk about it' or to see an expert.

Joan praised women's magazines for having introduced the anti-conception pill, and for still being an important source of sex education; she felt that women's magazines supported women's paid labour. In the period in which I interviewed her, however, she was trying to find a way out of a major depression that appeared to be related to the changes the birth of her son had wrought in her life, and she hardly read women's magazines. She did not have the concentration or an appetite for them. She made clothes, knitted and watched television. Her depression, the responsibility for the child, no longer having an income of her own, and being at home all day in a tiny apartment made her feel very vulnerable. Her fears focused on being a 'bad mother' and losing parental control. Television programmes seen by chance and newspaper items fed her fears.

> I had a very difficult time this summer; I was all tied up and physically unwell. Well, I thought, it might be good if I talk about it to an outsider. (. . .) And then my doctor suggested I might like to talk to a social worker? I felt positive about that, but I was very afraid that they would think me a bad mother, that I would be divested of my parental control – I don't know, that they would think I was bonkers or something. But it has all worked out since we moved. And because the doctor suggested it, I thought really hard about what was happening and I decided that I didn't want to be ruled by others. I chose for me, and I didn't need an outsider to talk to, after all. (. . .)

It was really a dip; sometimes I didn't dare leave the house for fear I would be ill again. (. . .) I had seen this film, you see, about this mother who lost parental control, and it made me anxious that they would think me a bad mother. (. . .) When you go to see someone when you have really serious problems, and things go other than you expected, you don't know whether you can still put a stop to it. Suppose that guy thinks that the child should definitely be removed from your care? Could you undo that? (. . .)

And there was this case in the media of parents of a handicapped child who had a fight over an operation with a surgeon, and it took years before the court case was closed. And that makes a big impression on me, I thought, yuck, others have so much power to decide over your life. (. . .)

During this really difficult period I thought, is this it? Did I do the right thing? You make these choices so consciously these days. While before you'd just have children and you accepted it. It was so difficult for me to lose my own income. I had a very good job and a better salary than Alex [her partner] has. (. . .) So after a while I started working again, to prove myself, maybe. (. . .) I like to take care of someone, but I want to choose for myself too from time to time. (. . .) Because you are really ruled by such a small one. (. . .) I feel so lucky that I was offered this part-time job. It's my independence. (Second interview)

Joan was very dismayed to discover that her conscious option for motherhood did not entail complete happiness or satisfaction. She did not link her disappointment to criticism of women's magazines and their individualist rhetoric of choice and happy endings. Given my mother's feeling of disconnectedness to the magazines in the period of the divorce, I have wondered whether Joan was in a comparable situation. Within a year she changed from being an enthusiastic reader of romances and women's magazines to a much more indifferent reader. Previously she liked to read magazines such as *Libelle* for the points of view of other readers: 'I used to like that, to see how others think about things. It helps form your own opinion.' Evidently she was not in need of opinions in the period after her son was born. Nor did she feel inclined to check women's magazines on the subject of post-natal depression, or the problems of young motherhood, in order to understand what was happening to her. To me, it does not seem entirely improbable that they would have had articles or advice on these things. Even though I do not think it would be a big help, through the repertoire of connected knowing and emotional learning you might pick up clues, or find examples to compare yourself with. Apparently this repertoire works only if you have some distance from the problems that are discussed, if you are able to slightly distance yourself from them and do not feel totally affected, or immersed in them. Women's magazines may offer comfort after you have managed to live through difficulties or if the disasters and problems you read about unfold at a safe distance from your everyday life. Where smaller, more manageable and less threatening problems, such as recurring headaches, are concerned, the situation is very different. Solutions are more likely to be found or some control to be gained. In such cases the repertoire of practical knowledge will be used, rather than the repertoire of connected knowing.

A last important point to be made, again on the basis of the interviews with my mother and Joan Becker, is that magazine reading is a subordinate part of everyday routines that one does not habitually reflect upon. All that both women said about women's magazines has been used in this chapter, most of it in direct quotes. The meanings women's magazines have, then, is very much dependent upon the context in which they read, upon existing values, ideas and norms that a reader has. These meanings, as Schutz (1962) argues, become defined only in looking back and, I might add, are subject to whether or not one wishes to look back in detail. My mother has strong memories of reading women's magazines in the first years of her marriage to my father but she does not remember much about them in the period of the divorce. Unlike my mother, Joan had never had occasion to look back and revalue her life when I spoke to her. When I asked her to evaluate what women's magazines meant to her, she felt that was a very difficult question, as did most of my informants.

Joke: When you look back on the periods in which you read many women's magazines, what comes to mind? Why did you read them?

Joan: I find that a very difficult question, you know? (. . .) Reasons for reading . . . that depends. With *Ouders van Nu* I had very clear-cut reasons for subscribing. Maybe because women's magazines have such a multitude of subjects, there is always something that you like. Because of the fashion . . . ? No. Because I don't go out and buy a specific magazine. Because there is a bit of everything in them. Sometimes it's cooking. Then I buy a magazine with different subjects. And what I like about *Libelle* or *Margriet* is that they don't force anything on you. (. . .) You can read them when you have children or when you don't have them.

Joke: And why do we stop reading magazines?
Joan: Because they repeat things. They'll have a story about a Down's syndrome child and then another time they'll have a slightly different story, but it is still about that Down's syndrome child. I had that with *Tip* (a recipe magazine). At some point in time you start to think, yuck, that sauce with oranges again. Sounds silly . . . but you think, I've had enough. (. . .) And, you know, there are so many magazines, and if you don't subscribe, you can buy it when it looks interesting. It can be *Libelle* and then it is *Margriet*. You aren't tied to one magazine. (. . .) There is one thing: you need time to read and you need to feel in the mood for it.

Readers change, magazines change

The interviews with my mother and with Joan Becker bear witness to the same style of women's magazine reading (easy to put down) and to the same repertoires (the repertoire of emotional learning and connected knowing and the repertoire of practical knowledge) that were found in the other interviews. Joan compared women's magazines to books and argued that '(. . .) women's magazines don't intrigue; you pass by things. It is nice to pick them up and it is easy to put them down again.' My mother, after not having read women's magazines for a considerable amount of time, went back to reading a particular domestic weekly, which informs her about how young women cope today, giving her occasion to review her own life and to come to a new understanding of it, and in which she values brief medical advice. In one case the medical advice page helped her to discover a reason for the trouble she was having with her legs. Although the medication she obtained for it through her GP turned out not to be particularly helpful because of side-effects, she felt better about her 'restless legs' because she knew what was the matter. The recipes are no longer a source of interest to her. The scrapbooks that she put together over a considerable number of years when I was in primary school have long since ceased to be a source of pleasure or a pleasurable duty to her. She gave them to me and I faithfully keep them, though I hardly ever use them, because 'you never know if they will be of use some day'.

Apart from recognizing the repertoire of practical learning and the repertoire of connected knowing – which my mother uses when she talks about getting a sense of what young women nowadays do – one may recognize another dimension to reading women's magazines in the contradictory attitude my mother and Joan Becker shared with many other women towards the value of the tips, advice and knowledge that the magazines offer. Like my mother, Joan collected copies of magazines, the booklets they regularly offer with knitting patterns, or medical advice, and threw them out again when she needed space or felt a need to clean out her house. Reading women's magazines, and especially collecting recipes, knitting patterns and advice booklets, is a way of establishing and defending boundaries to one's identity. Identities are never stable or fixed (Shotter and Gergen, 1989), they need continuing renewal. Being a housewife or being a mother, for my mother and Joan Becker, involves claiming access to specific semi-expert knowledges (cooking, health care, knitting) just as those who compile folders with reviews, or with ideas for where to go in foreign cities (such as are offered by the glossy magazines), maintain an identity of a cultured person. Evidently the pleasure is more in the collecting, in the doing than in using a collection. Hence quite a number of collections of magazines or magazine cuttings did not last long. Helen Carson's pile of magazines with knitting patterns, Marie Stemerdink's plastic bags with tips and recipes and patterns in the attic and Jeanne Rousset's hotel and restaurant reviews were exceptions to the rule. Despite the feeling of many readers that the information in magazines was basically valuable, only a few used them as reference books. May Han was one of those who did. In the interview she told me that she used her *Cosmopolitans* to look up their views on, for example, extra-marital relationships when a friend had landed herself in trouble. But at a later occasion she offered me her old copies, as did many of my informants, hoping they had found a respectable way out of their dilemma: they wanted both to be rid of them and to have the gratifying feeling that they would not go to waste or recycled paper.

Indeed, the way women's magazines are produced implies that the information they offer so abundantly must have low value. The recurrent themes, tips and recipes seem to be meant to discourage serious collecting. Clearly no publisher would cheer on readers like Joan who collect a year's copies of *Ouders van Nu* in the secure knowledge that the information will last her most of the childhood of her children. The repetitiveness of magazines, commented upon by many readers, is the reason offered most often for not reading them any more. The changes in my mother's life, and the consequences of those changes for her preferences in magazines and in the way she reads them, illustrate the temporality of reading women's magazines, which is the second major reason for not reading them any more. A third reason that is also mentioned by my mother is that there were periods when she did not have the money to buy them.

Reading women's magazines is part of some periods of one's life but not of others. Many women told me that they started reading women's magazines when they had small children. My mother is certainly an example. Joan may take up reading women's magazines again, once her life has settled down. Magazine reading has to do with having time on your hands, as well as being in the mood for it, having the financial means and finding enough of interest to keep you reading. In retrospect, it seems to me that my mother stopped reading women's magazines rather abruptly (though I am not sure whether that was the case). From what I heard at birthday parties and other occasions where I informally validated my findings by asking women and men about reading women's magazines, it is more usual to lose interest gradually in what the magazines write about. One woman in her seventies said, 'It doesn't seem to apply to me at all.'

From the interviews with my mother and with Joan Becker it also became clear that reading women's magazines may feed into imaginary scenarios, into imagining how things would be, or could go, just as collecting recipes or knitting patterns is an activity that is important in itself in that it sustains a particular partial identity. It is not as firmly attached to cooking or knitting as one would suppose it to be. In fact, although reading women's magazines is firmly situated in daily routines, their meaning and attractivity is predicated on a certain measure of distance.

Lastly, according to my mother, today's women's magazines involve other accents and issues than those of a few decades ago. The film stars have gone, as has the paternalistic tone and the strict timetables of good housekeeping. They have been replaced by another kind of advice and a liberal version of feminism. Comparing what my informants told me with Brinkgreve and Korzec's research on the advice column of *Margriet* (1978) and with Winship's reconstruction of magazines contents and their gradual investment in talking things out and in issues of women's emancipation (1987), I would hazard a guess that the repertoires I have found are very much of this time and place, widespread though they are. The repertoire of practical knowledge seems to be older, in fact, than the repertoire of emotional learning and connected knowing, which would seem to be connected with the realistic conventions of today's human interest reporting rather than with the more dramatic or romantic tones of reporting in women's genres of a few decades ago. The quest to understand human nature from a personalized perspective, on the other hand, is much older and certainly more widespread than the genre of women's magazines, and related to older oral traditions (see Bird, 1992; Ong, 1982). The particular form the repertoires take, then, is of today; but their roots go much deeper, and in the future they will doubtless crop up in new guises in relation to other genres and practices.

4

Reading a Feminist Magazine: Fantasizing the Female homo universalis

About Opzij

The feminist monthly Opzij *is the only remaining general audience feminist publication in the Netherlands. It resembles the German feminist magazine* Emma *and the British magazine* Spare Rib. *Being the only nationwide feminist magazine and contemporary feminism's most noteworthy means of expression in the Netherlands,* Opzij *virtually holds a monopoly position. According to its chief editor, Cisca Dresselhuys,* Opzij *is feminism's national 'headquarters' (Jungschleger, 1987).*

The first issue of Opzij *was published in November 1972. Wim Hora Adema and Hedy d'Ancona, who were involved in the liberal feminist organization MVM (Men Women Society), took the initiative. After its first year* Opzij *found a publisher (de Weekbladpers) who was willing to give practical and financial support. The editorial work was done in the evenings by a volunteer board. In 1980 de Weekbladpers took over* Opzij, *and since then* Opzij *has been a professional magazine with commercial goals. As a consequence the target audience was progressively broadened: from feminists, to those 'who are interested in feminism' (d'Ancona and Hora Adema, 1977: 2), and to those who 'care about emancipation' (Muyen, 1985: 34). On its cover* Opzij *has consistently called itself 'feminist monthly'.*

The covers of the first issues of Opzij *were professionally designed. Many readers objected and the covers became simpler and more in tune with then feminist lore. From the mid-eighties onward, the one or two special issues that* Opzij *has every year were given full glossy covers, and more recently all issues have had them. Covers use photographs that portray women (often women who are interviewed in the issue), cartoon drawings, collages or other artwork.* Opzij *carries personal and commercial advertisements, provided they fit within its policy of accepting only non-sexist material. At the end of the eighties the magazine started a more aggressive sales campaign, sold an impressive amount of copies (almost 50,000 a month in 1990, according to the NOTU Oplage Documentatie 1990), and changed its approach towards advertisers. Now advertisements include ecological make-up brands as well as expensive liquor, personnel advertisements for the Dutch army and for Nederlandse Spoorwegen (Dutch rail), national newspapers and so on. In fact, Opzij looks like and is priced as a glossy magazine, though with a difference: its advertisement as a rule present a more critical view of the environment and they do not portray 'perfect women' sprayed with expensive perfumes or dressed in unwearable designer clothing.*

In its articles Opzij has moved from a highly political accent and focus on articles that deal with politics, labour, law, social security, education and urban planning to a more personal perspective and articles that concentrate on love relationships, the body, psychotherapy, experiences and feelings. In the language of Opzij, it has changed from an 'outside' to an 'inside' perspective (see Schutgens, 1989, and also Hermes and Schutgens, 1991), because, as Dresselhuys put it almost ten years ago: 'Not all resistance [against feminism and women's emancipation] should be allocated in the male world outside, a lot of barriers are ingrained in women themselves. We have to do battle on all fronts: outside and inside' (NOTUschrift, 1983: 26). In 1992 Opzij published an anniversary issue for its twentieth birthday that addressed Freud's never answered question, 'Was will das Weib?' In its more than 160 pages, various articles also addressed the question, 'What do feminists want?' Although the content of the answers varies, one thing becomes very clear: 'feminists' do not want other things than 'women', according to the specialists and readers interviewed by Opzij, they simply want more (Opzij, December 1992).

When asked, many of the readers of different women's magazines genres I spoke to were not sure whether or not feminist magazines are women's magazines. The blurredness of women's magazines as a genre did not help them come to an answer. Feminist magazines apparently were a dubious kind of women's magazines, an odd one out. In terms of research outliers, the odd ones out, can prove to be goldmines because they can help to clarify on what grounds some magazines are called women's magazines and others are not (Miles and Huberman, 1984: 23–8). Moreover, how feminist magazines are read is an interesting question in its own right. Therefore, I decided to find and interview readers of the Dutch feminist magazine Opzij, the results of which are described in this chapter. (Another outlier, gossip magazines, will be discussed in chapter 5).

Hardly anyone reads *Opzij* because it is 'easy to put down'. Reading a feminist opinion monthly is associated with very different (more political and ideological) arguments from those connected with reading traditional women's magazines. As a result, how the magazine is used did not have a prominent place in the interviews. When this was discussed, it was in relation to one of the three interpretative repertoires that were found. There were not any specific descriptive repertoires that are comparable with the easily put down and relaxation repertoire discussed in chapter 2. Neither the easily put down nor the relaxation repertoire applies to *Opzij* (even if in the *Opzij* interviews examples were found of the 'easy to put down' theme regarding traditional women's magazines). Another difference between conversations about *Opzij* and those about other magazines was that far more was said about *Opzij* than about traditional women's magazines (which quite a few of the *Opzij* readers also read). The best way to describe both how *Opzij* is read and how the magazine becomes meaningful is to start with a reconstruction of the repertoires that are used to make it meaningful. As will be clear, *Opzij* becomes meaningful through three repertoires (the liberal-individualist repertoire, the vanguard repertoire and the repertoire of moral duty) that are not used for other women's magazines.

This suggests that *Opzij* is absolutely different from other women's magazines, which is not true either. The three repertoires a co-researcher (Véronique Schutgens) and I found that were specific to *Opzij* stressed the distance between readers and the magazine (and feminism), rather than closeness or a shared struggle. We found one other repertoire in the interviews with the *Opzij* readers, which foregrounded the relation between the reader and *Opzij*: the connected knowing and emotional learning repertoire, a repertoire that is also used to speak about traditional women's magazines (discussed at length in chapter 2). For some of those who read it, *Opzij* is truly a women's magazine.

One of the fourteen *Opzij* readers we interviewed not only used the connected knowing repertoire to talk about *Opzij*, she also used it to talk about (feminist) self-help literature, a genre I had already contemplated covering because of its textual likeness to women's magazines. The repertoire of connected knowing emphasizes the importance of articles about other people's personal experiences and problems from which readers may learn. It was a challenge to include a few interviews with self-help readers, since self-help literature, like women's magazines (especially the more traditionally oriented subgenres), offers such examples in abundance. Having interviews with self-help readers was also important because I was interested in the boundaries of women's magazines as an umbrella category and in the specific nature of the connected knowing repertoire. Four women who read self-help books were recruited through a personal advertisement in *Opzij*.[1] Their testimony will be found in the second part of this chapter. The interviews with the self-help readers make more than clear that for them self-help literature is related to but not part of the genre of women's magazines. Different fantasies, wishes and identity constructs were brought into play. Of course, four readers can hardly provide a representative view of self-help reading. Their accounts of their reading experience does, however, give another vantage point from which to check the validity of the repertoires that are reconstructed here.

The last part of the chapter, the afterword, deals with feminism as constructed in the interviews with all eighteen readers. Strictly speaking, it is not about how women's magazines become meaningful. Yet in relation to how the Dutch feminist monthly *Opzij* is read, it seems an important issue. Rather surprisingly, almost none of the '*Opzij* readers' (the eleven women and three men who were initially interviewed about reading *Opzij* by Véronique Schutgens and myself) were outspokenly in favour of women's lib. Feminism for them turned out to be a highly sensitive area. The 'self-help readers' (the four women I interviewed later on, who were recruited through *Opzij*), two of whom also identified themselves as traditional women's magazine readers, had far less trouble forging a feminist position of their own.

Reading feminist magazines

The vanguard repertoire

The vanguard repertoire provided a good means to stress one's politically correct, leftist view of the world. Strategically it consisted of attacking *Opzij* for its lack of political commitment and its growing commercial orientation, combined with demanding that the magazine fulfil its vanguard role. Note that it does not require that the speaker identifies with the magazine or with feminism, though it suggests that the speaker's heart is with the feminist cause. Rather, readers feel that a feminist magazine should be anti-commercial and radical.

Opzij isn't radical any more. In just a little while it'll be indistinguishable from *Margriet* [a Dutch domestic weekly]. (Beth Hansen)

Opzij has become a purely commercial thing that makes itself rich on what is easily brought together under a feminist label. (John Wiarda)

And then they will get a marketing firm and start to compromise their own views. (Art de Groot)

Opzij isn't militant any more. (. . .) Lots of subjects but nothing new. It isn't an assertive feminist magazine any more. They've chosen the road to the popular. I know a woman and for her *Opzij* was a revelation! I don't have that. I recognize things, but they're not new to me. Anyhow, there has to be a vanguard and that is the role of *Opzij*. (Antonia Jansen)

The vanguard repertoire partly covers the same domain as the liberal-individualist repertoire (see below), in that both portray the reader as discriminating and critical, even though the political position implied by both repertoires is rather different. In this case the fierce criticism of *Opzij* appears to imply heavy political involvement on the part of the speaker. To believe this, however, would be to misunderstand the relation between magazine and reader. Only Ingrid Meertens and Art de Groot mentioned political activities, the former in her capacity as a volunteer lawyer for Amnesty International, the latter in an action group called Loesje. Loesje produces billboard posters with often ironic, one-liner reflections on life, politics and so on. The group's aim is to make people laugh. They hold the view that if people were less serious and tense, they would be more open to social change. None of the other informants took part in politics directly, nor were they involved in the women's movement. Using the vanguard repertoire appears to be a means of portraying oneself, temporarily, as a political animal. It is a means of trying on an identity, rather than a mirror of an existing identity. In some cases the political tie between speaker and magazine was given a nostalgic slant, and was described as a remnant of sixties and seventies feelings of solidarity and commitment. Minnie Redding kept her subscription for that reason, even though, quite often, she never even opened a new issue. Antonia Jansen said,

'There's nothing else', to explain her criticism and her loyalty. John Wiarda gives a similar reason for retaining his *Opzij* subscription:

> Women haven't actually gained a thing [by the sexual and feminist revolutions]. Not when *Opzij* has a questionnaire about the most admired women and the results are Margaret Thatcher and Neelie Smit-Kroes [former Dutch liberal minister; the liberal party in the Netherlands is a right wing party] . . . And *Opzij* doesn't take up such a challenge! As general management I'd given the order [to the editorial board]: that is what we are going to write about [in *Opzij*] in the coming year. Is the only thing that emancipated women can achieve imitating those patriarchal bastards?! What are we doing, then? . . . Still, it is useful that *Opzij* exists. I still keep my subscription.

The repertoire of moral duty

Reading *Opzij* 'because there's nothing else', or because, as a good citizen, one wants to keep informed about non-mainstream perspectives, reading *Opzij* for one's work – all these arguments reflect the view that reading *Opzij* is a moral duty. Geraldine Bank felt it was very important to be an informed person and stressed that this is something to be achieved, something that has to be worked for.

> Well, I have my newspaper and my subscriptions. I can't manage novels as well. I read *Opzij*, *Hervormd Nederland* [a Christian opinion weekly], the church magazine, *Amandla* [leaflet distributed by the anti-apartheid movement], the Greenpeace mag, Amnesty's magazine,[2] but they all come monthly . . . I can keep up with that. I always read one or two articles. Wouldn't it be annoying for those who make these magazines if you just threw them out?

In her critical response to my and Véronique Schutgens's article about reading *Opzij* (1991) Geraldine Bank again emphasized that she wanted to 'spend her energy doing useful things. I read the [Amnesty magazine] because I know how much press coverage may help a prisoner' (letter of 12 January 1992).

Nancy Lemhuis reads *Opzij* partly 'because of her work' (she is a PhD student who also does some teaching), partly because sometimes *Opzij* has articles that she can relate to on a more personal level, such as the special issue on motherhood. She, as I interpret her statement, wants to make clear that she sees supporting *Opzij* as her moral duty:

> *Opzij* holds the middle ground between magazines you read for work or for relaxation. I don't have a subscription, I go by the cover. Many articles are quite heavy, not on the level of *Margriet* and *Libelle* [domestic weeklies]. Some of the articles in *Opzij* you can use for your lectures, but it is also relaxing because they pick up such themes as jealousy or other personal things . . . I think it's very important that *Opzij* exists as a counterbalance to all those voices that say that feminism is *passé*. *Opzij* stands for something.

Marieke de Bruin recorded that all reading for her has the character of moral duty: 'I read that thing [*Opzij*] from cover to cover. I do that with all magazines that I read – horrible habit, slightly neurotic – because I always think, at least I haven't accidentally skipped things I would have wanted to know.' Her obligations are not to feminism or to *Opzij* as a visible symbol of feminism, but to an abstract ideal of being well informed; not to other political causes or to obscure editorial boards she does not know, but to herself. She owes it to herself to read everything.

The liberal-individualist repertoire

The repertoire used most by these fourteen *Opzij* readers was the liberal-individualist repertoire. It centres around a typical liberal view, which defined *Opzij* as a special interest magazine. For instance, if you are interested in gardening, you will read a horticulturist magazine; if you are interested in 'women's point of view', you will read *Opzij*. A magazine in this repertoire represents a point of view on the world. The reader is pictured as a rational consumer who chooses to be informed by whatever point of view is of interest to him or her. Clearly there is a hierarchical relation between reader and magazine. Magazines do not affect readers or how they think. The reader is an individual who 'masters' the world surrounding him or her.

Opzij is seen as the authoritative source on feminism because it is the only available nationwide feminist magazine and because feminism is not thought of as all important, as an ideology that pervades all of one's life. Feminism is seen as a restricted area, one point of view among many. The repertoire, in fact, suggests that the speaker's lifestyle is that of a well-informed reader-citizen.

> *Opzij* reflects a part of reality, other magazines reflect other parts. I have additional subscriptions. I don't need to read about the Third World in *Opzij*. (Renée Groothuis)

> *Opzij* isn't a spineless leaflet; it looks at things from women's point of view. (Geraldine Bank).

> *Opzij* has very interesting articles on politics; they show more sides to a subject in a very realist and not really very feminist way . . . I like to read bits and pieces, to see how other people have another view of things. (Marieke de Bruin)

The description 'not really very feminist' is meant as a compliment here. For Marieke de Bruin feminism is a negative label that has to do with hating men, marriages breaking up and so on. That *Opzij* has another, balanced view of things is one of the magazine's good points. Or, as John Wiarda said: '*Opzij* gives aspects of a feminine approach to things.'

The liberal-individualist repertoire also stresses the difference between oneself and the magazine. As an individual one is able to have an overview of different perspectives on society; one never coincides with just one point of view; therefore, although one is a reader of the magazine, the difference between *Opzij* and oneself can (and must) be emphasized. Charlotte de Bouvry said, 'Some of the things in *Opzij* are so different from how I feel and the things that I do. But it makes me think, it gives me another point of view. *Opzij* is rather like a good friend who tells you what you're saying is rubbish . . . I don't always agree with *Opzij*, but then, I don't always need to be confirmed in what I think.'

To stress the difference between oneself and *Opzij* accords with the open mind, so cherished in liberal ideology. We might wonder, however, how these readers deal with feminism, with sisterhood and solidarity. Keeping one's distance *vis-à-vis Opzij* also means keeping one's distance from feminism. In fact, feminism does not appear to be very important at all to how *Opzij* becomes meaningful (see the afterword to this chapter). The three repertoires are a means for *Opzij* readers to picture themselves in different ways, not just for the benefit of an interviewer, much more for their own benefit. Which fantasies, then, are evoked by reading *Opzij*, and which partial identities are imagined?

Reading Opzij: *feminism as fantasy rather than lifestyle*

The content of these three repertoires suggests that they help the speaker fantasize about the different kinds of ideal persons they could be. Marieke de Bruin's description of her personal style of reading as a neurotic habit ('I read that thing from cover to cover . . . at least I haven't accidentally skipped things I would have wanted to know') can be read as a construction of such a temporary ideal self. Behind the slightly self-deprecating label 'neurotic' there is a female *homo universalis*: someone who keeps up with everything that is interesting, who is 'in' on all that happens. Marieke de Bruin is partly giving an account of her actual practice of reading, we may assume. The repertoire of moral duty in that case simply describes part of a lifestyle. It would seem, however, that repertoires encompass more than that. To explain how one reads could be done in a much more simple fashion than was the case in the interviews. The more important aspect of the repertoires seems to be that they allow speakers to construct new selves, to give voice to how they would like to be, to how they feel they ought to stand in the world and relate to it.

The repertoire of moral duty is a case in point. On the one hand it suggests that life is nothing but obligations, an almost Calvinist chain of unending duties: one has to be well informed, one has to help political prisoners, one has to read *Opzij*. But the seriousness of the *Opzij* readers also implies that they found pleasure in taking up these duties, that taking their obligations towards themselves seriously augmented their self-esteem. The grumbling about *Opzij*, their criticism, suggests that they have a responsibility, that they feel that it matters what they think.

The vanguard repertoire appears to build on to the same fantasy. Given that these readers are not overwhelmingly politically active (in other ways than reading *Opzij*), one cannot speak of a lifestyle. Rather, it suggests they take pleasure in imagining themselves as responsible citizens and in working on how they understand the world intellectually. This involves constructing ideals or fantasies of perfect versions of oneself. I believe such fantasies to be constitutive of who we feel we are. Like the domestic weeklies and the glossies, feminist magazines (or at least this one) are used in highly personal dialogues that are conducted with widely available cultural systems of terms and meanings.

Opzij readers differ from those who do not read *Opzij* in that they are less apologetic and less ironic about their particular fantasies. One way to legitimate reading domestic magazines is to point out how very handy and useful the tips and recipes are. In chapter 2 I interpreted the use of this repertoire as involving a dream of perfect professional home-making and household management. Many readers added, ironically (or, at times, sincerely) reflecting on what they had said, that often tips are forgotten and that recipes can never be found again. *Opzij* readers did not do that. Marieke de Bruin's apologetic description of her 'neurotic habit' is an exception. As the other quotations show, the *Opzij* readers usually felt very good about taking up strong views. Until, that is, the subject of feminism was broached, to which I will return in the afterword to this chapter.

Opzij and the repertoire of connected knowing

The above interpretation of how *Opzij* becomes meaningful is exclusively based on the three strongest repertoires found in the interviews. On the basis of these quotations, one would have to conclude that *Opzij* has nothing in common with other women's magazine genres at all. There is even less reason to group *Opzij* with other women's magazines if what the *Opzij* readers said about traditional women's magazines is anything to go by.

Criticism of domestic weeklies was put thus: 'I've never been interested in *Margriet* and *Libelle* . . . I can't be bothered' (Antonia Jansen); 'The solutions given on the problem page are always so obvious . . . too thin . . . too much emphasis on babies' (Nancy Lemhuis). Art de Groot thought traditional women's magazines were 'overly snug' and portrayed 'set sex-role patterns'. Charlotte de Bouvry thought they were 'too fussy and there's really very little to read'. Marwil Sluiter told us how she scolded her German lover for not 'broadening her outlook on life and continuing to read *Der Bunte*', a German general audience magazine. Traditional women's magazines were sternly berated for their focus on home and hearth, on babies and motherhood, and for their reluctance to change with the times. The above quotations illustrate, for one thing, that it is easy enough for women to use male-associated comments: 'couldn't be bothered', 'rubbish', 'limited outlook'. Gendered discourse is not fixed to a sex, but, depending on the context, may cross over.

Positions initially taken up regarding women's magazines often changed later on in the interviews. Some of our informants occasionally enjoyed reading traditional women's magazines. Marieke de Bruin recalled how she used to swoon over romantic stories of the Mills and Boon kind in *Margriet*. Charlotte de Bouvry every now and then bought herself a French *Marie Claire* to indulge herself. Note how she carefully dissociated herself from *Libelle*, clearly assuming that any right-thinking person knows what being 'too much like *Libelle*') means: 'I buy *Marie Claire* because I studied French. It's good for my French and it's very cosy. I buy it to indulge myself. I wouldn't buy the Dutch *Marie Claire*, far too much like *Libelle* for me.' Nancy Lemhuis, though critical of the lack of depth in traditional women's magazines, had greatly enjoyed reading *Margriet* and *Libelle* while spending the weekend with her (former) parents-in-law. Antonia Jansen, who said she could not be bothered about them, later on in the interview admitted to browsing in a *Margriet* now and then. 'I like a *Margriet* just once in a while. I don't find it very absorbing. But, a nice recipe, I don't find that in *Opzij*.' Charlotte de Bouvry stopped her subscription to *Margriet* when she found that it took her ten minutes to read the entire magazine, it did not mean that she had lost all interest in it.

> I read *Libelle* and *Margriet* when I see them lying around at someone else's and she's making coffee. (Charlotte de Bouvry)

> I used to read [*Libelle* and *Margriet*] at my parents-in-law's and I really loved that – just, you know, relaxation. You seem to enter a totally different world. I loved dieting stories, women who'd suddenly lost 40 kilos and how happy they were, I loved that. But there's also a column, in *Margriet* I think, written by a woman who has lost her husband, a year and a half ago. She writes a diary and I always thought that very gripping. So, I'd browse more than I'd read. Relaxation, but also a particular image of how you're supposed to live. On the one hand that was really contradictory. But on the other hand I loved to lose myself a little. (Nancy Lemhuis)

Clearly readers may have access to very different reader identities. These identities, one might add, are highly contextually determined. They are particular to specific times and places, even if they can be talked about outside those specific contexts.

Not only did five of the fourteen *Opzij* readers 'confess' to reading traditional women's magazines, some of the *Opzij* readers also used the connected knowing repertoire – the only repertoire that under-lines the value of traditional women's magazines as a unique genre – to talk about traditional women's magazines and to talk about *Opzij*. In this respect, then, *Opzij* at least for some readers is a women's magazine. The repertoire of connected knowing pictures reading as a form of learning by reading about the experiences of others, which is thought to prepare one for the vagaries of life. Geraldine Bank was one of those who used it (one is tempted to say, 'in an unguarded moment', which is probably not true) to explain why she reads *Opzij*: 'You read things [in *Opzij*] and you know they could happen to you.' Nancy Lemhuis quoted *Opzij*'s special issue on motherhood as an example of the kind of issue that she buys and likes to read. This led her, towards the end of the interview, to more general reflection on the career woman's predicament (having a career and having children): 'Maybe in ten years' time I will have a job as a lecturer and then I'll have an enormous reaction. What is all this good for [I will ask myself], there were other things that were important, weren't there? That was part of my dream. What has happened to it? Yes, I do expect that that is going to be difficult.'

Since repertoires work at the level of fantasy rather than at the level of everyday organization and reflection, readers are, at times, slightly dumbfounded about the contradictions in their feelings regarding, in this case, reading *Opzij*. Charlotte de Bouvry looked forward very much to when the new *Opzij* came out, but then read it dutifully and without any enthusiasm. She indicated that she felt *Opzij* was to blame for her disappointment. Renée Groothuis got depressed and angry, though she also wanted to be informed about the injustice and the social wrongs done to women: 'I think that's why I also read *Viva* [a young women's magazine] – I have a life beyond feminism, try to do other things . . . For that is how it is when I'm reading *Opzij*; I stamp through the house very aggressively.' Renée Groothuis was the kind of ideal informant whose suggestions help a researcher to understand reading and what it means. What she refers to as 'having different lives' I have translated into fantasizing about different (ideal) selves by using different repertoires. I think we are talking about the same thing. Renée Groothuis is also the *Opzij* reader who suggested the value of self-help literature in terms of the connected knowing repertoire. She used this particular repertoire for traditional maga-zines, *Opzij* and self-help literature. Like a sizeable portion of the self-help readers I later talked to and heard from, she turned to the genre of self-help literature after a nervous breakdown. *Opzij* too was a help: '*Opzij* was an eye-opener when I was in trouble. It taught me to be a big, strong woman. On the other hand I enjoy their interviews with famous women, they can be surprisingly vulnerable. I am not the only one to have doubts and women's fears.'

Opzij is different from traditional women's magazines in many respects. There is a connection, though, between both women's magazines subgenres (the feminist and the traditional). The repertoire of connected knowing is one of the repertoires used by readers to make both subgenres meaningful. Since self-help literature is apparently also made meaningful through this repertoire, I shall now turn to its readers.

Reading self-help literature

Familiar arguments crop up when self-help readers explain how and why they read this genre of non-fiction books. Like women's magazine reading in the repertoire of connected knowing, reading self-help books is understood as a quest for understanding; reading about the experiences of others means learning about your own. Martine Spanier, when answering my question about which magazines she reads, turns from magazines to books:

Martine: And [*Avenue* magazine] described women's books too. I had a bout of reading women's books in large quantities, nothing else, and they wrote about that. (. . .)
Joke: What kind of women's books did you read?
Martine: I wish I could remember. Very well-known ones (. . .), you know, those well-known feminist . . .
Joke: Dutch authors? Renate Dorrestein, Anja Meulenbelt, Hermine de Graaf . . .
Martine: Yes . . . Meulenbelt and that book of hers that was admired so much – that one, that was a kind of bible to me, a terrific book, in which she . . .
Joke: *The Shame is Over Now*?
Martine: Yes, I thought that was a wonderful book. Everybody is in it, your mother, your sister, yourself . . .

Martine talks on about other authors she likes and ends up talking about a book she is reading at the moment:

I am reading something by a man called Langevelt. (. . .) It is called *Sensitive People*. (. . .) It lies next to my bed. I have a stack of books next to my bed. [She laughs and explains the subject-matter of the book.] But it says things that make me think, I have that, I feel that too, I recognize this.

Somehow the conversation drifts on to reading tarot cards. Using a little force, self-help books again become the topic of discussion.

Joke: Did I understand correctly that you started reading self-help books when your children were small?

Martine: Well, it started because I didn't understand why my father drank. And the answer to that question was given by the book *My Name is Wieters. I am an Alcoholic.* Have you read it? It answered a lot of old questions. (. . .) And then, of course, you can settle your account with it.

Later on in the interview the subject of self-help literature came up again, and Martine recalled:

When I had my children, you started with Spock. I don't know whether Spock is still there, but. (. . .) And then you buy other books about children or about special things that your child has. (. . .) And once you have started that, you keep looking for them because you can always pick up bits and pieces (. . .) If you knew, if you could learn a couple of practical methods from your parents or school, and if you didn't feel life was so difficult and such a struggle, then you wouldn't need these books, but you do. (. . .) People expect too much from one another.

Martine Spanier uses the connected knowing repertoire to explain how she reads self-help literature. Like the other self-help readers I interviewed and as reported in the letters of the self-help readers who wrote to me, Martine has a habit of gathering information from diverse sources, picking up bits and pieces here and there, which helps her to (temporarily) come to terms with personal problems. Occasionally she finds texts that appeal more to her than other texts. She treasured Meulenbelt's novel like a bible. Other readers used the same metaphor. The word suggests that the books are something to grasp hold of. Carolien van Essen's and Trudi Fransman's 'little bible' had been Louise Hay's *You Can Heal Yourself*.[3] Carolien van Essen also used another metaphor to describe what a good self-help book should do for its reader: 'A book like *The Words to Say It* [by Marie Cardinal],[4] I don't know whether others have told you about it? It's about an analysis, a psychoanalysis. And when you are pondering whether to go into analysis, something feels wrong, then you buy a book like that to see whether it would be a good idea. Like a kind of mirror.' Renée Groothuis, one of the fourteen *Opzij* readers, used the mirror metaphor to express what she sees as her debt to *Opzij*. She valued *Opzij*, she said, for holding up mirrors of the different identities she has, which indicates that reading *Opzij* is a way of learning about yourself by comparing who you are with women portrayed in the magazine.

Like Martine Spanier, Carolien van Essen prefers reading snippets here and there to 'official' forms of learning:

> You take bits and pieces and you hold on to what you can use. Sometimes it disappears and sometimes it becomes part of you. You wouldn't know from which book it came. That is how I have worked alternately on my physical condition and my mental condition [after a period of serious depression]. And that holistic influence, it's almost Salvation Army. I don't feel comfortable about it, but . . . [Louise Hay's book] was next to my bed as a kind of bible. I needed to learn to see the world in a different light, to free things and give it room. And the funny thing is, I started to find information that helped me to know myself.

Carolien goes on to explain about another book that has been important to her, by a psychologist named Alice Miller. Miller has helped her to understand what it means to experience oneself as a centre rather than to experience the world through others: 'Everybody said to me: take what *you* want seriously instead of doing what others would like . . . I didn't know what that was. I could say, I'll start with "me", but I didn't know what that was. By reading that book I suddenly understood what they meant and, I have to say, I felt liberated. Of course, things may go wrong again, but I do think that this depression is over.'

Recognition is the central good that reading self-help literature is about, which is exactly what other interviewees brought forward with regard to reading women's magazines. Trudi Fransman and Martha Janssen both enjoy reading traditional women's magazines; in some ways, according to them, it compares with reading self-help books. In the middle of the interview we started discussing women's magazines. Martha Janssen described herself as an omnivore. I asked her to explain something she had written in her letter to me: 'women's magazines carry self-help articles'.

> *Flair* [a Belgian/Dutch domestic weekly] recently had an article about sexuality and they write about that quite thoroughly, about a

few aspects, that is, in short blocks of text, very accessible. What I see as self-help is that readers may recognize themselves in that. I think that it . . . [helps] a lot of people. It's not that if you recognize it from another person or from a written text you are automatically helped but it is the kind of thing that makes people think, 'aha, they have the same thing, others have the same thing I have, I am not that strange, I don't have the aberration I thought I had.' (. . .) And almost all women's magazines have problem pages for medical and relationship problems. I imagine that questions about (. . .) illnesses you have yourself, or that a child or a partner has, help. It wouldn't have the effect of a self-help book. It's not like Nancy Friday's *My Mother and Myself*. But if you read an article in *Libelle* about three daughters who describe their relationship with their mother . . . the best thing would be if they had one with a good relationship, one with a normal relationship and one with a bad one. But it is always a bit coloured. The way Nancy Friday writes, you won't find that in *Libelle*. (. . .) [Women's magazines are] always a bit on the positive side. Although they also have dramatic stories about illnesses and death and I don't know what. (. . .) If you read that, it might help you a small step further. It might make you think, 'that's how it was for me', or 'no, for me it was really different', but it makes you think again.

[A bit later] Anyhow, I like to read about different kinds of things and about how people have solved things.

I asked Trudi Fransman outright whether she felt that articles in traditional magazines are comparable to self-help literature.

Joke: Would you say that feature stories in *Margriet* in which they describe what it is like to live with someone who has cancer – you know, the kind of article with lots of examples – would you say they can be compared with self-help books?

Trudi: Well, I think so.

Joke: Did you ever read them like that?

Trudi: I think so. You can also recognize things in them. Or if you are in a certain situation, you might think, it can be done like that too!

Joke: Reading a *Margriet*, you wouldn't really be searching, but you'd get a lot of small pieces of information that you didn't know beforehand you were going to get.

Trudi: Maybe there is a difference between having a subscription and buying single copies. (. . .) If you don't get them every week, automatically, you'll check what subjects they have. That could work a bit like me and self-help books. When my relationship is

not going well, I'll go to the library and see what they have. (. . .)
It's a bit like buying a copy of a women's magazine after checking
what's in it.

There are similarities in reading women's magazines, *Opzij* and
self-help books. Books, like magazines, are sampled, what one has no
use for is skipped and highly personal reconstructions of what ails the
reader are pieced together. The self-help readers I have spoken to are
convinced that reading will lead to a better understanding and
ultimately to a solution of their problem. Trudi Fransman chooses the
magazines she buys in almost the same manner in which she chooses
self-help books in the library. She skims them for relevant subjects.
The underlying repertoire of connected knowing and emotional
learning is the same for traditional women's magazines and self-help
books: by reading about other people's problems you can learn about
yourself and prepare for what may befall you.

Reading self-help literature, however, is usually not inspired by
mere curiosity. It is a more focused activity than reading women's
magazines. Most of the self-help readers I spoke to and who wrote to
me define themselves as someone who has a problem or a heavy
burden to carry for which official psychotherapy offered no relief or
for which it was simply not enough. One of my respondents was
trying to recover from the damage done by years of incestuous abuse
by an older brother. Self-help books were a relatively secure and
private means of exploring her feelings. Moreover, she could give
books to her partner to read, which was easier than telling him the
whole story herself. Martine Spanier felt that her life was not easy:
she had coped with an alcoholic for a father, two divorces and a
diabetic child. One of the others said, 'I am always fighting an
elementary insecurity that has to do with being a woman and the fact
that I was brought up to think, you're only a woman.'

All four self-help readers were 'self-made' women. They had taken
evening courses to enhance their professional qualification, or had
started new careers while no longer young. Somehow these
interviews left me with the impression that they saw themselves as
fighters. Even when they spoke of their insecurity, or confessed that
they did not have the heart to have an 'official' therapy again because
they felt uneasy about mental health institutions, they also conveyed
that they felt they had done fairly well for themselves and managed
to be their own experts. This impression may have been strengthened
by the fact that the self-help interviews and letters showed much
more 'literacy' than the interviews about *Opzij* or any of the other

women's magazine genres. I was given many examples of titles and arguments. Evidently the social use of this genre is markedly different from the social use of magazines, for the literacy in these interviews certainly did not extend to women's magazines, whose content was usually described rather vaguely.

Are feminist magazines women's magazines?

Does the subgenre of feminist magazines (here represented by *Opzij*) become meaningful through repertoires that are shared with other women's magazine subgenres? It seems to be the case that the more important repertoires for making sense of *Opzij* (the vanguard repertoire, the repertoire of moral duty and the liberal–individualist repertoire) are not used to make traditional women's magazines meaningful. The fantasy of being the perfect responsible and politically committed citizen is not built through, for example, the repertoire of practical knowledge. *Opzij* and self-help literature, however, together with traditional women's magazines and glossy magazines, are made sense of through the repertoire of connected knowing. Like traditional women's magazine reading, reading *Opzij* did not appear to be much reflected on or to lead to strong involvement, which makes both of them different from self-help literature.

Used in relation to traditional magazines, the repertoire of connected knowing is predominantly focused on taking care of others. The fantasy involved seems to be that of the perfect caretaker and mother, who keeps her family together in good (mental and physical) health. When it is used by *Opzij* readers, or a *Cosmopolitan* reader such as May Han (quoted in chapter 2), the connected knowing repertoire becomes self-directed. It leads to fantasies of being an ideal partner in such respects as not being jealous or possessive, of being someone who is totally in touch with her deeper feelings and ambitions: someone who is willing to learn and build on to her personality.

When the repertoire of connected knowing is used in relation to self-help literature, a new self-image crops up, linked to fantasies of a perfect self, stripped of the scars left by problematical relationships, incest, depressions: the image of the fighter. The fighter is a person who may not be seen as successful by others (and by critical others within herself); she may not have all the right certificates and qualifications, but she will eventually get where she wants to be. To do so, she is not highly critical; she will read everything to see if it can be of help. Clearly there are elements that connect women's magazines (including feminist magazines) to self-help literature. The difference between both genres seems to be the extent to which one is involved in them as a reader.

A last point that needs to be made is that the repertoires discussed here (and in the other chapters) do not exist as such. They are my reconstruction of common themes that form the cultural system of making sense of a feminist magazine, traditional women's magazines and self-help literature. Readers do not wittingly refer to the four repertoires (vanguard, moral duty, liberal-individualist, connected knowing) discussed in this chapter. Since the repertoires are referred to in highly personal dialogues, they remain in the background and are never made explicit.

To underline the personal quality of readers' involvement in these repertoires, let me quote Renée Groothuis once more. She pinpointed the identity play involved in women's magazine reading by comparing it with looking in different mirrors that are held up by the magazine. She clearly did not think other *Opzij* readers would read the same way, using the same cultural sources that she used. Of *Opzij* readers she said, 'I can readily imagine that *Opzij* readers belittle readers of traditional women's magazines, you know, as if they were housewives hung up on junk.' Renée Groothuis, like some of the other *Opzij* readers, portrayed herself as someone who sets store by political involvement. Like the self-help readers, she also set store by another self construct and found pleasure in feeling there are no general solutions to personal problems, one has to piece together particular, individual solutions from divergent sources. I interpret this pleasure as being derived from a fantasy of being able to build yourself by shedding old problems like old skins and by believing that deep down in oneself there is a new happy you to be found, who does not have problems, neuroses and so on. The partialness of reader identities is illustrated once more: seeing oneself as a politically involved person – and thinking in terms of collective subjects ('women') and general conditions ('oppression') – can exist side by side with a totally different, radically self-centred fantasy.

Afterword on feminism

In the interviews no one spontaneously described herself as a feminist. The *Opzij* readers' criticism of traditional women's magazines suggested implicitly that they would see themselves as feminists. But almost none of them did. In fact, quite often feminism, the women's movement and women's clubs were seen as frightening or very radical, possibly lesbian. Feminist women, stereotypically, were thought of as being overly provocative and out to find fault with everything. This surprised me very much (*Opzij* labels itself 'feminist monthly' on its cover) and also alarmed me, because I feel strongly about feminism and its value as a critical social perspective. Therefore I shall discuss the particular place feminism was given in the interviews in this afterword, which is also intended to clarify further the repertoires that have been reconstructed in this chapter.

Marieke de Bruin said of feminism:

> It is important that women occupy equal positions in society, that we have the same rights and duties. I find it difficult to define that. Feminist . . . I think how people feel about feminism has to do with having arguments over everything and going out in the streets [to demonstrate]. And, you know, claiming the right to your own body. That's what they talk about, feminists. While it is really a basic right to do that [have an abortion]. That doesn't have anything to do with feminism. It is a basic human right.

Antonia Jansen told us that many people think that *Opzij* is a lesbian magazine. She thinks that has something to do with the personal advertisements and that people who say this do not read *Opzij* all that closely. Like the other readers Véronique Schutgens and I talked to, she connected feminism in general with demonstrations and struggle, which she herself had never been involved in. Feminism and women's lib are quite often related to bra-burning and radicalism. The readers we talked to preferred to label themselves as 'emancipated'. Antonia was one of the exceptions, and called herself a feminist. 'I don't really do much about my feminism, it is so self-evident to me. My mother worked outside the home. And neither am I the kind of person who stands on the barricades. But I do think of myself as feminist.'

Antonia Jansen's careful explanation and other *Opzij* readers' hesitance make one wonder why they answered the newspaper advertisement asking *Opzij* readers for interviews. A mixture of pride, curiosity and defensiveness seems to have motivated them. They wished, perhaps, to dispel popular misconceptions about reading *Opzij* and 'feminism'. *Opzij* readers' fantasy or imaginary selves are not fighters, guerrillas or frightening women. Ingrid

Meertens voiced a comparable wish to influence stereotypical images: 'I answered your ad because I didn't want you to think that *NRC Handelsblad* readers [a Dutch liberal quality newspaper that is similar to the *Independent* but has a reputation like that of *The Times*] don't read *Opzij*.' To be fair to her, and to her male partner and a woman friend whom she persuaded to join in the interview, they were careful and precise about being feminist rather than obverse to being called thus. Ingrid would rather not be seen as a stuffy liberal, while her friend Marga Koster stressed that for her the magazine was a secret power reserve that helped her to do a tough job. She would not want to come across as a feminist and 'shock' people, however, because that would ruin her chances of bringing about any changes in the educational institution where she is a women's emancipation officer: 'As an emancipation worker you'd better not come on as a Joan of Arc. You'll turn people against you instead of emancipating them . . . You cannot tell everybody you're a feminist . . . it would lead to those hopeless discussions.'

The four self-help readers were not more political or less personally oriented in their reading than the *Opzij* readers, yet their strategy when talking about feminism was totally different. They sharply criticized the women's movement for its dogmatic character, which enabled them to claim feminist identities that were not tainted by negative definitions of feminism. Martine Spanier has a successful business in which she employs many women and a few men who work in an easy atmosphere of camaraderie and companionableness.

I am a feminist in my own way. I stand up for women. (. . .) I really am fed up with being the first woman to do market research. (. . .) In the firm I had with my husband, I did a man's job. I did a project for the Ministry of Economic Affairs. No one could imagine a woman doing that job and I wasn't even technically qualified for it. (. . .) And now the bon-bons. (. . .) I am the only woman in a buying group of confectioners. [I am tired of being the first or the only woman] because they really don't give you an honest chance. (. . .) It is such a petty-minded small world. I'll save you the insults I have had to take. (Martine Spanier)

When I had just come to live here I did a course called 'Women Orient Themselves in Society'. I was not brought up according to the stock sex-role pattern whereby girls don't need an education; we had to learn. Feminism, in a way, felt very natural to me, but then it started to live for me with the feminist wave. And that is how I started reading self-help books. (. . .) Fifteen years ago [in the mid-1970s] I started reading feminist books, about power relations between men and women. (. . .) [Trudi had a period in which she read many romances.] Of course, ten years back it was a mortal sin to read romances as a feminist. (. . .) That was one of the things that made me kick at feminism for a long time. Because . . . who can decide for me whether something is or isn't good for me? (Trudi Fransman)

I was born before the feminist revolution. (. . .) I find feminism such a charged word. Not everybody knows what you mean by it. I have called myself a feminist but not in the sense of the Amsterdam feminist movement, with the groups and the women's cafés. I was a feminist in my mind, so to speak, but I was recalcitrant and militant. (Carolien van Essen)

I would describe myself as a feminist as regards how I think and how I act. I don't belong to a movement. I don't identify with the feminist community that is talked about. There are things I find interesting, but some of it makes me think, sorry, but this is not for me. Especially when they were very rigid, it was almost a faith. (. . .) They were like the Reformed Church, it was Reformed Feminist. (. . .) But I would call myself a feminist now. (Martha Janssen)

The self-help readers were critical about what they perceived as the rigid dogmatism of the women's movement of the late seventies and the early eighties. Trudi Fransman went to a women's club, hoping to find a safe place to have fun, but felt very unwelcome because, she thought, she was not serious enough and was 'too fluttery' in the eyes of the other women. Possibly as a consequence of their outspoken criticism of the women's movement, coupled with their conviction that they were feminists in their own right, the self-help readers were more straightforward in their criticism of *Opzij*.

Martine Spanier said she thought *Opzij* dull. Three times she had started reading an article that seemed interesting and three times she had fallen asleep. Trudi Fransman, on a sudden urge, had taken a cheap introductory subscription to *Opzij* and forgot to cancel it in time. She said that not much of the content remains with her. Carolien van Essen appreciated *Opzij* a good deal. According to her, it is the professional magazine for emancipated women. She likes to read it for arguments to use in discussions. When I asked her whether she also felt critical of *Opzij*, however, she agreed the magazine has what she called a, 'distant, from the outside' semi-academic style. Martha Janssen appreciated that *Opzij* had become more separate from the women's movement, implying that she enjoyed reading it less a couple of years ago. Such is the irony of history: *Opzij* prints and sells more and more copies while becoming less and less recognizably a feminist magazine.

5

Reading Gossip Magazines: the Imagined Communities of 'Gossip' and 'Camp'

About gossip magazines

Printed gossip has a long history in the form of cheap populist newspapers and broadsheets (an example is the yellow press, popular at the turn of this century; see Kobre, 1964) but also in, for example, biographies (see Meyer Spacks, 1986). Contemporary gossip magazines such as the Dutch Privé *and* Story *or the British* Chat *and* Hello! *do not have such long histories. The Dutch gossip magazines were launched in the mid seventies, to cater for a group of female readers, who – according to publishers' market research – were not reading the women's magazines then published. The popular domestic weeklies had become more serious (partly, I assume, because of second-wave feminism) and were writing less than before about film stars, celebrities and royalty. Surprising publishers and critics alike, there turned out to be quite a large market for magazines that did (see Bardoel and Vasterman, 1977). In Britain* Chat *and* Hello! *were introduced a decade later. They too apppear to be commercially successful. All these magazines print practical advice, horoscopes and so on, alongside articles about celebrities, stars, TV personalities and royalty. Articles are mainly made up of pictures accompanied by a little text and suggestive headlines. The royalty magazines concentrate on royal families around the world.*

In order to elucidate the kind of gossip that is printed in the magazines my informants talk about, it is helpful to distinguish between three different varieties of gossip in gossip magazines: malicious gossip and scandal, friendly stories about celebrities (usually with a focus on babies) and stories about royalty. Most of the gossip magazines reader I spoke to have a preference for one of these three areas. The British magazine Majesty *and the Dutch magazine* Vorsten *(Sovereigns) differ slightly from other gossip magazines in their more expensive look; they are also older. They write about the trials and tribulations of royal families, most of whom have lost their empires. Kings of dubious East European countries that have not existed since the First World War abound. Magazines like the British* Chat *and the Dutch* Story *are friendlier and more focused on celebrities having babies than a magazine like* Hello! *or the Dutch magazines* Weekend *and* Privé. *Or, as Eduard Spaans, one of my informants, said:*

> Story *is more baby-oriented, full of Vanessas [Vanessa is a Dutch singer][1] who have babies, and it is sillier and on a smaller-scale. (. . .) While* Privé *is bent on scandals, really. Abortions, Sonja Barends' [chat-show host] wrinkles hugely enlarged.* Story *would never do that. [Would they have stories about very young girls having children?] That would never be in* Story, *or they would immediately have a Mother Mary, or a convent who takes care of the girl, they'd have a happy ending. It always ends more or less well. No drug-addicted artists in* Story *who die. They do have the funeral, but not as closely photographed. In* Privé *they have funerals, including the very last tear [and close-ups of the grieving] widow. (. . .).
> [On dramatic occasions]* Privé *will have pictures of everyone who was moved, while* Story *would write: 'They had a singer and it was nice.'*

Gossip has a bad reputation. It is considered a typical women's pastime and is often taken to be highly malicious talk about persons who are not present. Academic sources underline that gossip creates in-groups and out-groups and that it is a social menace. Anthropologists have presented many examples of gossip's dire consequences. Marlene de Vries, for example, researched gossip in the Turkish migrant community in the Netherlands. She suggests defining gossip as 'talking in an informal manner, with a certain satisfaction, about third persons who are not present in a more or less unfavourable vein; conveying to others a perhaps exaggerated version of specific unfavourable things one feels one knows about someone' (1990: 48). Her main conclusion is that gossip serves as an informal control of young women, especially as regards going out and seeing Dutch men, which makes it virtually impossible for them to do so, out of fear of having their entire family ostracized. Gossip thus serves to tie the Dutch Turkish community together and to discipline young women.

Gossip does not always have the consequences it has for the young Turkish women in the research of de Vries. I find the reputation of gossip somewhat harsh and one-sided. Gossip can also be a highly pleasurable experience for those involved in it and it does not necessarily influence other people's lives and choices. Patricia Meyer Spacks (1986) has taken up the cause of gossip, based on her own experience and on extensive literary research. She defines gossip as a continuum. Her description is so apt and altogether complete that I will quote it at length, to show how gossiping and reading gossip magazines may be a pleasurable, intimate pastime rather than a force of social control:

> At one extreme, gossip manifests itself as distilled malice. It plays with reputations, circulating truths and half-truths and falsehoods about the activities, sometimes about the motives and feelings, of others. Often it serves serious (possibly unconscious) purposes for the gossipers, whose manipulations of reputation can further political or social ambitions by damaging competitors or enemies, gratify envy and rage by diminishing another, generate an immediately satisfying sense of power, although the talkers acknowledge no such intent . . . More common is gossip issuing not from purposeful malice but . . . from lack of thought, the kind of gossip accurately characterized as 'idle talk.' It derives from unconsidered desire to say something without having to ponder too deeply. Without purposeful intent, gossipers bandy words and anecdotes about other people, thus protecting themselves from serious engagement with one another . . .
>
> At the opposite end of the continuum lies the gossip I call 'serious', which exists only as a function of intimacy. It takes place in private, at leisure, in a context of trust, usually among no more than two or three people. Its participants use talk about others to reflect about themselves, to express wonder and uncertainty and to locate certainties, to enlarge their knowledge of one another. Such gossip may use the stuff of scandal, but its purposes bear little on the world beyond the talkers except inasmuch as that world impinges on them. It provides a resource for the subordinated (anyone can talk; with a trusted listener, anyone can say anything), a crucial means of self-expression, a crucial form of solidarity. (1986: 4–5)

Reading gossip magazines may be a form of 'serious gossip'; it may serve to enlarge the reader's private world, and to create moral community. In this chapter I shall argue that printed gossip, like oral gossip, may serve (unconscious) needs for the reader. Reading gossip magazines may involve building fictions that are comparable to the intimacy and the stories that spoken gossip spins. In the case of both spoken and printed gossip a sense of community may be established.

While spoken gossip is built on learning about the other speaker through what she or he says about 'third persons who are not present', written gossip tends to create closeness or familiar faces in a wider world by helping the reader to bring celebrities into her or his circle of family, friends and acquaintances and by inviting readers to share in a moral universe that is at times petty, and at times rich.

During the first set of interviews it became clear that many readers regard gossip magazines as women's magazines. I would have thought them to be a genre in their own right, but it is true that gossip magazines, like women's magazines, write about people's emotions. Excluding the royalty magazines, most of them have a problem page, a medical advice section, a crossword. Some of them have recipes. But, as in the case of the feminist magazines, gossip magazines' resemblance to women's magazines in some respects makes the differences in other respects stand out strongly. Gossip magazines write about famous people rather than about anonymous women and men who could be 'living next door'. When those who read the subgenre talk about gossip magazines, the difference between gossip and women's magazines becomes even more pronounced. Gossip magazines inspire strong feelings, as much among those who would not define themselves as readers as among those who do. The quotations in this chapter come from both kinds of readers. They are considerably longer than the quotations about other women's magazines, which faithfully reflects the time readers took to talk about gossip magazines as compared with the time they took to talk about, for example, domestic weeklies. A second important difference between gossip magazines and other magazines with regard to how they are read and talked about concerns how gossip magazines become meaningful. The repertoires I found point not so much to fantasies of perfect selves, as was the case with traditional and with feminist magazines, as to 'imagined' communities, to use Benedict Anderson's (1983) term.

This chapter roughly divides styles of reading and talking about gossip magazines into two categories: serious reading and camp reading. This is the unintended result of the fact that in my search for readers I happened upon two widely divergent groups that enjoyed gossip magazines. The larger group consists mainly of women, who speak more or less seriously about gossip magazines. The other group consists mainly of gay men, who never seem to speak seriously about gossip magazines (nor about other popular media genres). Some of the men were found when searching for male readers of women's magazines in general, and some of them were on the list of names a research bureau I hired to find respondents came up with after a computer-aided telephone search. One, Eduard Spaans, was interviewed with the clearly stated goal of finding more information about reading gossip magazines, 'camp' and the gay community. First I shall turn to 'serious reading', describe the pleasure readers in general derive from these magazines, and then explore whether any specific repertoires were used to talk about gossip magazines and, if so, what they were like. I shall then turn to 'unserious reading of gossip magazines', discuss irony and camp as strategies that readers may employ, to then show how gossip magazines have an important role in gay subculture. Ten women are quoted at some length in this chapter and four men. Brief quotations from another four women are also included. Some of these readers have already been quoted in chapter 2.

'Serious' reading of gossip magazines

The pleasure of reading gossip magazines

Generally speaking, reading gossip magazines is very much like reading traditional women's magazines: it is pleasant to look at pictures, to read photo captions, the more so because the pictures are of people we are familiar with through television. Some of the women's magazine readers introduced in the previous chapters, who would not define themselves as gossip readers, do occasionally read gossip magazines (Jeanne Rousset and Mrs Dobbel) and enjoy their unpretentious, undemanding stories. Others are fascinated, but express puzzlement at their fascination or defend their taste for this low-valued genre by making it clear that they are aware of this low status and that they are not taken in by the magazines and what they write (Joan Becker).

> Every now and then [I read] *Story* and *Privé*. (. . .) I don't know what I find in them, but I read them at my hairdresser's. (. . .) That kind of thing, when you have to wait, or something, and then it's lovely. I'll flick through them and read small bits and pieces . . . Usually it's more looking at pictures and the captions [than reading]. (Jeanne Rousset)

> *Story* and *Weekend*, that's looking at pictures. [When the collection of magazines comes] usually *Story* is the first I pick up, 'cause it is

nice to leaf through, you don't have to really read it. (. . .) It's looking at pictures, I don't get anything out of it. (Mrs Dobbel)

My mother reads herself silly with that *Privé* and *Weekend*. (. . .) When I visit her, I dive into her magazine basket and I'll look for them. With a lot of scepticism. (. . .) I really hate those magazines, but I have to look through them. Not that I believe them. (Joan Becker)

They are stupid stories, but you are curious. You buy it. (. . .) When you see them on the counter, you think, 'I won't buy it, I won't.' But when you get home from work, have a cup of coffee, and there's something to browse through . . . you buy it. (Marion Gerards)

Apart from describing the simple pleasure of browsing through these magazines or stressing critical distance, however, gossip magazine readers would often also enthusiastically describe the different forms their attachments to the genre take. An important aspect of the pleasure in gossip magazine reading, for example, is to feel involved with the stars and celebrities the magazines write about.

Things on the front page, well, I want to read that. When a couple breaks up, and it turns out to be not true . . . you thought so, but you do want to check. (Tina Poorter)

When I read about Mies [Bouwman, a chat-show host] and I see her swollen face . . . That happened to me too, when I had that medication. (. . .) If *Story* wrote about strangers, you wouldn't be interested. (Christine Klein)

I do want to know who has been married and who is going to divorce. (Joan Becker)

[They are called gossip magazines] because they are about famous people. [Domestic weeklies] are also about people, but they aren't well-known. These are all really well known, from television; it's twice as interesting to know something about them or to read about them. (Ina Dammers)

Reflecting on what my respondents told me, there appear to be different kinds of pleasure involved in reading gossip magazines. The pleasure of reading about celebrities is a pleasure both of vicariously enjoying the world of glitter and glamour and of gaining a 'secret', inside knowledge that may confer an imaginary sense of power over the rich and powerful. Then there is the pleasure of extending your family by including the stars, as well as a kind of pleasure that is akin to the pleasure of puzzle solving. Since some of these pleasures have been described in relation to other popular genres, I shall briefly turn to work on soap opera, before returning to my readers.[2]

Maarten Reesink (1990), speaking from a dual perspective as student of popular culture and as gossip magazine aficionado, likened reading *Privé* to watching soap opera. Just as the soap opera viewer follows the ups and downs of a large cast of characters through highly diverse plots, reading a gossip magazine engages one in the lives, or 'plots', of the rich and famous. Gossip magazines appear to offer the pleasure of fiction in the guise of journalism, reminiscent of how Kim Schrøder (1988) typified what makes watching the prime-time soap opera *Dynasty* worthwhile and pleasurable. Schrøder proposes that part of the fun of watching the series is to be engaged in a 'fictional jigsaw puzzle, constantly on the look-out for new pieces, imagining what they look like, tentatively fitting them into gaps in the narrative structure or character relations, and experiencing triumphant gratification [when one] succeeds' (1988: 63). *Dynasty* viewers forecast how relations between characters will develop. Part of the fun of reading gossip magazines, likewise, is to ferret out the extent of truth in what the magazines write about stars, princes and television personalities, and to put together who is involved with or pregnant by or breaking up with whom.

Defending one's credentials

That reading gossip magazines involves (or may involve) intellectual exercise in hypothesizing about relationships, based on a trained intuition, is not a generally accepted view. As a rule reading gossip magazines is condemned as a silly waste of time, something that mindless women engage in. The alleged untruth of most of what is written is one of the grounds on which reading gossip magazines is criticized. Although the gossip magazine readers I spoke to did not mind sharing their enthusiasm and ideas about the genre with me, they also told me that they, in turn, were critical of the fact that reading gossip magazines is not approved of. They suspected many people who condemn them of hypocrisy and suggested that those who say they happened to have seen a copy at their hairdresser's read them secretly at home. They also made clear that they were certainly not the silly women gossip magazine readers are made out to be. Christine Klein, quoted below, has just sarcastically remarked that all those people who disapproved of gossip magazines tend to grab them, first thing, when they come to visit her. Moreover, they appear to be well informed about the trials and tribulations of the stars, one of her favourite topics for talk and speculation. She herself holds the view that a practised reader may learn much from careful reading about the stars she feels connected to and will be able to tell true from false information, for example by comparing the information in different magazines.

> Gossip or not, there is always a kernel of truth. When they write, 'Martine is divorcing her husband' [Martine Bijl is a Dutch singer and performer], she'll leave, that's for sure, but how? . . . Then you search, the other magazines write slightly different things . . . People are so negative about that. If I want to talk about something, I talk about Martine Bijl. That is what I like. (Christine Klein)

> They do print a few lies, but you still read it. You see these people often on television and you know a little bit more about them. You know it is a lie sometimes, but you do read it . . . Gerard Joling [popular singer] is supposed to be gay. It is hard to believe that. (Solema Tillie)

> You don't have to believe everything, but I do like to read them. (. . .) I often think, they add a little to it, to make a good story. But [since it is about these well-known people] I always think some of it must be true. (Ina Dammers)

> When I tell my husband about something I've read, he says, 'you read it in *Privé*, didn't you? I don't understand why you believe all that.' Well, there are things that I don't believe. (Tina Poorter)

Tina Poorter occasionally disputes the gossip magazines' interpretation and comes up with her own. So does Solema Tillie.

> Part of it is true, but I don't know. (. . .) They write quite a lot now about [a celebrity whose name could not be transcribed.] But they say she has been partying all night. They say it without thinking. You don't know how they [famous people] live; she could be having a miserable time – she is only human. Yeah, what do I care whether she parties all night? They don't have to write about that

for me, I won't read it anyway. They [famous people] have their lousy times too. Those bags under her eyes don't have to come from just partying. (. . .) I think they simply like to write filth about a person like her. Sometime I think it is just to drag a person through the mud. I hate it when people say things about me that aren't true at all. That is why I don't believe everything. (Tina Poorter)

What Rob de Nijs [popular singer] did, with that girl, he saved her from becoming a prostitute. [Apparently de Nijs brought a South Asian girl to the Netherlands and made a video with her.] I don't think they were lovers. (. . .) They rescued that girl from poverty and gave her a few nice days here. I really like that. (Solema Tillie)

The extended family repertoire

The pleasures of reading gossip magazines – the soap opera like pleasure of puzzling over what is 'really' happening in the lives of the celebrities the magazines write about, vicariously enjoying the world of the rich, gaining a sense of secret power, a scandalized sense of outrage, or simply of things happening – are reported on and legitimated through two main repertoires: the extended family repertoire and the repertoire of melodrama. The extended family repertoire has been referred to above. On an imaginary level it helps readers to live in a larger world than in real life – a world that is governed by emotional ties, that may be shaken by divorces and so on, but that is never seriously threatened. Sociological realities such as high divorce rates, broken families, children who leave home hardly ever to be seen again are temporarily softened.

Tania Modleski (1984) has put forward a similar argument about soap opera based on an analysis of soap opera's narrative structure. Whatever may happen to the enormous cast of characters who are all lead characters (though from time to time less prominently so), they tend to come back to the family, the hospital or small village in which the story is set. Modleski claims that it is reassuring for viewers to see that, whatever happens, families do not fall apart. Gossip magazines hold the same kind of attraction, even though the extended family in question is more loosely structured than the fictional families in soap operas. Tina Poorter likes to read about artists she has been following for years. Joan Becker said, 'I want to know who has been married and who is going to divorce'. Christine Klein professed her deep and personal liking for Martine Bijl (a performer) and Mies Bouwman (a TV-show host). Solema Tillie spoke of the artists she likes to read about with much feeling and in great detail. Like some of the others, she stresses that she feels she knows these artists because she sees them on television. In point of fact, some of those she mentioned have not been on television for a long time, though over the years they seem to have become heroes of Dutch popular culture. Given all the years of bits of information, one might well feel one knows these people and address them by name.

The extended family repertoire is a relatively simple and straight-forward repertoire. It engenders a highly personal form of address in which solidarity and connectedness resound. In the interviews the extended family repertoire tended to be mixed with a disapproval that was clearly savoured, with a sense of outrage and a wish to reset the societal power balance, if only through the pleasure of knowing things about the high and mighty, with a relish for misery and tragedy. These I consider traces of another, much more complex repertoire, which has been called the repertoire of melodrama because of its exaggeration and revelry in states of great emotion. Tina Poorter used the extended family repertoire when she said she liked to read about how 'Gert and Hermien [singers who midway in their career "saw the Lord" and changed their repertoire, and now, it seems, have changed back again] are doing, haven't heard from them for years. They had such difficult times', as if these singers were acquaintances she would like to have a good chat with. But Tina Poorter also enjoyed 'a bit of sensation', and used the repertoire of melodrama (see below) to give an example of other stories she likes, such as a celebrity drinking outrageously heavily, something she claims she did not hear about among her friends and acquaintances. Joan Becker, who did not consider herself a gossip reader, mixed the two repertoires when she explained that she wants to know 'who has been married and who is going to divorce'. She loves and loathes the stars as well as the magazines.

The repertoire of melodrama

Some readers hardly used the extended family repertoire at all. Dot Groeniers, for example, emphasized that she enjoyed it when the rich and famous were put in their place by their share of misery and unhappiness: 'I like [it] when things go really badly for those [people]' (full quotation below). She predominantly used the reper-toire of melodrama, which focuses on misery, drama, sentimental-ism, sensation and paying for daring to rise above other people or for being filthy rich. Melodrama is associated with a fascination for misery, sorrow, heartbreak and so on. As an art form it consists of 'a sensational dramatic piece with crude appeals to the emotions and usually a happy ending', according to the eighth edition of *The Concise Oxford Dictionary*. The joy, for readers or spectators, is to wallow in the sorrow and misery of others, rather than in one's own. Life is a vale of tears. Life in the repertoire of melodrama becomes grotesquely magnified.

Whereas the extended family repertoire is centred around a certain kind of content (a usually benevolent interest in a cast of well-known people and how they are doing) and does not evaluate, measure or condemn, the repertoire of melodrama is as outspoken in its indignation as in its sentimentality. It questions what makes life worthwhile, though normally not by rational reasoning, but by emotional appeal or outrage. Thus, the repertoire of melodrama may provide solace for individual readers. The misery of others may either make them feel better about their own lives or allow them to have a good cry over frustrations and sorrow they choose not to analyse more closely. In chapter 2 I quoted Elizabeth Veenstra, who cried her eyes out over a story of a seriously ill child that dies. There is a certain satisfaction in being able to do so, to experience a deep sense that the world is not just, not only to the child and its parents but, of course, also to you yourself. The sense of injustice that is at the heart of the repertoire of melodrama also points at a more collective sense of social inequality. To enjoy it when things go badly for 'rich and famous people' is a way of imagining cosmic (rather than political) justice taking its toll, it is a moral stance.

To illustrate the repertoire of melodrama, first a quotation is offered about how 'enjoying the misery of others' can be a way of displacing injustice we feel we have suffered.

> I noticed that when I was in a rotten mood, I wasn't reading those magazines for cheerful subjects and I thought, you want to read about others having an even worse time than you're having. [For] they mainly write about misery. [Later during the group interview Tina Poorter remarked that when you read about the woes of others, your own troubles do not seem so bad.] That's what I mean, that comfort, when I read about other people's trouble, I think, I am not doing all that badly. I'm doing fine, really. (Martha Steenman)

The melodrama of the repertoire of melodrama can be found as much in the subjects it deals with (emotions of the stars over divorces, heartbreak and dead children or, to the irritation of readers, dead pets) as in the suggestion that the speakers have a hard life themselves. 'I'm not all that badly off' was never said smugly. Rather, it was meant to denote constraint in not complaining about one's life. Interestingly, in the group interview with Tina Poorter, Martha Steenman and Marion Gerards this constraint fell away. While they announced ritually that they did not mean to complain, they all talked at length about hardships in their lives: divorce, illnesses and loneliness. The sphere of melodrama, conjured up by talking about gossip magazines, stretched to envelop the personal lives of the three speakers. For a change, they were interviewed, they held centre stage, and they used the codes of the genre in the way it had meaning for them. Melodrama was as prominent in Marion Gerards's story about her lonely life as a sailor's wife as it was prominent in what Tina Poorter said about her mother (who had to have psychiatric help after a period of loneliness and the breaking up of a relationship) or about the partners of gay celebrities. The drama, sensation, misery and wretchedness readers talked about often concerned not their own lives, but the lives of people they knew. The quotations below attest to the *frisson*, the commiseration and the indignation that reading about other people's misery may give.

You wouldn't usually hear about it. I mean, I wouldn't. You read sometimes about someone who's given to drink. That wouldn't happen around here. That's why it's nice to read. It's sensation, really. (. . .) They have these stories about artists. Not the kind of thing that would happen in my daily life. (. . .) And they had this piece about Jos Brink [gay performer and television personality] and André van Duin [humorist, also gay], about their partners who they had to keep in the background. And that Jos Brink came out and when he went to a party, someone else would come with her husband (. . .) and his boyfriend would have to keep out of the way in those ballrooms . . . It's the kind of thing that gets you thinking . . . that those people had really difficult times. (Tina Poorter)

I really read [instead of browse in *Story*], I like that . . . All that happens in those [circles]. (. . .) People like that don't live in this village. (. . .) They just have nice stories about those stars. (. . .) I really think I'm not doing that badly when I read some of those things, divorces and so on. That is what I read, what I like, when things go really badly for those [people] . . . It's nice to read because you wouldn't hear about it otherwise. (. . .) I like *Weekend* for their real life stories about girls of twelve years old who have babies, or girls of nine years old. A child has a child, they then write. (Dot Groeniers)

... and the misery. You often think for those people, on television or wherever, that life is all roses. When you see them, they are always looking so fine, but it gets you thinking they may be unhappy in some other way. (. . .) Their lives aren't as easy as you might think. Maybe because of the kind of circles they live in. This one is carrying on with that one, and that one is carrying on with that one. Then I think, but that's not right. They have a totally different kind of life. (Ina Dammers)

In what Ina Dammers and Tina Poorter say there is more than just the thrill of partaking in sorrow, or seeking sensation, there is also a strong moral feeling. Their basic moral assumption seems to be that all people are equal and that all have their crosses to bear, their portion of grief to deal with. Obviously such moral assumptions are closely linked to how those who are not rich or well-to-do, experience social inequality. Money does not set one free of sorrow, nor ought it to bestow privileges. Like Ina Dammers, both Tina Poorter and Christine Klein criticized the fact that apparently those who are very rich, or have much social prestige, may live above laws of morality. Christine Klein felt very strongly about the corrupting powers of money. 'We stayed honest,' she says, 'because we didn't have any money.' Her other strong claim is, 'Money can't buy happiness'. Happiness, friendship and her close-knit family are her riches.

I have had an awfully rich life. Very rich. I have been ill a lot, but I can say that I've always had a load of fun too. (. . .) Money is the problem. Money is the biggest evil in society. You need it, I know, you need money. But when you have too much, you start spending it, children get spoiled. I have known poverty, real poverty; because I was ill, you know. Back then, you couldn't just go to hospital, we had to pay. (. . .) Money is the biggest dirt that exists. (. . .) Friendship is the richest thing one has. Like my youngest son, who was born and brought up here, he still goes on holiday with a friend [he was at school with] for three weeks every year. And my other son still sees his first friend. And my daughter is still friends with a girl from the house we lived in before this one. They live in Australia now and have invited her over. Those are friendships. I have friends myself whom I met fifty years ago. (Christine Klein)

Christine Klein has a sharp eye for social inequality and for the different rules on behaviour that apply. She is very much aware that whereas a film actress might wear funny hats, she would not be able to do so, because 'the whole street would be in an uproar'. Her strong belief in friendship and having fun is an alternative system for evaluating what life is worth. Tina Poorter is more conventional in the moral systems she recognizes. She mixes a need for 'a bit of sensation', or, as Patricia Meyer Spacks (1986) would say, 'the living breath of event', with a firm belief that all women and men are equal, and with 'the good citizen's' outcry: they are spending my tax money!

[Those soccer players] they're young, they earn a lot, they do what they like. They live [in Italy] and they come to Amsterdam to go out. What that must cost! (. . .) But they are all ordinary people for me. You do find that out. You thought some of them were really special, I used to think that, but they are all ordinary people, just like us. Beatrix, the queen, or a minister, they are all just like us. (. . .) They have their fiascos. On the one hand you think, they earn a lot and they can do everything they want to do, because you read about that. And you start to think about it and you think, they are close to the fire. They have jaunts abroad. They have to go to do this or that, but they turn it into a junket . . . I get angry at that: why do they need to do that? It's my tax money they're spending. (Tina Poorter)

The (moral) community of gossip

In their own ways the extended family repertoire and the repertoire of melodrama betoken a wish for and a forging of community, a quality that, I would argue, is inherent in all gossip. The extended family repertoire in its friendly manner simply draws a wide circle of people into a person's private life by discussing them intimately. On an imaginary level, this creates a form of community. Going by hints and sometimes open remarks made by the readers I spoke to they also use the extended family repertoire in conversations with friends. Christine Klein finds talking about her favourite stars a comfortable way of spending her time with other people. Gossip draws speakers together in their sharing and evaluation of 'news' about 'third persons who are not present'.

The repertoire of melodrama creates community in a different manner. This repertoire comes into play when readers are indignant, when they are shocked or deeply moved and wish to evaluate explicitly what they have heard. By either reading gossip or talking about what they have read with friends they appeal to and thus construe shared standards of morality (with an imagined community of other gossip readers, or with other readers who are present in the flesh) that alternate between disapproval and understanding. Gossip brings together by creating an intimate common world in which private standards of morality apply to what is and what is not acceptable behaviour. It is about basic human values and emotions, about the fact that, in the end, all human beings are equal, whether they are rich or poor, whether they live in the glittery world of showbusiness or whether they only read about it. Going by the two repertoires I found, reading gossip magazines revolves not around fantasies of perfect selves but around fantasies of belonging: to an extended family or to a moral community. Moreover, in interpreting the gossip magazine text readers use and validate their own personal knowledge and experiences. Solema Tillie (a proud mother and grandmother), for example, drew upon her own experiences to challenge what was written about the Dutch queen mother Juliana:

> In Surinam I used to read a lot. I remember reading about when that girl Christina [the Dutch royal princess] had a bad eye, and her mother [then Queen Juliana] had gone to see a clairvoyant. And I read that there was a scandal about that in the Netherlands. The woman worked in the palace or Queen Juliana had her called in (. . .) And I wondered whether that girl couldn't be operated on for her eye. Maybe a doctor had said that that was impossible and that's why her mother went on. Even if you are a queen, it is about your child. When you hear that someone may help, you'll try. Whatever you are, whatever title you have, you'll try. She is a mother. She didn't think, I am the queen, she thought, I am going to try and see if it works. (. .] .) When it concerns the health of your child, even if someone is fooling you, that's not what you think of, you'll always try. [The 'clairvoyant' was a kind of faith healer called Greet Hofmans. She was thought to inspire communist ideas in the Queen, which at the height of the Cold War, at the end of the fifties, gave rise to a huge political scandal.]

'Unserious' gossip reading: irony and camp

Stereotypically, women are thought of as gossipers, whereas men are not. A close second, as far as stereotypes are concerned, are gay men.

And, indeed, although I did not initially set out to find gay gossip magazine readers, a first interview with a male reader about gossip magazines strongly suggested that reading gossip magazines for him was part of an 'act', a playful way of showing off and playing with other people's cultural values and judgements – the kind of act, in fact, that some gay men like to use in confusing others and enjoy among themselves, often labelled as 'camp'. All four male gossip readers who were interviewed to some extent used irony or camp when talking about women's magazines. Only one of them (Eduard Spaans, the last to be interviewed) was asked with the explicit goal of talking about the relationship between gossip magazines, camp and the gay community. Before I go on to explore how gossip magazines relate to yet another kind of imagined community (the camp fantasy world of appearances and superficiality, of living a public image rather than a life), let me explain about camp and the difference between camp and irony.

Camp and irony

Camp is notoriously hard to define and, according to some, 'in appalling taste – because camp defined no longer is' (Schiff, 1984: 65). Camp is mainly to be found in the male homosexual community. Camp mocks existing standards and perverts them by turning them upside down. It is camp, for example, to make a top ten of 'the worst films that have ever been made' and to flirt with knowing them back to front. 'To perceive Camp in objects', according to Susan Sontag, 'is to understand Being-as-Playing-a-Role. It is the farthest extension, in sensibility, of the metaphor of life as theater' ([1964] 1982: 109). Camp divides the world between those who are 'in the know', *cognoscenti*, and those who are not by offering those who are in the know a different, supplementary set of standards (p. 114).

Andrew Ross (1989) takes a slightly different and somewhat exalted but interesting view of camp. Ross sees all culture as a product of power relations. Camp, in particular, he sees as containing 'an explicit commentary on feats of survival in a world dominated by the taste, interests, and definitions of others' (1989: 144). Camp is not a fixed category. Rather, in the words of Thomas Hess, it 'exists in the smirk of the beholder' (quoted in Ross, 1989: 145). Camp, according to Ross, involves 'a celebration, on the part of cognoscenti, of the alienation, distance, and incongruity reflected in the process by which hitherto unexpected value can be located in some obscure or exorbitant product' (1989: 146). Quoting Mark Booth, he goes on to say that: 'far from being a "fugitive" or "ineffable" sensibility, camp belongs to the history of the "self-presentation" of arriviste groups. Because of their marginality, and lack of inherited cultural capital, these groups parody their subordinate or uncertain social status in a self-mocking abdication of any pretentions to power' (p. 146).

There is a difference between camp and irony. The first concerns, for example, gay readers of gossip magazines, who aggressively flaunt their 'bad taste', their 'being different' to the world. Ross would call them the marginal camp intellectuals, who 'express [their] impotence as the dominated faction of a ruling bloc at the same time as [they] distance [themselves] from the conventional morality and taste of the ascendant middle-class' (1989: 146–7). Irony, on the other hand, is parody rather than outright subversion on the part of groups outside the homosexual community. It is a much more defensive stance on the part of those with enough cultural capital to feel sure that they will distinguish themselves as 'cultured' by admitting that they feel critical about the system of taste and the exclusiveness of high culture.

Whereas camp is a means by which to immerse oneself in low taste, to enjoy thoroughly 'the bad taste of yesterday', as a friend says, irony is a way of distancing oneself from low culture, of laughing it away, as it were. Joppe Boodt (1992), one of my co-interviewers, concentrated on male readers of women's magazines (including gossip magazines) and found that among them there are two dominant ways of talking about women's magazines, one serious and involved, the other ironic. Irony, he argues, following Bourdieu (1980), is a highly effective way of distinguishing oneself. Irony is a means of detaching oneself from what one reads (or watches on television). Irony indirectly confirms cultural competence. One shows one has knowledge of what is and what is not Culture or Art by commenting on one's occasional bouts of bad taste. Irony suggests not only duplicitous knowledge, but also that since one knows how bad it is, one is surely inoculated against it. Cultural competence, according to Bourdieu (1980), is the result of class background and education. Boodt found that education was, in fact, a fitting explanation for the difference between the two groups of men (the involved and serious readers versus the ironic and detached readers) he found among our respondents.

The seven respondents with a university education all thought *Privé* amusing, they were not irritated by the magazine. The other men [with lower-level education] stressed that they found both the content and the journalistic method employed by the gossip magazines objectionable. The same mechanism was found for other magazines. The men who did not have much education did not use irony when they occasionally read magazines they did not particularly appreciate (*Cosmopolitan*, for example). They got angry when they talked about them, they were not at all amused. (Boodt, 1992: 10).

To talk seriously about gossip magazines is to argue that it is legitimate to want to know how one's favourite stars are doing, the low cultural status of the genre notwithstanding. To speak of reading gossip magazines ironically is to underline that occasional indulgence in low culture is legitimate for the cultured. Camp, though, dismisses out of hand the question of the legitimacy of enjoying low culture. Camp talk makes fun of the magazines, and of the stars and celebrities the magazines write about and about the speaker as reader. Camp is to 'adore *and* to jeer, to be sucked in *and* then to pull back in derision' (Schiff, 1984: 65, my italic). Serious reading may be intent on ferreting out the particles of truth that articles must be based on. Camp reading is not interested in whether or not what is written is 'true'; life is a farce, a comedy of manners, which is nowhere more clear than in gossip magazines.

Camp is not strictly confined to the gay community. Some women (regardless of their sexual orientation) sport the same affected tone. Generally speaking, however, irony and camp were less important in the interviews with women. Comparing all women with all men, it would seem to be the case that women tend to talk more seriously and more respectfully about women's magazines and gossip magazines. To some extent women with more education tended to be more distanced from and more ironic about what they read, a difference in cultural capital that has also been found by other researchers (see, for example, Gray, 1992).

Fun and exaggeration

Irony and camp are alike in that both use and parody available repertoires to talk about gossip magazines. Frederik Paulsen alluded to the extended family repertoire during a group interview with Ingrid Meertens, his partner, and Marga Koster, a friend. In the middle of a discussion about a cover story about black women in *Marie Claire*, a glossy that had just been published in a Dutch version, and about the level and critical potential of such stories, Frederik felt the need to confess, a broad grin on his face: 'I have to say, on the other hand, that I was sailing with friends and what did we buy? *Panorama, Story* and *Privé* and we had a wonderful time reading that in the sun. [Everybody laughs.] I could pretend to be better than I am, but I really loved that. And I'll think, whatever happened to Hans van der Togt [a newsreader]? Really blissful.' Lies Machielse, who does not and never did read women's magazines, employed the same strategy when we happened on the subject of gossip magazines: 'Well, *Privé* I find delightful, too. [This was said in a slightly mocking tone of voice.] All that dirty gossip about royal families, I really love it. And then that awful van der Meyden [editor-in-chief of *Privé* and a national celebrity and television personality himself], that piece of scum, I like that [page of his in a right-wing daily] too. I would never buy [*Privé*]. I see it on the counter when I'm buying cigarettes: Willem-Alexander [Dutch crown prince] with a beautiful lass'. Joan Becker (a self-trained secretary) made fun of her fascination for gossip magazines (and also criticized them for their unethical methods), Christine Klein (who is seventy–four), crossing over from serious reading, used both the extended family repertoire and the repertoire of melodrama when she characterized *Story* and *Privé* as 'tasty garbage': 'There is no real sorrow in those two [magazines], you have to take them with a pinch of salt. (. . .) [Later on in the interview, laughing] Ahh, Ron Brandsteder [good-looking chat-show host], well, I'm too old for him.'

Irony, I agree with Boodt, in general seems to be the weapon of the 'cultural capitalist'. It is not always perfectly clear whether one is dealing with irony, with unwitting forms of camp or with simply making fun. To make such distinctions based on the few quotations above would be risky. Suffice it to say that reading gossip magazines, for all readers, is to some degree shot through with reservations about their truthfulness, with the fun of speculation and with the pleasure of gaining 'forbidden' knowledge, both in the sense of scandal and in the sense of partaking in low and almost illegitimate culture. When reading seriously we may experience the added pleasure of moral indignation and an equally moral sense of connectedness, while reading ironically bars others from questioning our taste: we can enjoy what is deemed 'bad' without enabling others to hold us responsible for what we read.

Camp comments occasionally surface in interviews that are otherwise serious and/or ironic in tone. True camp sensibility that extended far beyond gossip magazines, however, seems to be so much a part of specific communities that it is very different in style (though not so much in content) from other ways of talking about gossip magazines. Camp turns reading gossip magazines (and, I would imagine, gossip itself) into a performative art. In doing so camp, like irony, poaches the extended family repertoire and the repertoire of melodrama. The interview with Charles Vlaming provided examples:

Which one do I get first? Do I really have to answer completely honestly? [Yes, you do.] *Privé*. [He laughs.] I enjoy gossip immensely, I really like to read that. *Privé* is really aggressive, so that is the one I get first. (. . .) I'll look over what subjects they have and then I start to leaf through it. I wouldn't be looking for a specific part, you'll get there anyhow. I'll read like: 'Ooh, she has adopted three children again' [parodying woman's voice]. (. . .) [Which parts do you think are 'tastiest'?] Hmmmm, the misery, the misery. Especially the misery that you know is absolutely untrue. It sounds funny, you know; a friend of a star or a well-known acquaintance of that star said something and you think, aha, that kind of story. People with unhappy marriages . . . We make fun of it at the sports centre, 'Have you read . . .?' You know? Like that, as if you yourself know her. They become your acquaintances. Like: 'I told her that she shouldn't . . .' That kind of thing. We make it into a game. (Charles Vlaming)

Charles easily extended his camp style of reading to the domestic weeklies *Margriet* and *Libelle* which he also talked about quite seriously in terms of learning, using the repertoire of connected knowing (see chapter 2):

I do read the problem page. [For the problems or for the answers?] For both, really. The problems people see themselves confronted with! And then, really, those answers, I split my sides laughing about those. Really! For example, a woman writes her life story and it is very, very sad [sad tone of voice]. And she is answered, 'Come on, girl' and 'Do let us know how you are doing.' And I'll think, oh, my God!

The contact with other people at the sport centre where Charles Vlaming works for a few hours per week and where he trains bears all the hallmarks of a small community that enjoys camp games. Others find similar enjoyments in the gay community. That was made clear particularly by Eduard Spaans, who is quoted at length below.

Camp and the gay community

In constructing a common frame of reference regarding taste among a relatively small group of insiders camp creates community. It 'offers a subversive response to mainstream culture, and provides both in-group solidarity and an opportunity to express distance from and disdain for the roles most gay people play most of the time' (Gross, 1989: 143). Although all community, ultimately, is imagined (Anderson, 1983) and exists as a notion and a loyalty among those who feel they belong to it, the kind of community camp creates is closer than most forms of community. One might speak of a subculture, in the sense that camp functions 'to win, or at least contest "cultural space" for [its] members; [it] also generate[s] and confirm[s] important modes of both collective and individual identity and orientation towards the dominant values of wider social and cultural order' (O'Sullivan et al., 1983: 231). Camp not only creates community in its imagined sense, it also creates community in a more material, subcultural sense through play-acting in clubs, for instance. Debby Olders told me about a gay disco she regularly visited where a group of other guests organized contests in replaying episodes from the prime-time soap opera *Dynasty*.[3] From the following quotations from the interview with Eduard Spaans it will become evident that for him a particular kind of parodying investment in gossip magazines is very much part of interaction in the gay community in Amsterdam.

Eduard Spaans says that he enjoys gossip magazines because they are all bluff and pretension. Part of the fun is that others, apparently, are fooled by the magazines. His involvement with the gossip press started as a joke:

> I was in London some time ago and they have all these posters and postcards of the British royal family, really garish, on every street corner, really shameless, and I took four of them home, bought them with money that was left over or something. We had a noticeboard in the corridor and people saw that and started sending me cards. Now no one sends me normal postcards any more, I only get royal families. And I get magazines (. . .) those French magazines on dynasties that have long ceased to be dynasties. That is very funny to read. They keep saying 'Roi de France' and who knows who else is in those magazines. (. . .) Maybe the Bourbons

are still kings of France. One that hasn't been decapitated. And there are still several houses who claim the throne and so on. I don't know, they are very busy playing that game. (. . .) It is funny because it is really silly. (. . .) It's funny. A dynasty . . . it is no more than a function now, nothing much else. They haven't got much to show for it. And what makes it extra funny is all the brouhaha that is made about them. It is so interesting because there is nothing that is really interesting. They blow it up out of all proportion and that is amusing. (. . .) I read gossip to see how other people are fooled and how they fall for it too.

Eduard Spaans and Frank Stevens, who is also gay, both share their pleasure in the make-believe world of gossip and royalty magazines and television programmes with others.

A friend of mine works in a library as a typing goat – that is what he calls himself – but he says he always has to explain to people at his workplace that *Glamourland* [a televised version of a gossip magazine] is persiflage. And it is fun to talk about that with him. (Eduard Spaans)

Frank Stevens, a teacher, and a colleague of his like to embarrass others by flaunting what outside the codes of camp is seen as bad taste.

I have noticed that you can really shock [others by talking about royalty magazines]. And then I do it on purpose, of course. 'Ha, the new *Vorsten* [Sovereigns] has arrived.' People react furiously. When I say in the staffroom, 'I had such a good time reading *Vorsten* yesterday', [they say] 'Do you read that? Ridiculous', like that. Well, then I put on an even stronger act. Although I do enjoy it genuinely. (. . .) It is my kind of romanticism, I think. [I have heard the royal family is really an object of interest in gay circles?] Oh, yes, that's true. I have a gay colleague and we share this interest, so we always take time to talk about the new *Vorsten*. He doesn't subscribe – he is too stingy – but his old mother has a subscription, so we discuss what was in the latest issue.

To embarrass others, to shock them and provoke them into showing their disapproval of what you happen to like, in my experience, is one of the favourite ploys of the gay scene towards the outside world. Reading gossip magazines is made into a provoking and noticeable mark of difference as well as a sign of 'membership' (that extends to those outside the gay scene who are also 'in the know'), apart from being something to enjoy genuinely. To prize what are considered worthless cultural objects and prove that what is deemed valueless by dominant culture is a matter of rules and conventions rather than inherent value is also a means of protesting against the continuing ostracization of homosexuality. Camp is as much a political weapon as it is cultural enjoyment. Of the objects camp chooses to cherish the most favoured are actresses and singers past their prime, bad films and the transparent pretensions of gossip journalism, and kings and queens whose titles, if not their countries, are wholly imaginary. A part of camp is serious and based on real drama, which it recognizes but also relativizes. Camp enacts the pain of playing a role that does not suit, of trying to be who you are not. Camp is the at times bitter mockery of having to try to be someone you are not. It is laughing at one's own expense and at all those who cannot distinguish the fiction from facts, the blatant untruth from real sorrow and real suffering.

This interpretation is more political and dramatic than the reports of readers were. It is borne out, however, by the work of Sontag and Ross and by informal inquiry among friends. All agree that gossip is very much part of the male homosexual community, in printed and oral forms, as is a sense of (melo)drama. Eduard Spaans enthusiastically changed from the status of respondent to that of an informer in the true gossip sense and confirmed the status of gossip in the gay community:

> I used to see a lot of Paul de Leeuw [gay cabaret artist] and people often asked me, 'Is it true that . . .?' They doubt it a little, but they believe it too. [What did they write about Paul de Leeuw?] Well, they recently had a ridiculous piece about him, saying that he wanted to have children with a girlfriend. [They wrote that] he lived with a boyfriend and they even gave the boyfriend a name. And it was a boy he had had an affair with, but three years ago, and they suggested that they were living together. And he wanted to have children and raise them with this boyfriend. How all these people related to one another, they left out of the story. Was that woman supposed to give birth to that child and then give it up? But the funny thing was that there were all sorts of real, true things in that story. That he was going to act in *Les Miserables* and that he was going to go to New York. That is really scary. They had spiced the story with things that seemed to give it truth content. (. . .)

I know a guy, well, not really, that man [name of journalist] who gets taken to court all the time. He is gay too. You know, he writes about the royal family . . . Maybe Paul was drunk and got talking with one of those guys. [It really is a gossip circuit, isn't it, the gay world?] That's true. Because all those gossip journalists are gay too.

Eduard Spaans is not a walking caricature. He gossips, he laughs about gossiping and gossip magazines, is awed by the frightening mixture of half-truths the magazines print, but he also feels everyone, including gossip readers of any kind, deserves respect: 'My mother is in a nursing home at the moment and she hates it that all those women don't have anything else to do but [to read gossip magazines], and she condemns that a bit. She doesn't respect them or that they might want to have their own kind of pleasure'.

Community, solidarity, criticism

Whereas the repertoires that are used to make other genres of women's magazines meaningful stress dreams of perfection, control and mastery, the repertoires that are used to make gossip magazines meaningful seem to do something completely different. In so far as the repertoire of melodrama and the extended family repertoire betray specific fantasies or dreams, they are fantasies of belonging, of imagined communities. In a more direct sense, gossip magazines have a special place in communities that are held together by a shared camp sensibility, which can be read as a form of protest against prevailing norms and values. In fact, the discussion of camp reading of gossip magazines has made clear that 'serious gossip reading' and 'camp gossip reading' are not so very different from each other. Both recognize and confirm the realness of drama and sorrow as part of the everyday. Camp talk uses the same repertoires serious gossip readers use, though in a more exaggerated and parodying fashion.

Generally speaking, printed gossip is not all that different, then, from oral gossip. It serves an unconscious need to belong and it also serves a need to address social inequality, whether through creating moral standards or by challenging 'good taste'. Like serious, intimate oral gossip, printed gossip is a resource for the subordinated: it can be a means of self-expression and solidarity (the male homosexual community and camp); it can be a means of sharing judgement of an unequal society as well as a source of sentimental enjoyment and thus the confirmation of what is usually considered 'low taste' as a taste culture in its own right. 'Low taste' is, of course, an aesthetic criterion that precludes the possibility of recognizing that everyday experience could have any value whatsoever.

Gossip magazines have even lower status than other women's magazine genres. Marie Stemerdink defended her reading of gossip magazines to her daughters: 'The children don't like it, but I cull from them what I want to know.' Tina Poorter manoeuvred around a critical husband. Naturally, readers themselves were critical of the magazines too. Criticism of their journalistic methods and their highly suggestive style of writing was often expressed by informants. Eduard Spaans, Solema Tillie and Frederik Paulsen all qualified their enjoyment of the magazines (however incidentally in Frederik Paulsen's case) by criticizing how gossip magazines dig around in other people's lives. I suspect their complaint is partly sincere and partly evidence of their added enjoyment of what is deemed to be scandalous and absolutely not done. Others, such as Pam Gradanus and Ina Dammers, were critical of the pretensions of gossip magazines. For readers criticism of the magazines often appears to go hand in hand with enjoying them. Mona Brooks made fun of gossip magazines with Natacha Cuellar and Tina Smart, and they shared their embarrassment about their mothers who read them:

Natacha: I mean it [*Hello*] has got lots and lots of pictures, but it's articles about pictures, you know, absolute rubbish. I mean, like the second son of this Jew, someone you've never heard of, couldn't give a damn about anyway. You know, how he went on holiday to Portugal . . .

Mona: My mum reads the one that talks about, you know, TV personalities . . . Nasty things you hear about them – she holds them against them for the rest of their lives . . . I think it's *Chat* she reads.

Becky: My mum does that. She points out . . . whoever went with who, you know.

Referring to the music magazines, which also carry much gossip and personal information about celebrities and which she still likes (though less than when she was a teenager), Mona said: 'You get a buzz from it somehow, I don't know why. You feel more alive'.

Conclusion

Looking back on four years of work, the experience of interviewing stands out strongest. It is as if I have been playing with weighted dice against crafty opponents. I wanted to know how women's magazines became meaningful for readers and readers told me that women's magazines have hardly any meaning at all. They are convenient, my informants said, easy to put down when other things need to be done, but of little cultural value and therefore not very meaningful. They would also point out that while women's magazines have little cultural value, they do have practical value: all those tips, recipes, dress patterns. What more meaning would a medium need than to be of such practical use? Although reading women's magazines is a complex activity that certainly has more than one side to it, readers would mainly speak of its cultural insignificance. It was as if we were throwing dice that would fall with their 'cultural insignificance' side up and sometimes roll on to the opposite side, which said 'practical use'. While they were rolling, an occasional glimpse showed other sides of the dice, the daily routine related pleasure of picking up a magazine, or the fantasies of control and perfect selves that reading women's magazines also occasionally gives rise to.

The point I want to put forward in this conclusion is that a genre study based on readers' stories has special merits. It effectively counters stereotypical views of readers and it also counters the pervasive view in popular culture research that texts are always deeply meaningful. Of course, this view prompts questions regarding the place that should be accorded to textual criticism, a second item on the agenda of this conclusion. Lastly, I would like to go back to a feminist evaluation of women's magazine reading.

The merits of researching a genre through the eyes of its readers

The research consisted of interviews with eighty informants, analysis of those interviews and a long journey to a theoretical understanding of how women's magazines become meaningful. I started out by categorizing informants in terms of their choices and opportunities (housewives, career women, young women), and in terms of the magazines they read. Commercial market research would lead you to believe that each category reads a particular kind of magazine, but they do not. Home-makers do not necessarily read domestic weeklies, and high-powered executives do not exclusively read expensive glossies. Nor is it the case, as chapter 4 has shown, that a feminist magazine is read by people who would define themselves as feminists. Rather, readers read unpredictable and changing combinations of magazines. From time to time they stop being readers altogether. Clearly categorization cannot encompass the shifting preferences and practices of use that characterize everyday women's magazine reading. The commercial research that categorizes readers works from the assumption that women's magazines provide additional information concomitant with a person's lifestyle. But lifestyles are never uncomplicated, one-dimensional or unchanging. Lifestyles change. Moreover, women's magazines may be full of all kinds of information, but that does not say much about how readers use that information.

My first real find was when I realized that the most important aspect of women's magazines for readers was not that they are so full of practical information, even if that is a common justification for spending money and time on them, but that they blend in easily with other obligations, other duties and activities. Women's magazines as a text are not highly significant, but as an everyday medium they are a means of filling a small break and of relaxing that does not interrupt one's schedule, because they are easy to put down. The use to which they can be put largely converges with the meaning women's magazines have for readers. A second, less manifest aspect of reading them is that women's magazines offer material that may help you imagine a sense of control over your life by feeling prepared for tragedy, or a more perfect version of yourself by supposing that you would be able to answer any question regarding the difficult choices in life someone else might ask. These fantasy-investments are not of astonishing proportions, but for many readers they are enough to sustain an interest in women's magazines, and a sense of loyalty and appreciation. As was argued in chapter 2, the practical tips, the recipes and the advice on the one hand and the features about relationships and stories of having a child with cancer and the like on the other may temporarily empower a reader. Even if you do not do anything at all with the recipes or the practical advice, you can imagine baking a perfect pie, or managing your boss so that she or he will feel you cannot be missed. The stories that deal with the wide area of human emotion, from a discussion of secret love affairs to a sad tale of accepting the death of a child, can help you feel prepared in case such a thing happened to you, or more knowledgeable about human nature in general, which may give a satisfactory sense of being a 'wise person' or bolster your professional confidence.

I have assumed that uncoerced friendly conversation about everyday media use will reveal traces of how a specific genre becomes meaningful. These traces indicate how a genre is used (the experience of reading), how it is interpreted (whether it speaks to our experience in general, to our identities) and also what its cultural value is understood to be. In short, these traces can, for analytical purposes, be named repertoires. Repertoires are not available at the level of everyday talk; they are the researcher's reconstruction of the cultural resources that everyday speakers may use (dependent upon their cultural capital and, thus, the range of repertoires they are familiar with), based on fragments from interviews with different readers, that can be recognized as collective themes and understandings. Some repertoires are broad and predominantly descriptive (the relaxation and easily put down repertoires); others, such as the repertoire of connected knowing, or the repertoire of moral duty, interpret the media text in relation to how we perceive ourselves, our ideals, ambitions, obligations and anxieties.

The theoretical value of the approach employed in this book may also be measured in future research. I have proposed that women's magazine reading is an example of everyday media use: other forms of everyday media use can also be fruitfully examined following the same procedure. Research of radio and television use that starts from the repertoires listeners and viewers use to explain and describe may also find that much of the radio and television text never acquires substantial meaning. The repertoires that listeners and viewers refer to will probably encompass only tiny bits of the original text. Repertoires may do even less than that and refer to no more than the activity of radio listening or watching television. To follow radio news programmes, for example, may evoke the image of a politically involved person, just as the vanguard repertoire evokes images of committed left-wing views, and just as the repertoire of moral duty and the repertoire of practical knowledge acknowledge the taking up of the content of feminist magazines or traditionally oriented magazines but hardly the letter of the text.

In general, I wish to conclude that reader repertoires are shaped historically in interaction with a multitude of sources, texts, experiences. Repertoires are not specific to media genres, though specific repertoires may be used predominantly for a particular genre. The repertoire of moral duty, for example, extends far beyond reading a feminist magazine (as is indicated by the quotations given in chapter 4); likewise the repertoire of practical knowledge extends beyond reading traditional women's magazines. Using the same repertoire, you could watch a food programme on television or browse in a do-it-yourself manual. A combination of repertoires, however, can be specific for a certain genre. Thus, the extended family repertoire and the repertoire of melodrama together describe reading gossip magazines fairly well. As has been stated above, the repertoires that readers use give meaning to women's magazine genres in a way that to a quite remarkable extent is independent of the women's magazine text. Readers construct new texts in the form of fantasies and imagined 'new' selves. This leads to the conclusion that a genre study can be based entirely on how women's magazines are read and that it does not need to address the (narrative) structure or content of the text itself at all. Given the strong influence of literary traditions in cultural and media studies, such a point of view might raise eyebrows.

Text analysis and everyday media use: the art of 'listening through' texts

I do not wish to recommend that all popular culture research should base itself entirely on audience reactions and views. I have no objections to textual criticism in itself, for, in so far as media genres shape contemporary culture and are its bearers, analysis of their form and content can contribute to cultural critique. Our role as intellectuals in that case resembles the role of the court jester: we hope to enlighten, to open eyes, to stimulate critical imagination, but our position is never unquestioned, our audience may be no more than a small elite. The role of the ethnographically inspired reception analyst, ideally, is a different one. It is based on trying to understand how texts make sense to others, in the context of their lives. Again ideally, in that case we can be what Gramsci (1971) called 'organic intellectuals' – not so much in that we speak for others as in that we know how to listen and how to translate everyday knowledge and common sense into academic and critical knowledge and interventions, as well as how to bring back some of that knowledge to those who were interviewed, and possibly to wider audiences.

From the position of such an 'organic intellectual' – and I apologize for how presumptuous this sounds – I wish to take a stand against doing only text analysis. Far too often criticism of the text has been extended to its readers; it has led to horrifying stereotypical views of women's magazines' heterogeneous audiences and portrayed them *en masse* as silly housewives. I hold the view that it simply is not possible to read characteristics of an audience from the surface of a text: there is no single text that has the required monopoly position to exert such influence. All texts are used in the context of other media texts and genres; all readers bring their social and cultural backgrounds to texts; reading can be a fleeting, transient pastime that does not leave much of a trace.

Text analysis on its own has no way of dealing with how readers emotionally invest in texts, and it particularly lacks understanding of the superficiality of much media use. Reception analysis on its own may also run into trouble, despite the merits – sketched above – of such an approach, because it does not always help one formulate particular kinds of cultural criticism. One might end up overstretching what one actually knows about the readers who were interviewed or going back to the 'effect' rhetorics one had intended to leave behind.

Where text analysis is still required, I would plead for it to be textual criticism of an 'enlightened' kind, by which I mean a self-reflexive criticism that is aware of its limitations. How is such a criticism to be combined with audience analysis? I would hope it would be hermeneutical in the sense established by Gadamer ([1960] 1986). Gadamer held the view that 'we understand the meaning of a text, work of art or historical event *only in relation to our own situation* and therefore in light of our own concerns. In other words we understand it only in light of its significance' (Warnke, 1987: 68). Necessary to a research that would combine audience and text analysis would be what Gadamer called a 'fusion of horizons', which does not involve 're-experiencing an original understanding but rather the capacity to listen' (Warnke, 1987: 69). At this moment, however, I should think there are still enough reasons to concentrate on readers rather than on both texts and readers, especially when it concerns so-called women's genres – that is, as long as what I have called the fallacy of meaningfulness is guarded against.

To recapitulate briefly, with the exception of the work of Ann Gray (1987, 1992) and David Morley (1980, 1981, 1986), most of the recent reception analyses, which share the point of view that meaning is not a property of texts but constituted in the interaction between readers and texts, are subject to the fallacy of meaningfulness. They suggest, as I have argued in chapter 1, that the outcome of interactions between media texts and readers always leads to the production of meaning: in other words that texts are always significant. The fallacy of meaningfulness is the result of two unintended condensations. First, specific texts are lifted from the stream of daily life and media use, and given special status. Secondly, researchers have been drawn to knowledgeable readers and viewers and to fans, whom they have presented as average readers. Thus, media and cultural studies research and theories about the use of popular texts have become overburdened by their attention to fans and to the reading and watching experiences that readers are enthusiastic over, to the detriment of theorizing (the mundaneness of) everyday media use.

The canon of popular culture research as it has recently emerged (critics coined it 'New Audience Research' and a collection of research monographs and articles have since become a tradition – see, for example, Corner, 1991) has not, as yet, taken up the Gadamerian invitation to listen 'through' the text for the resonance of its everyday use. In its enthusiastic depiction of the popular culture 'fan' it has created miniature high culture connoisseurs, which does not in any sense undermine the division between high and low culture of which it is critical. The only way to do so is to take everyday media use seriously, including the small and not highly significant pleasures it gives rise to. The significance of everyday media use has to be sought mainly in the routines it sustains, the experience of which may, for example, be reassuring, an unnameable pleasure rather than a liberating event. To fight the division between high and low culture effectively and to take everyday media use seriously, the media text has to be displaced in favour of readers' reports of their everyday lives.

Repertoire analysis is especially suited to analyse these reports because it does not impose academic standards since it does not require textual closure or consistency. It respects and works with what John O'Neill has called 'the intrinsic generosity of the platitudes of common sense values and knowledge of the social world' (1974: 20). Even though a single quotation can be shallow and not a brilliant interpretation of women's magazines or women's magazine use, a sample of quotations may show that single quotations are linked by common interpretative frameworks. Common sense is not lay theory, but it yields far more when closely looked at than one would expect. Moreover, in the context of an entire interview vague remarks can come to have specific meaning. If it is repeatedly stated that women's magazines are liked because they are easy to put down, such a phrase may come to signify far more than its direct, literal meaning.

Feminism and women's magazine reading

This book is not only an intervention in the media and cultural studies debate on the meanings and significance of media texts and how this is to be researched, it is also a feminist intervention on behalf of women's magazine reading. The first item on my agenda is emancipatory in nature. The field of research concerned with women's media, and in particular with women's magazines, confirms at a glance that it is a marginal area that is neglected by mainstream academic research. Virtually all the research (with the exception of commercial market research) is done by women, most of whom are feminists. Others, evidently, do not feel they have to bother with women's magazines. Women's media use is important, though, and it needs to be made part of accepted and respected social research.

Then there are the insulting stereotypes. Contrary to stereotypical male genres, such as sports programmes on television, women's genres are consistently denigrated, while sport, for example, is associated with heroism, team spirit, loyalty and other grand values. This denigration of women's magazines and especially of their readers (a group to which many women, as well as a considerable number of men, belong from time to time), is based on elitist and inaccurate stereotypes that assume readers are not capable of assessing the value of the text and are completely taken in by it. It turned out that my informants regarded women's magazines as being of little significance. The repertoire of connected knowing, however, reconstructed from examples they gave, made clear that women's magazines also offer opportunities for 'emotional learning'. The testimonies and life stories related in features offer readers material for comparison, which may reassure them or help them to define themselves as 'not such a bad mother' or 'colleague' at all. To me, those are valuable resources for those who are in vulnerable, because low-valued, social positions.

In her study on supermarket tabloids (an exceptional book that combines text and reception analysis) Elizabeth Bird ends by saying that she has stressed that 'stereotypes of tabloids and their readers are offensive and elitist, based largely on a conception of what people "should" be interested in and the correct style in which such media should be presented. I have tried to help tabloid readers break the stereotype in their own words; in fact, I have tried to show them as more than "tabloid readers" ' (1992: 208–9). Although she is cautious about a celebratory optimism that has stressed the 'playful' reader, and aware (quoting Jim Grealy) that tabloids are the 'site of a symbolic order within which the subordinate class lives its subordination' (1992: 209), Bird argues that readers give a wide spectrum of meanings to a text, which that text is not of itself able to contain. The very same arguments hold for this study, even though I would put less emphasis on the 'playfulness' of readers, which I think is more typical of genres that engage readers' imaginations directly (for example, fiction genres or non-fiction genres that tread the thin line between the believable and the unbelievable, such as tabloids or gossip magazines) than of such women's magazine genres as domestic weeklies or feminist magazines, or, say, newspapers. I would also emphasize more strongly that it is important to understand the meanings a genre gives rise to in relation to how readers perceive its significance. By giving much room to my informants, I have shown that they are neither cultural dupes nor silly housewives.

To interview both male and female readers is also a way of disproving the theory that women's magazines directly influence gender identity or turn one into a housewife. As became clear in chapter 2, men do read women's magazines and they may use the same repertoires as women use (even if it is also important for some of them to keep their distance from the genre by ironizing their use of it). The obvious point for a feminist evaluation of women's magazines is that, although it is the archetypical women's genre, it is also read by men. As Liesbet van Zoonen (1991) has put forward, the point may be obvious, but it has been taken up in neither feminist nor mainstream research. Most of the work on media consumption and gender has concentrated on women and still does so, thereby unwittingly reflecting the more general bias in society that women are the problematic sex (see Ang and Hermes, 1991; Coward, 1983).

The postmodern feminist views to which I adhere are often criticized as leading to an uncritical celebration of texts and of forms of (playful) resistance. However, the opposition between concern and celebration in the field of women's genres and media use is singularly unproductive. Feminist criticism needs to be interested in the wide variety and diversity of women's lives and, as part of that, in their media use. Concern and celebration, in small doses, may be part of that interest. But feminism's overriding motivation should be to respect women and women's genres, and to demand respect for them from the world at large.

In the case of women's magazines that is a simple command (given that women's magazines are all looked down upon, though for slightly different reasons) and a hard task, which needs to depart from the point of view that 'being a women's magazine reader' is a temporary identity that women as well as men may take up in highly diverse ways and that therefore concerns many of us. It needs to recognize, as has been argued at length above, that the repertoires readers use to make women's magazines meaningful are dictated not by the text, but by a changing fund of knowledges that readers may draw on, which changes because it is used by different people under different circumstances. Paraphrasing Jana Sawicki's argument about sexuality, feminist criticism's goal 'requires that we continue to provide detailed historical analyses of the ways in which [media consumption is a target in strategies of domination]. The purpose of such consciousness-raising would not be to tell us who we are, but rather to free us from certain ways of understanding ourselves; that is, to tell us who we do not have to be and to tell us how we came to think of ourselves as we do' (1991: 44). The division between high and low culture, the neglect of everyday media use and the eternal putting down of women's media are all strategies of domination that define us, as users of those genres and even as their researchers. Those definitions ultimately designate the battlefield for feminist media criticism to fight on.

Following Sawicki, reading women's magazines should be understood and described as a series of locally and historically specific practices that change with time and according to context, within the constraints of the dominant order. Likewise, it would be a misconception to expect that readers of such an everyday genre would be especially enthusiastic, even if the existing popular culture research were to seduce one to do so. In fact, as I have extensively shown in chapter 1, the interviews did not seem to yield much information about women's magazines at all.[1] Partly because of that, I see no reason to celebrate women's magazine reading, in so far as the fantasies readers forge are about control, and authority and strength. Also, to celebrate these fantasies would all too easily overlook their lack of choice (to take care of children on your own leaves little time or energy, and accordingly narrows down your choice of media to relax with, to learn from or to be diverted by). On the contrary, since it is my main argument that readers deserve respect, their view that everyday media use is not highly significant needs to be taken seriously. And if one takes their point seriously, then concern has no place in one's reconstruction of women's magazine reading.

To summarize, feminist criticism should do its utmost to emancipate marginal fields such as women's magazine research. It should try to counter existing abusive and degrading stereotypes of readers. In the actual research practice, concern, celebration and overbearing strong views will not be of much help. Rather a critical feminist view should start from respect and the knowledge that everyday media use is a highly complex phenomenon, made up of routines and constraints, of wishes and fantasies. It is on the cutting edge of these investments, constraints and daily routines that women's magazines have meaning. Moreover, feminist research should be sensitive to the fact that readers' investments in texts are not, of necessity, directly connected with the narrative structures of these texts. For example, reading a feminist magazine does not necessarily mean that you identify with feminism (or with the magazine); it can also be part of your idea of what a well-read, cultured and responsible woman should be informed of and thus feed a fantasy of being an all-round intellectual.

My rendering of and recommendations for feminist research and media criticism are motivated by the expectation that women's magazines will continue to exist. But will they? Watching *The Oprah Winfrey Show* on television, it struck me that the repertoire of connected knowing and emotional learning, women's magazines' strong suit, might come to be more specific for television than for women's magazines. Never before has there been such a supply of true life stories, confessions and testimonies on television. On the other hand, although television sets are easy to leave on when other activities take priority, a programme one is watching is not all that easy to pick up again later, whereas women's magazines are not only easy to put down, they are also easy to pick up again.

Appendix 1
List of Informants

The ages given date from 1990. All names are pseudonyms. Any information that could betray an informant's identity has been left out. All informants were advised that they would be quoted, and no one had any objections.

Terry ATKINSON (thirty-nine), a black woman, teaches at a university and lives with her son. She is not a regular women's magazine reader, but has 'binges' and buys trendy glossy magazines, such as *Marie Claire*, *Vogue* or *Elle*. We met at a seminar.

Geraldine BANK (twenty-six), a white woman, reads *Opzij*. A mathematician, she lives in Amsterdam and teaches at a university. She answered my advertisement in the newspapers asking *Opzij* readers for interviews.

Joan BECKER (thirty) is a white woman, with a young son, who lives near Amsterdam. She has a part-time secretarial job. We met at a group interview about romance reading organized by students as part of a course. When I asked her for an interview about women's magazines, she readily agreed.

Menno BOTTENBURG (twenty-six), a white man, is a film producer. Joppe Boodt, who interviewed him, was introduced to him through his personal networks. Menno lives with a female partner who buys various glossy magazines.

Charlotte de BOUVRY (forty-eight) is a white woman. She trained as a social worker and is currently studying sociology; she lives in a small village with her family. She answered the *Opzij* advertisement. She occasionally browsed through the French *Marie Claire* and, when she saw them lying around, domestic weeklies. She was interviewed by Véronique Schutgens.

Mona BROOKS (nineteen), a black woman, is a cultural studies student and spent a semester in Amsterdam. She and two friends were happy to discuss English women's magazines and what they were about. She herself has a preference for music magazines, but reads women's magazines (mainly the glossies) when she comes across them.

Nathalie BROOKS (forty-four) is a black woman and Mona Brooks's mother. She lives with her younger children in Birmingham. She is a housewife and does a little catering work. She likes to read *Prima* magazine, but is most of all a romance enthusiast. I met her through Mona.

Marieke de BRUIN (forty-two), a white woman, reads *Opzij* and answered the newspaper advertisement. She lives in a village with her husband and children, and works as a skin specialist. She was interviewed by Véronique Schutgens.

Helen CARSON (seventy-four) is a white woman. She is a retired child-care officer who lives with the last of her 'children' in London. She used to buy domestic weeklies for the knitting patterns, but is not very interested in them any more. I met her through Terry Atkinson.

Mary CROSTON (sixty-two), a white woman, is a widow and lives in Birmingham. She has held a long string of jobs; she worked as an usherette, when there still were neighbourhood cinemas, and in a factory. She lives off her pension now and does some cleaning work for elderly people. She likes women's magazines (especially the domestic weeklies) and *Reader's Digest*, but hardly ever buys them. Neighbours and the people she works for pass their magazines on to her. She is the neighbour of a friend of a good friend.

Natacha CUELLAR (twenty-five) is a white woman. A cultural studies student, she spent a semester studying in Amsterdam, which is how we met. She used to read young women's magazines, such as *Just Seventeen*, and found great pleasure in discussing all sorts of magazines, from gossip magazines to glossies, which she reads when the opportunity arises, though she does not often spend money on them.

Ina DAMMERS (forty-eight), a white woman, reads domestic weeklies and gossip magazines. She lives with her husband and one of her daughters in a city in the eastern part of the

Netherlands. She has a part-time job helping retired people. Her name was on the computer-compiled list of magazine readers ordered from a market research firm.

Mrs DOBBEL (forty-one) is a white woman who lives on a farm with her family. She reads domestic weeklies and gossip magazines. From time to time she and her husband raise young bulls, which she takes care of. She described herself as a traditional housewife. Her address was on the research firm's list.

Annie DUINDAM (thirty-nine), a white woman, lives with her daughter and has a job as a management assistant. She reads *Cosmopolitan*, which she also uses as 'interior decoration' by leaving the magazines open at pages she likes and placing them around the house. She does not do that with the other magazines she reads, among which are traditional women's magazines and gossip magazines. I met her at the *Cosmopolitan* group interview arranged by the respondent agency.

Valerie van EIJCK (fifty-seven), a white woman, is my mother. She used to have a secretarial job but stopped working. She lives with her husband and six cats in a small town. She reads the domestic weekly *Margriet* and the feminist monthly *Opzij*.

Carolien van ESSEN (forty-eight) is a white woman. She is a journalist, and lives with her male partner in a small city. She reads *Opzij* and answered my advertisement in *Opzij* asking for self-help readers. She used self-help books to guide her in times of personal crisis. She saw *Opzij* as the journal for the professional woman who wanted a quick read.

Trudi FRANSMAN (thirty-three), a white woman, is training to become a social worker. She reads domestic weeklies and *Opzij* and answered my advertisement asking for self-help readers. She lives with her husband in a village in the north of the Netherlands.

Marion GERARDS (forty-three) is a white woman, and has a part-time job as a coffee-lady. She lives with her husband (who is a sailor and is away three quarters of the year) and her nearly grown-up son. She likes to read gossip magazines. She was one of the women in the group interview about gossip magazines organized by the respondent agency.

Pam GRADANUS (thirty), a white woman, works as a police officer and lives with her husband and two children near Amsterdam. She was on the respondent agency's list for the gossip magazine group interview. Since she had to work later than she had expected, she could not make it on time and I interviewed her at a later date. She was on the brink of changing from gossip magazines to reading domestic weeklies because the gossip magazines were starting to bore her.

Dot GROENIERS (twenty-six), a white woman, lives with her husband and child in a small village. She likes to read gossip magazines and occasionally domestic weeklies. Her name was on the computer-compiled women's magazine readers list ordered from the research firm.

Art de GROOT (twenty-four), a white man, does administrative work, lives in a big city and is a member of the playful political group Loesje. I thought he answered my advertisement in the newspapers asking for female and male *Opzij* readers, but it turned out that a Loesje news bulletin had carried various small advertisements, and mine had been one of them. Art thought another Loesje member was doing research.

Renée GROOTHUIS (thirty) is a white woman. An unemployed academic, she lives in the Bijlmer, the south-east part of Amsterdam, with her female partner. She reads *Opzij*, but also *Viva*, and answered my advertisement in the newspapers asking for *Opzij* readers.

May HAN (thirty-five) is a Chinese-Indonesian woman, an academic and a friend who used to live in Amsterdam. She was a *Cosmopolitan* reader (preferably the American edition) when I interviewed her and felt greatly cheered by the solutions the magazine provided for almost any relational problem. She also loved to do the quizzes. When we discussed magazines again, a little less than a year after the interview, she confided that she had completely lost her interest in *Cosmopolitan* and that she did not buy it any more.

Mrs HAN (sixty-four) is May Han's mother, a Chinese-Indonesian woman who studied in the Netherlands and went back to Indonesia, but had to go when the political regime changed. She read the domestic weekly *Margriet* when her children were young, but was no longer interested in it. She lives with her husband and youngest son in a small town.

Yao Hua HAN (thirty), one of May Han's brothers, is an artist. He had a habit of going through May's *Cosmopolitan*s when he visited her and, based on that, May thought I might want to talk to him. He turned out to have a vast collection of glossies and a few young women's magazines. He looks at the art work and generally enjoys browsing through them. He lives in Amsterdam with a female partner.

Beth HANSEN (thirty-two) is an Irish woman who lives in Amsterdam. She answered our *Opzij* advertisement. Véronique Schutgens interviewed her and reported that she seemed rather taken aback when it became clear that we would not pay her for the interview. She lives in a women's commune and is a mature O-level (Mavo) student.

Antonia JANSEN (fifty-one), a white woman, has had occasional jobs, but trained as an art teacher. She read *Opzij* and answered our advertisement; Véronique Schutgens interviewed her. She lives with her daughter in a big city and has a 'living apart/together' arrangement with a male partner.

Martha JANSSEN (thirty-five), a white woman, lives in a middle-sized city with her husband and young child. She has a job as an administrator. She answered the advertisement in *Opzij* asking self-help readers to write. She also liked to read domestic weeklies and detectives.

Leo de JONG (thirty-seven), a white man, is a physiotherapist who lives in a small village in the eastern part of the Netherlands with a partner and their three children. At the group practice where he works there is a collection of magazines. When he has to wait, he browses through the domestic weeklies and he likes to take out tips and ideas for outings. Sometimes he reads his wife's magazines. His name was on the computer-compiled list ordered from the market research firm.

Christine KENTER (twenty-four), is a white woman. I met her at a group interview about *Cosmopolitan*, arranged by the respondent agency. An economics student, she lives in a village near Amsterdam with her parents. At her invitation I also interviewed her there. She in not a fan of women's magazines in general. Her favourite genre is thrillers.

Christine KLEIN (seventy), a white woman, lives with her husband in Amsterdam. She is a friend of Martine Spanier, who introduced me to her. She loves to read gossip magazines, and also loved to talk about her children and grandchildren.

Margot KLEIN (fifty-seven), a white woman, is the mother of a very good friend. She does not read women's magazines, and has never done so. She lives on her own in a big city with her two cats.

Marga KOSTER (twenty-eight), a white woman, lives in a big city with a male partner. She works as an emancipation worker. She answered my advertisement looking for *Opzij* readers because her friend Ingrid Meertens has specifically asked her to do so.

Felicia LANDMAN (thirty-five), a black woman, is disabled, and we met through her therapist, who is a friend of mine. She lives with her male partner in a small city north of Amsterdam. She likes to read domestic weeklies. Reminiscing about her childhood in the Antilles, she made fun of how, based on what they read in the Dutch domestic weeklies that were sent to them by family and friends, people would fantasize about meeting the queen and how the Netherlands was the 'Land of Plenty'.

Nancy LEMHUIS (twenty-seven), a white woman and PhD student, answered my advertisement asking for *Opzij* readers. She had also enjoyed reading domestic weeklies and was a 'weepies' addict: she loved old, melodramatic films.

Lies MACHIELSE (sixty-three), a white woman, is a good friend and lives in a village; she teaches French and has also worked as a social worker. She holds firm views on almost anything, and one of the them is that reading women's magazines is not for her. She was one of my two 'non-readers'. She told me that she had briefly read women's magazines when her children were small, but had always felt that she had sunk beneath the standards of good taste by doing so.

Ingrid MEERTENS (twenty-nine), a white woman, is a senior civil servant. She also does volunteer work as a lawyer for Amnesty International. She saw the advertisement for *Opzij* readers in her newspaper (*NRC Handelsblad*, the Dutch equivalent of the *Independent*) and immediately decided that it was important I should not think that *NRC* readers did not read *Opzij*. She asked her friend Marga Koster and her partner, Frederik Paulsen, with whom she lives, to write too. I interviewed the three of them together. They also read traditional women's magazines and were highly conversant with, for example, the new glossies (*Elle* and *Marie Claire*), which at that time had only recently been introduced on the Dutch market.

Karel MESSING (thirty-one), a white man, is studying to be a social worker and has a part-time job in a day-care centre for children. He answered Joppe Boodt's advertisement asking for men to be interviewed on the subject of women's magazines. He reads domestic weeklies and young women's weeklies and exchanges them with his mother and sister. Joppe interviewed him.

Paul MORTIER (thirty-two), a white man, works as a maintenance engineer in the offshore industry. He lives in a village with his wife and child. He reads the domestic weekly his wife buys.

Debby OLDERS (twenty-eight), a white woman, is a freelance journalist and works as a bartender. I met her through a mutual friend. She read the young women's weekly *Viva* as a teenager, but had become very critical of traditionally oriented women's maga-zines. She sometimes read *Opzij*, but preferred the underground feminist press. She takes a look at the domestic weekly her mother reads too from time to time, and attacks her on that score. She lives in a commune in a city in the southern part of the Netherlands.

Mrs PARRY (sixty-two), a white woman, lives with her husband and one of her three daughters near Birmingham. She has held a variety of jobs (as a factory worker, as a sales assistant in a newsagent's). She used to read *Woman* and *Woman's Own*, but finds them 'too mushy' now and prefers *Me*, *Bella* and *Best*. Her daughter is an acquaintance of a friend.

Frederik PAULSEN (twenty-eight), a white man, is a company lawyer. He is the partner of Ingrid Meertens, with whom he lives. He started reading *Opzij* because Ingrid read the magazine; he also reads the glossy magazines they occasionally buy.

Ard PENNINGS (twenty-three), a white man, is a student and part-time ski instructor. Joppe Boodt found him through his personal networks and interviewed him. He likes to buy women's maga-zines and young women's magazines occasionally.

Tina POORTER (forty), a white woman, was invited for the group interview about gossip magazines by the respondent agency. She lives near Amsterdam with her husband and children. I inter-viewed her for a second time on her own. She used to have part-time jobs, but is not employed at the moment.

Rebecca PRIEST (thirty-four), a white woman, lives not far from London with her husband and daughter. She runs a flower-shop and likes to read a broad range of domestic weeklies. She describes herself as an enthusiastic consumer, which is one reason for reading the magazines. I met her through a mutual English friend.

Minnie REDDING (fifty-two), a white woman, is a women's magazine journalist. She still subscribes to *Opzij*, though she hardly reads the magazine any more. She came to interview me about the research project and in exchange told me about how she reads women's magazines.

Jeanne ROUSSET (forty-two), a white woman, lives with her husband and children in the southern part of the Netherlands. She reads glossy magazines and describes herself as a 'lady of leisure'. She travels a good deal with her husband, who is a businessman.

Marwil SLUITER (forty-four), a white woman, lives with her daughter in a small town. She is on indefinite sick leave and used to be a sales representative. She has a 'living apart/together' relation-ship with a German woman. She reads *Opzij* and answered the advertisement in the newspapers. *Opzij* meant and means much to her in terms of personal growth. Véronique Schutgens interviewed her.

Tina SMART (eighteen), a white cultural studies student, sometimes reads but is mainly appalled by the magazines taken home by her mother, who picks them up in doctors' waiting-rooms, thereby hugely embarrassing Tina. She was in Amsterdam along with Natacha Cuellar and Mona Brooks.

Peter SMIT (thirty-three), a white man, is a psychologist and the brother of a good friend. He lives with his wife and children. He reads the domestic weeklies and *Opzij*, which his wife buys.

Eduard SPAANS (twenty-seven), a white man, is studying law. He lives in Amsterdam and is a fan of gossip magazines and other 'camp'-related objects. His brother told me about his collection of 'royalty' postcards, which led to an interview.

Martine SPANIER (fifty-five), is a Jewish woman who lives on her own in Amsterdam and has a business. She saw my advertisement in *Opzij* asking for self-help readers and decided to write since she had worked in market research and knew how difficult it can be to be dependent on others to talk to you. We discussed self-help literature, *Opzij* and why there was not a magazine that catered for professional, independent women like her.

Tineke SPOOR (thirty-four), a white woman, lives with her husband and daughter near Amsterdam. She is manager of a temporary-work agency. She reads a wide diversity of women's magazines, I met her at the *Cosmopolitan* group interview organized by the respondent agency.

Martha STEENMAN (thirty-four) is a white woman on indefinite sick leave who lives with her daughter. She reads all kinds of women's magazines, but was selected by the respondent agency for the group interview about gossip magazines.

Marie STEMERDINK (fifty), a white woman, lives with her family in a small city. She loves to read the domestic weeklies *Margriet* and *Libelle* and deplores the fact that there are only two 'real' women's magazines. I was introduced to her by the parents of one of my friends.

Frank STEVENS (forty-seven), a white man, is a secondary school teacher and is part of Joppe Boodt's family network. He likes to spoil himself with chic magazines; sometimes he uses women's magazines for his classes. He also dearly loves to talk about reading *Vorsten* (Sovereigns). He lives with a male partner in a small city. Joppe interviewed him.

Lodewijk van STRATEN (twenty-six), a white man, is a civil servant who answered Joppe Boodt's advertisement asking for male readers of women's magazines. He was rather surprised to learn that it is not at all common for men to read or admit that they read them, a fact of which he became aware when the subject came up during a work break. He likes to read the domestic weeklies his wife buys. He lives in one of the new garden cities.

Lauren TERBERG (thirty-two), a white woman, lives with her son in Amsterdam. I met her sister at a lecture and was given her address. Lauren likes to read domestic weeklies and occasionally a glossy. Most of the magazines she reads are passed on to her by a good friend. She lives on social security and cannot afford to buy them. Her mother from time to time gives her a copy of *Opzij*. I interviewed Lauren twice.

Solema TILLIE (fifty), a coloured woman, lives near Amsterdam and takes great pride in her children and grandchildren. She does cleaning work for an elderly lady. I met her through her son-in-law, who is an academic. She enjoys reading, she told me. She has a preference for gossip magazines and true story magazines about mother love, but she also likes to read domestic weeklies for the handy tips.

Elizabeth VEENSTRA (thirty-five), a white woman, lives with her children in Amsterdam. She was doing a silversmith and jeweller's course in the period in which I twice interviewed her, but was not employed. She passes on her magazines (domestic weeklies, mostly) to Lauren Terberg, who gave me her address.

Charles VLAMING (twenty-six), a white man, works as a nurse in a centre for mentally disabled children and as an aerobics teacher. He lives on his own in a small southern Dutch city. He reads gossip magazines avidly, mainly at the sports centre where he teaches aerobics. With the visitors and staff he likes to make fun of the magazines. He also likes to read thrillers and biographies of popular stars. I was given his name by the research firm I asked to do a telephone survey to find (male) readers.

Tom VONK (forty-eight), a white man, is head of a secondary school and lives with his wife and their daughters near a big city in the southern part of the Netherlands. He likes to read domestic weeklies, which he finds cosy and 'human', but he also reads the feminist monthly *Opzij*. He was one of the men on the computer-selected list ordered from the market research firm.

Pauline van der VOORT (forty-four), a white woman, works as a commercial manager in a small firm and lives near Amsterdam with her husband and family. She reads *Cosmopolitan* and other glossy magazines. I met her at the *Cosmopolitan* group interview organized by the respondent agency.

John WIARDA (sixty-two), a white man, answered the newspaper advertisement asking for *Opzij* readers. At the time of the interview he lived in a big southern city in the Netherlands. He had been a sales representative and had had a business of his own, but after his divorce he lived on left-over money and later on social security. He keeps in touch with his children and still, in a sense, lives a 'hippie' life. *Opzij* is part of his left-wing, critical universe.

Carla WILLEMS (thirty-one), a white woman, lives with her male partner in a small village. She works as a security officer. She took part in the *Cosmopolitan* group interview organized by the respondent agency.

Karen de WIT (twenty-four), a white woman, is studying law. She is a friend of Linda Zijlstra, who invited her to come to the interview. I interviewed her again a year later. She liked to read *Cosmopolitan* and various other magazines in a coffee-shop she visited, though far less so at the time of the second interview. She said she had become bored with the magazine and that she finished reading it in no time at all. Karen lives in Amsterdam on her own.

Linda ZIJLSTRA (twenty-four), a white woman, is a law student. I met her when she was working in a newspaper shop. I asked her about who bought what kind of magazine and we went on to talk about women's magazines in general. Linda agreed to be interviewed and asked her friend Karen de Wit if she would join us. Linda reported that she had periods in which she was a fervent reader of the young women's magazine *Viva*, though at other times she did not read it at all. I interviewed her again after a little less than a year. Linda lives on her own in Amsterdam.

Twelve informants have not been quoted in the text.

Five women took part in a *Cosmopolitan* group interview of which the tapes were unusable because the tape recorder did not work properly.

An English former nurse and mature cultural studies student has not been quoted, though her memory of reading women's magazines at work fits entirely in the 'easily put down' repertoire.

A young woman who took part in the group interview with the English cultural studies students has not been quoted because she did not say much apart from assenting with the others.

A young man who read car magazines has not been quoted because he had nothing to say about women's magazines.

The interview with my mother's friends (who hardly read women's magazines) was valuable in that it pointed out that many have knowledge of women's magazine content, even if they do not regularly read them or have long stopped reading them. One of them, for example, had memories of reading women's magazines when she and her family lived on Curaçao, where her husband was then employed. They exchanged magazines with other Dutch families living there as a way of keeping in touch with the homeland. These informants were not quoted because introducing and explaining their points would have taken up more space than it was worth in terms of informational value.

I had one interview with a self-help reader who did not read the feminist magazine *Opzij*. Again, this was a very valuable interview that validated my view of the difference between self-help literature and women's magazines. Since it fell foul of the categories I formed to be able to divide my material over different chapters (I interviewed no other readers of self-help literature and traditional women's magazines), however, it was not quoted.

Appendix 2

The Women's Magazine Market in Britain and the Netherlands

No attempt has been made to give a full overview of all women's magazines in Britain and the Netherlands, though all women's magazines mentioned in the text have been included. The years to which the figures apply were chosen on the grounds that they correspond as closely as possible to the periods in which interviews were sought and held with readers in the Netherlands and in Britain.

Table 1 Circulation of British and Dutch magazines

Title	Owner	Circulation
Domestic weeklies		
Bella	Bauer	1,202,229
Best	Gruner and Jahr (UK)	658,441
Essentials	IPC[a]	750,000
Libelle	VNU[b] (Spaarnestad)	704,900
Margriet	VNU (Geïllustreerde Pers)	551,303
Me	IPC	–
Woman	IPC (Odhams)	716,758
Woman's Own	IPC (Newness)	732,348
Woman's Realm	IPC (Odhams)	454,730
Woman's Weekly	IPC (Fleetway)	905,095
Young women's weeklies		
Flair	VNU (IUM)[c]	187,780
Just Seventeen	Emap Metro	210,871
19	IPC	190,218
Viva	VNU (Geïllustreerde Pers)	128,645
Yes	VNU (Spaarnestad)	141,698

Glossies (women's monthlies)

Avenue	VNU (Geïllustreerde Pers)	65,000
Company	National Magazine Company	220,972
Cosmopolitan (Dutch)	VNU (Geïllustreerde Pers)	128,634
Cosmopolitan (British)	National Magazine Company	472,480
Elegance	Elsevier	65,513
Elle (Dutch)	Hachette	85,000
Elle (British)	Hachette	190,227
Good Housekeeping	National Magazine Company	391,449
Marie Clarie (Dutch)	VNU (Geïllustreerde Pers)	76,201
Marie Claire (British)	IPC (European Magazines)	222,671
New Woman	Murdoch Magazines	238, 236
Prima	Gruner and Jahr (UK)	738,871
She	National Magazine Company	283,731
Tatler	Illustrated Newspapers and others	64,689
Vogue	Condé Nast	181,912

Feminist monthlies

Opzij	Weekbladpers	41,949
Spare Rib	Spare Rib Ltd	–

Gossip magazines

Chat	Publishing Developments Ltd	584,424
Hello!	Hola	444,257
Majesty	Hanover Magazines	69,178
Privé	Telegraaf	500,240
Story	VNU (Spaarnestad)	424,685
Vorsten	VNU (Spaarnestad)	62,659
Weekend	Kontekst	220,771

[a] International Publishing Corporation.
[b] Verenigde Nederlandse Uitgeversbedrijven.
[c] Internationale Uitgevers Maatschappij.
Sources: circulation figures for British magazines are official sales figures from the ABC (Audit Bureau of Circulations) for July–Decemeber 1991, with the exception of sales figures for *Chat* and *Majesty*, which are ABC figures for January–June 1987, culled from Braithwaite and Barrell, 1988; figures for *Essentials* are the publisher's own estimate; for *Bella*, for which no ABC figures were available, registered figures were provided by the publisher. Ownership of all British magazines except *Hello!* was also taken from Braithwaite and Barrell (1988); information for *Hello!* came from the magazine itself.

Circulation figures for Dutch magazines are official sales figures taken from the NOTU (Nederlandse Organisatie van Tijdschrift Uitgevers) *Oplage Documentatie 1988*. Figures for *Elle* and *Mariel Claire* were taken from the *Adfomedia Handboek* no. 4 (October 1992) as no NOTU circulation figures were available. Ownership of Dutch magazines was found in the magazines themselves and in the *Adfomedia Handboek*, no. 0 (November 1990).

Table 2 Readership of Dutch magazines in the Netherlands

Title	Percentage of total population	Percentage of women	Percentage of men
Domestic weeklies			
Libelle	29.3	43.8	14.2
Margriet	24.3	36.4	11.6
Young women's weeklies			
Flair	6.2	9.9	2.3
Viva	5.4	8.6	2.0
Yes	4.8	8.0	1.5
Glossies			
Avenue	4.8	6.7	2.8
Cosmopolitan	4.8	8.0	2.9
Elegance	4.0	6.3	1.6
Elle	–	2.2	–
Marie Claire	–	2.3	–
Feminist monthlies			
Opzij	1.6	2.2	0.9
Gossip magazines			
Privé	18.8	24.4	12.9
Story	19.0	25.4	12.4
Vorsten	1.4	–	–
Weekend	10.3	14.1	6.4

Sources: for *Vorsten*, SUMMO (Samenwerkingsverband voor het Uitvoeren van Multi-Media Onderzoek) figures for April–July 1990 have been quoted (*Vorsten* is a relaunched merger of two 'monarchy' magazines). For *Elle* and *Marie Claire*, SUMMO readership figures have been taken from the *Adfomedia Handboek*, no. 4 (October 1992). For all other magazines, readership figures are official SUMMO figures for April–July 1988.

Appendix 3

Example of Interview Transcript and Analysis

Below are a few pages from the interview with Mary Croston (sixty-two). A widow, she lives on her own on a small pension and on her earnings from part-time work with elderly people. She is the neighbour of a Birmingham friend, here named Christine. The full transcript (of approximately an hour's interview tape) takes up thirty pages, of which pp. 1–5 and 19–21 are reproduced. Before and after the part of the interview that was taped we talked and had tea.

Analysis of the interviews proceeded as follows. All fragments that dealt with women's magazines were marked and summarized (to reduce the data and make them manipulable). The full transcript was read several times, but each reading was part of reading a series of interviews (the series in this case were all the British interviews and interviews with older women). The summarized fragments were then used to find common themes, and to theorize tentatively, how magazines become meaningful. Armed with a theoretical view, I went back to the full interview fragments and formulated the interpretative repertoires that I recognized as holding together different fragments and themes.

In the following text fragments dealing with women's magazines have been printed in bold. When essential other information is given in brackets.

Pages 1–5

Joke: What do I want to know? A couple of things. What I'm interested in and what I've asked people in Holland, and now a few here, about is which magazine they'd usually read today: and, you know, you told me you usually get them from others who pass them on to you and you pass them on to others, or that sort of thing . . . I'll repeat the questions, you don't have to remember them, I just tell you about it first and then . . . No, I won't be eating, that'll save time. Not a good idea [I am refusing a biscuit] What I want to know about is sort . . . When would you read a magazine, when would you feel like it, what does it mean to you? Sort of its place in your daily life. So, therefore I'd also like to know, you know, a bit, the sort of work that you do, how you spend your days, just to get an idea.

Mary: Yes, I would say, yeah, ehm . . .

Joke: That's about the idea.

Mary: But . . . **I don't read during the day. It's at night-time, when I go to bed, I always** . . . I do always love a read, always have done. **And it is only magazines that I read. I have got some books, you know, but ehm . . . I very rarely read in the daytime, it's usually at night-time.** And then it makes me tired, you see, to read. But then, you can say, **I don't buy magazines as such. Because, I say, they're too expensive.** But they are . . . I say, expensive. They're not . . . it's all right if you have the extra money coming in, sort of thing. But, I do have to watch my pennies, sort of thing, you know. And, eh, **but I have some. I do often get them and then I always pass them on to somebody else, you know, like that. So, it's more that I can't afford them, so it's mostly the old, you know, folks, that I pass them on to.** Like Mrs Brown, who I work for, down the road. She is ninety-three, and – ninety-five, sorry, she is ninety-five. **And some friends come in and bring her magazines and then she will pass them on to me. And then I – Quinny, next door but one, is eighty and I give her some . . . And I also take them down to the neighbour from my brother. She is eighty-six and she takes them, then reads them and she goes to a club, the Darby and Joan.** Have you heard of Darby and Joan? That's for the old folks.

Later on in the interview Mary repeats that she reads magazines in bed. I have used the first bit of this fragment to introduce the quotation in chapter 2. It reads: 'I don't read during the day. It's at night-time, when I go to bed . . . And it is only magazines that I read. (. . .) Just have trouble sleeping, which everybody does, and that is what started me reading in bed . . . to put me to sleep.' The parentheses denote that interview text in between has been left out. The second part of the quotation does not come from these pages.

Joke: Oh, I see.

Mary: You know, yeah, and she takes them down to the club **and then they swap them all round down there**. So really, they get used, they just don't . . . **I hate to throw them in the dustbin**, you know. You know, I know some of them are very old, that I get, but **there's little stories in and that . . . but I miss, when I haven't, like that, it's the serials in them. You know, if I start to read one and then I can't carry on, sort of thing, you know, that's . . . So, I don't read serials so much, unless I've got the full amount, you know to, eh . . .**

Joke: Would you sometimes get, sort of, half a year's of women's . . .

Mary: That's right, yeah. Well, then, people, eh, Mrs Brown, her nephew and his wife come down, well, she has this eh . . . *Woman's Realm* and that . . .

Joke: Oh right, I know that one . . .

Mary: **And the *Woman's Own* and the *Woman* . . . and if she brings them down, you see, she brings a pile 'cause they don't come very often, so I'm able to read a serial right through, which is very nice, you know. I like that.** I do. But anyway . . . read, we get through it, don't we? Do you read and that? Well, I suppose you have to.

Joke: For my work, of course. I read books, lots of books . . . but I also like to read for pleasure as well. When I was a very small child too. I still do and all sorts of things, really. Ehm, you know, *Mills and Boon*. I have read those . . . ehm, occasionally I read magazines. Not often, really. I like books better. But it's the same thing you have with the serial. It's nicer to have a sort of longer story, to know the people in it and . . .

Mary: Yes, that's the way I found it. Well, **these little story things, I enjoy them, but, ehm, nevertheless**, I, eh, I mean Christine gave me a book, that big, thick book there, about women when they grow older.

Joke: This one?

Mary: That one underneath. Christine gave me that one and it is ever so interesting, it is.

Joke: You have been reading this one?

Mary: Yeah, I, you know, I'd read little bits here and there, sort of thing, you know, and, eh . . . when I read something, I go read, and tell the old folks, you know, I'll collect the stories about bones to shrink and things like that. [she laughs.]

Joke: So, how old are you?

Mary: I've had a real long laugh with that book, you know, with some of the old folks that . . . It's usually if I tell Quinny next door, won't

she say, 'Don't tell me no more, I don't want to know', you know.
[She laughs.]

Joke: Well, I can imagine that.

Mary: Hmm, she said, it was, Christine was in there, when I was looking after the cat. I used to go and sit with the cat sometimes, better for it, like. And I'll pick up that book, you know, and I started reading it at Christine's, and I told Christine about it, you know, and then she lent it to me and then I'd give it her back. Anyway, she finally gave it to me in the end. I wanted to . . . have a look at it, you know, and she'd say, 'Do you want it back?' And I'd say, 'I definitely want it back!' [She laughs.]

Joke: [I laugh.] Yeah, so can I ask you how old you are?

Mary: Me? I will be sixty-three in October.

Joke: So you're a Scorpio?

Mary: That's it, yes! Yes it is, yes. When you pinch, they say, when you pinch, they bite! [She laughs.]

Joke: I know, my father is a Scorpio.

Mary: Is he?

Joke: Yes.

Mary: We're all good teachers, Scorpios! [She laughs.]

Joke: Do you read things like that, you know, the stars and . . .

Mary: Oh yes, **I always read my stars, I do**. I've been to twenty fortune-tellers, you know, I have been with people and that, and they'd say to me, 'Well, you know, we'll pay for it, pay for you, if you come with us', sort of thing. Some of them are six pounds a day! I said I would not waste money on that you know. **But, eh, anyway, I like the stars. I like to read the gardening in the . . . I do like the gardening. I don't do any knitting, but I crochet.**

Joke: Oh, right, that's a kind of embroidery, or . . . ?

Mary: I do, I used to do embroidery, crocheting is different. Crocheting . . . you do it with a crocheting pin.

Joke: And is it . . . you make a sort of lace?

Mary: That's it! Like old lace, look . . . this . . . here. That's crocheting, it is, yes. I make, eh . . . you make cushion covers and blankets and things like that, you know. And **if there are any crocheting patterns in, I like to have a look at those, sort of thing.**

Joke: You take them out? Do you take the patterns out of the magazine?

Mary: **Sometimes, it depends on what I want, you know, things. Some things are beyond me, you know.** [She laughs.]

Joke: Yeah.

Mary: **Some of the time they put these little lace mats in, that you do, crochet with cotton, well, they are beyond me now, with my**

eyes, so, my eyes are not so good as they were. You know. I have to wear glasses and things, you know, for reading and anything, like I do now. I mean I could see you all right, you know . . . [She laughs.]

Joke: OK, well, then, it's OK. [I laugh.]

Mary: But it's close, I'm short-sighted, in other words. So I use my glasses, I have to wear glasses for that. So, if it's this big stuff, like that, you know, I can do it. I used to do, like embroidery, you know, and **I have saved the patterns from time to time. I had to. But . . . but, of course, with my eyesight now, I can't do it.** Ehm, well, I can do it, but I make so many mistakes and I have to keep unpicking it, you know, so . . . it's no fun doing it any more. So I don't do that now. But, ehm, I say, **I like crocheting and, eh . . . you know, medical stories in the book and things like that, I do. And I like reading the letters.**

In chapter 2 the fragment above has been edited into: 'If there are any crocheting patterns in, I like to have a look at those. (. . .) Sometimes I take the patterns out. It depends. Some things are beyond me. (. . .) These little lace mats that you crochet with cotton, they are beyond me now, with my eyes. (. . .) I make so many mistakes and I have to keep unpicking it, you know. It's not fun doing it any more.'

Joke: The letters to the magazines?

Mary: Yes, you know . . . People write to problem pages, the problems, you know, in . . . and, ehm . . . **I like to read those, and then this, the doctor gives advice, ehm, different medical things, I like to read those. So I get my money's worth out of the magazine! I do! [She laughs.]**

To get your money's worth out of a magazine you have never even paid for is, of course, a joke. It also ties in, however, with the theme of thrift, and whether or not a magazine is 'good value for money', which cropped up in other interviews. Interestingly, my mother's memories of thrift as a value of good housewifery is very different from Mary's. My mother recollects that it was a disgrace to borrow magazines. Thus, while both share the same value, for a middle-class person such as my mother it meant something completely different from what it meant to Mary Croston, who has a working-class background.

Joke: Oh, I think so, yes I do, sure. So what do you think makes these problem pages so interesting?

Mary: **Oh, yes, I love the problem pages, I really do.**
Joke: So, why do you think it's so interesting to read these things?
Mary: **I think that it's the answers more or less.** I always think, if somebody wants to ask you a question like that, you know, the people that send the letters, I think, they must, somebody wants to ask me a question, you know, and I sort of knew what they, the editors, put in, you know, auntie . . . they call them aunties, you know, I think without, well. I might be able to tell them what they said, you know, because it does give you a better outlook, you know. But that's, ehm, why I like to read in, like they said the things. I do.

In chapter 2 this fragment has been edited into: 'I love the problem pages, I really do . . . It's the answers. I always think, if somebody wants to ask you a question like that . . . and I sort of knew what they, the editors, put in . . . I might be able to tell them what they said . . . because it does give you a better outlook.'

Joke: Can I ask you something about yourself? Do you come from Birmingham?
Mary: Birmingham, yes, I was born in Birmingham, I was . . .

Mary goes on to tell me about her parents, where they used to live, about her family, the war, the jobs she has held, about reading books, bingo and gambling and one-arm bandits.

Pages 19–21

Joke: So, when you were just married and still working at the cinema, did you have magazines of your own then? Could you buy them or read them?
Mary: Yes, but I was in rooms. I had two rooms, and I had a room downstairs and a bedroom upstairs, and the **lady who got the house, she used to have the** *Woman's Weekly,* **so she bought it one week and I paid for it the next week.**
Joke: I see, so you've . . .
Mary: **So we used to do it that way then. You see. 'Cause we wasn't very flourishing in them days, you know.**
Joke: No, no.

Mary: We were just getting started and having the money to pay for, buy, to get a home together and things like that, but we used to do it that way and then we left. And we moved into the flat. I didn't have any books for a long time. I didn't. **I didn't buy any magazines for a long time and then, who started . . . There was a Mrs Parks who used to live down the bottom and she used to give me some occasionally. She used to say, '[Mary], do you want some magazines?' or something like that, and I said, 'If you've got any', and then I got so used to that. 'You want them back?' And she used to say, 'No, when you're finished, put them in the dustbin.' I used to take them over to my mother-in-law and she used to read them. And her house was converted into two flats and there was a young couple upstairs that hadn't got very much money, so she used to let them read them as well. I don't know what happened to them after that, you know.** But I know my mother-in-law used to read them and she used to give them to the girl upstairs and she used to read them.

Joke: And in those days you read the same sort of [article]?

Mary: Yes, ehm, **the books, since then, really haven't changed all that much, you know. They've got more open on sex, that's the only thing that has changed. That's it, it is the only thing. When before there was nothing much in it about that, but now it's more open, you know. But apart from that, there used to be serials in them days and then it's in patterns and crocheting patterns and the letters in the back, so they haven't really changed all that much at all.**

Like many other readers, Mary sometimes uses 'books' and 'magazines' interchangeably. Those with working-class backgrounds do this far more often and appear, implicitly, to assign value to all reading matter and to reading as an intellectual effort. Middle-class informants would sharply differentiate between high culture (books) and popular culture (magazines) and not put both in one diffuse category.

Joke: No, right, and they – I have to turn this thing round . . . [I turn the cassette.] So, and were you interested in recipes and things? You know, tips for doing this and that . . .

Mary: Oh, yes, **cooking tips! Yes, I cut some of them out sometimes. I've got a book outside, well, it's an old cookery book. And if I see any tips in them, you know, I cut them out and keep them all together right there. Yes, I do that, I do. Mind you, I do that with some of the gardening sometimes. When I go to look for them, I can't find them!** [She laughs.]

In chapter 2 this fragment has been edited into: 'Oh, yes! Cooking tips. I cut some of them out sometimes. I've got an old cookery book and if I see tips in [the magazines], I cut them out and keep them all together right there. Mind you, I do that with some of the gardening tips sometimes. When I go to look for them, I can't find them! [She laughs.]'

Joke: I know, that's always the problem, isn't it? You see these very interesting things and then you forget or you don't know where you put them or . . . I know.

Mary: **Oooh, yes, and, you know, when it comes to Easter and Christmas, they put some, the cookery, put some extra nice things in, you know. So, I do cut some of them out, not as I do much cooking these days, you know.**

Joke: No, being on your own, then, or whatever . . .

Mary: Well, being on my own, and then I usually have to get Mrs Brown a meal, 'cause she's not . . . So, I'm not in on Mondays, Thursdays and Fridays and I stay up there till lunch, you see, and I go, I take some lunch down to my brother's and cook him a lunch, Sundays and Wednesdays. So, I'm only in on, like, Tuesday and I do my shopping and then I have to go back, up to Mrs Brown, you see, and fix her up, you see, and that. So, I'm not really in the house a great deal of time.

Joke: No, no, you aren't.

Mary: No, I'm out. I'm out more than I'm in, I am.

This reads like a fairly straightforward description of magazine reading, with much emphasis on the clever exchange systems that Mary and the people she works for or is friendly with use. It does not become very clear, however, what it is specifically that makes women's magazines meaningful. (And this is not particular to the interview. Indeed, I chose this interview because it is a more lucid account than most.) In relation to the other interviews, though, the story about the problem page letters and the little anecdote about losing the recipes and the gardening tips suggested Mary Croston and other respondents were referring to two particular repertoires through which magazines become meaningful: the repertoire of connected knowing and emotional learning (to be able to advise others on what to do, to acquire insight, of 'a better outlook'); and the repertoire of practical knowledge, which does not simply have to do with learning, or 'picking things up', as others put it, but also with a pleasurable fantasy of doing certain things, which need not be acted upon to give one a good feeling. Examples are gardening tips that get lost but provided ideas about the garden, recipes that are never made but looked attractive, crocheting patterns that take you back to the crocheting work you did when younger.

In the repertoire analysis I have not paid much attention to the exchange systems some groups of readers have. As I remarked in the text, passing magazines on accords with the value of thrift and is therefore an extra source of pleasure in itself. It also appears to be more typical of the working class than the middle class. Although it would be interesting, and indeed important, to tease out differences between groups, I interviewed too few readers to find significant differences. A class-based analysis could, of course, also be a part of a more properly ethnographic project (in which case one would need to interview fewer informants, spend more time with them and have more textual space in which to describe them). I did not select informants because of their class status, however. Rather I sought to interview at length as varied a group of readers as possible, since I had decided (in the second stage of the project) that the structure of meaning underlying women's magazine reading was more strongly connected with different kinds of magazine subgenres than with groups of readers. Finding readers of different class and ethnic backgrounds (for each magazine subgenre) and interviewing men as well as women therefore served the goal of quality control.

Appendix 4

The Research (as) Process: a Methodological Account

Not many methodological accounts of ethnographic interviewing in media and cultural studies research are available. It seems important, however, to shed as much light as possible on how a researcher comes to a theoretical evaluation of how others interpret and use popular media, based on participant observation of and interviews with these others. As has been stated, my goal was to understand how women's magazines become meaningful for readers in the context of their everyday lives. I followed different routes to find an answer. The most important route consists of the interviews I held with readers. The other, complementary route that was of singular importance has been reported on in chapter 1. It involved looking for comparable research on other popular media. The two routes are parallel and interlocking strategies.

When I found out, after the first set of interviews, that readers did not have much to say about reading women's magazines, I concluded that women's magazines are not highly significant texts for readers and that they do not appear to be highly meaningful. Rather, women's magazines are convenient texts that are easy to pick up and easy to put down; their meanings are alluded to in few interview fragments. This finding led to an additional question: how can we properly research and theorize everyday media use and its meanings and significance for readers? As mentioned, I evaluated existing theories of meaning production to find a preliminary answer. Based on this evaluation, in chapter 1 a possible research scenario is presented and illustrated, here and there, with examples from the inteviews. This appendix describes how the methodological foundations were laid to come to a viable theory of how women's magazines, and everyday use in general, become meaningful through what Glaser and Strauss (1967) called 'grounded theorizing', which is to say, through a particular form of empirical research.

Glaser and Strauss developed the grounded theory approach to defend the idea that qualitative research has merit over quantitative research when it comes to theoretically understanding social phenomena as opposed to merely testing existing theory by trying to falsify it. Grounded theory is organized in stages of data gathering and evaluation. In each stage relatively small sets of data are sampled on theoretical grounds, starting from a broad spectrum and then progressively narrowing the focus. Thus, a relatively open research question is sharpened and specified until a satisfactory theoretical explanation is found. Theoretical sampling is what sets the approach of Glaser and Strauss apart from other forms of qualitative research, which tend to be more descriptive. Glaser and Strauss hold that the theoretical knowledge a researcher has should be used, including the theoretical intuitions that are fed during data sampling and evaluation. This leads to new theoretical assumptions that can be put to the test with small new samples, until a theory can be formulated. The aim of grounded theorizing is theory rather than representativeness for large populations. My search through existing literature thus fed into methodological decisions on, for example, who to interview and what to ask, and how to analyse the interview material. Field experience led to the conclusion that *everyday* media use had not been theorized at all. A truly chronological account of this process would be unreadable, not to say dreadfully boring, so in this book the process is split along the conventional criteria of theory versus methodology. This appendix deals with the methodological and ethnographic sides of coming to a theory of women's magazine use.

Before I give a rough outline of the stages in this research project and explain the different questions and goals that were involved, it must be said that although this project was inspired by and set out to be an ethnography, the final result is hardly a 'true' ethnography. Small-scale ethnographic research, which would contain much more descriptive material and give a fuller sense of readers' cultural backgrounds, has little legitimacy in media research, which I regret. It seems to be a consequence of the fact that there is a strong tradition in media research of doing surveys. Because of institutional pressure, I extended the method upon which I had decided (lengthy interviews) to interviews with eighty readers, which presented me with an enormous amount of material, much of which has not been used in this book.[1] The good side to having access to so much material is that I feel I can make a strong case for my interpretation of how women's magazines become meaningful. Although it is not representative for any population, it is theoretically generalizable to other forms of everyday media use and it covers in depth the different ways in which magazines have meaning.

Since this piece of work, though ethnographic in orientation, is not a classical ethnography, one might wonder about its 'truth' value: how does a reader of this text know that my account is truthful and recognizably connected with women's magazine reading? How did I know that what readers told me was true? Do I know whether they accurately described their practices of media use, since I did not spend more than half a day to a day with each informant, during which time they certainly did not follow their normal routines? In point of fact, I do not know. In the book numerous quotations are given. Beyond that I can only offer David Morley's comment on his research practice (as reported in Morley, 1980 and Morley, 1986):

> In the case of my own research, I would accept that in the absence of any significant element of participant observation of actual behaviour beyond the interview situation, I am left only with the stories that respondents chose to tell me. These stories are, however, themselves both limited by, and indexical of, the cultural and linguistic frames of reference which respondents have available to them, through which to articulate their responses. (1989: 24)

To which he adds that all behaviour leaves open the question of interpretation.

> Should you wish to understand what I am doing, it would probably be as well to ask me. I may well, of course, lie to you or otherwise misrepresent my thoughts or feelings, for any number of purposes, but at least, through my verbal responses, you will begin to get some access to the kind of language, the criteria of distinction and the types of categorizations, through which I construct my (conscious) world. (p. 25)

I shall not return now to my informant's verbal responses. Here I wish to explain how the interviews were done, which criteria were used to select informants and, in a later stage, which criteria were used to select interview fragments. The three sections of this appendix deal with the three main stages that structured the research.

The first stage (after some experiments with other research forms, such as street interviews in a railway station and an attempt to do participant observation in a hairdresser's shop and a doctor's waiting-room) consisted of ten pilot interviews with readers who differed in age (early twenties to late fifties) and who read different kinds of women's magazines (domestic weeklies, glossies and a feminist magazine). Although their incomes diverged (as far as that can be deduced from their occupational status, clothes and homes), their class background tended to be more middle class than working class. The main goal of the interviews was to find out what informants generally had to say about women's magazines when encouraged to talk about them. Theoretically, I was interested in finding out if and how reading women's magazines related to how readers constructed feminine identities for themselves. Given that informants liked the interviews but had little to say about women's magazines, there was not much material to use in an interpretation of women's magazine reading as part of specific constructions of femininity. There was, moreover, significant danger of tautologically interpreting constructions of femininity from magazines that were read, and interpreting a choice of a magazine as evidence of a particular construction of femininity; besides which, many readers read magazines from diverse subgenres. More interesting was my impression that, despite differences of social class and preferences for different magazines, there were comparable elements in the interviews concerning women's magazine reading that pointed to a possible common structure of understanding women's magazines among different readers and across different magazines.

The second stage, therefore, was organized to check whether differences among readers and differences in what individual readers said about women's magazines were related to, on the one hand, magazine subgenres and, on the other, readers' positions in the social formation (structured, for example, by their gender or ethnicity). The question was, could a broad theory of women's magazine use be developed and justified despite differences among readers and the variability (and sometimes inconsistencies) in the interviews with individual readers? Thus, moving from 'central' women's magazine genres to 'outlier' genres, I interviewed ten readers of *Cosmopolitan* magazine (domestic weeklies had been relatively extensively discussed in the pilot interviews), ten readers of gossip magazines, fourteen readers of a feminist magazine and readers of a genre that is closely related to women's magazines, self-help literature (four women). Since by then I had interviewed women from different class backgrounds (though very few upper-class readers), I sought to interview coloured women and male women's magazine readers (seven coloured women were interviewed, four Dutch women and three English women; sixteen men were interviewed). Looking for readers, care was taken to move away from Amsterdam, where I live and work, to the periphery (the less urbanized and industrialized southern and eastern parts) of the Netherlands, where I interviewed ten informants (three of them men, some of whom were interviewed about gossip magazines). Since almost all the existing theory and research I had found was British, I decided, as a check on the Dutch material and so that I could place the theoretical work I had been using in its context, to interview British readers too (eleven women were interviewed, eight with working-class backgrounds and three with middle-class backgrounds; their ages ranged from eighteen to seventy-four). As a last check two women who did not consider themselves ever to have been women's magazine readers were interviewed. Differences that were particularly useful in coming to a broad theory of women's magazine reading were focused on: female versus male readers; traditional women's magazines versus feminist and gossip magazines. Focusing on readers of particular women's magazine titles was not very productive; nor was focusing on ethnic difference. Underlying meaning structures, in the case of women's magazines, are evidently not the property of specific social groups or categories.

When I felt I had acquired sufficient material and overview, I moved on to the third stage, which consisted solely of analysis and theory building. My aim then was to come to an understanding of how readers construct, negotiate and interpret women's magazines and women's magazine reading, and thus make the practice of reading as well as the texts meaningful.

The first stage

The first stage of the research was only generally focused. My research question was, what do women say about the magazines they read? After a little trial and error with different methods, I decided to find readers to interview in their homes, where they would feel at ease and I would be able to get a better sense of who they were by studying how they lived. I believed that it would not be very difficult to find informants since so many people read women's magazines, and during the first stage it was not. Because fieldwork accounts and ethnography handbooks stress that entry into the field and making contact with informants can be a difficult and frustrating phase, I decided to recruit informants by 'snowballing' or 'friendship pyramiding' (see, for example, Kitzinger, 1989: 87). Thus, I asked a woman in my karate class if she knew any women's magazine readers I could interview, which resulted in two interviews; I used work contacts and asked friends to ask friends. I also decided to interview my mother, who, I hoped would refresh my memory as to which magazines we had at home when I was a child. This interview led to a group interview with three friends of my mother and herself. Her friends did not consider themselves to be magazine readers, but felt it was important that they, as non-readers, also had a say. In total I did ten interviews, one with two women and one group interview. With six of these women return interviews were held after a little less than a year.

To avoid embarrassing myself in the first interviews I used a sheet of paper with a few key issues and questions (see below). Later on I dispensed with the paper, though the open, only minimally structured interview method remained the same. I started the interviews by introducing myself, the project and three topics to talk about: their reading history (from as early on as they could remember), the women's movement (since feminism has made rather a difference as to how women especially can, or feel they have to, legitimate their choices in life as well as in what they read), and, if it applied, professional opinion. A non-stated goal was to find out as much as possible of the personal history of the person, to provide information about the kind of daily context in which she read and had read women's magazines. The three topics broke down to a series of informative questions. Which magazines do you read? Do you buy them or borrow them? Are they given to you, and if so by whom? What do you like to read especially? Do you browse or really read? Can you remember women's magazines from your parents' home? Which ones? When did you read them? And so on. The women's movement raised such questions as, how do you feel about feminism and emancipation, and how, in your opinion, do women's magazines write about feminist topics? I also asked informants about their 'professional opinion' of women's magazines, as an academic, a journalist, a bookseller, or simply as an informed reader. What kind of readers do different subgenres attract? These questions were used to broach the different subjects. They led to answers and new, more specific, questions, which varied, depending on what readers had to say.

All the interviews were taped.[2] The tapes were transcribed by the administrative staff at the Communication Department where I work and by students, who were paid out of my research budget. I then checked the transcripts against the tapes. The transcripts served as the basic data. All statements about women's magazines and about femininity were coded, following a procedure that was quite similar to one I later found in a qualitative research handbook by Catherine Marshall and Gretchen Rossman.

Marshall and Rossman (1989) advise, as one of several research strategies, asking questions of one's data. To analyse the pilot interviews I made two lists of questions that specified the two parts of my research question at that stage: what was said about 'reading women's magazines', and what was said about 'being a woman' (that is, constructions of femininity)? Statements about women's magazines (whatever the point of view from which an informant was talking, either as a professional, a private individual or as an observer of others) from each informant were sorted into the different categories that are recognized under the umbrella term 'women's magazines' (see the introduction) and two non-women's magazine genres (numbers 5 and 6): (1) traditional women's magazines (which included domestic weeklies and magazines for young women); (2) glossy magazines (traditional and upmarket glossies, such as *Cosmopolitan, Elle, Marie Claire,* all of which are monthlies); (3) gossip magazines (relatively cheap weeklies); (4) feminist magazines; (5) porn magazines; (6) other magazines.

I was asked remarkably often whether magazines that, in my view, were clearly not women's magazines were also included in the research. For most informants women's magazines are a 'blurred' genre. Karen de Wit, for example, was not quite sure whether her definition of women's magazines concorded with my supposedly 'official' definition (even thought I had explained I had no standard definition and was interested in her definition). Like many others, Karen simply asked what I thought of it.

Joke: Do you regularly read women's magazines?
Karen: I read *Cosmo* and *Viva* and I go to this coffee-shop where they have all these magazines. So I browse in them every week, though not all that often in *Margriet* and *Libelle.* Only when I really feel like it and I have done all the others.

Joke: Which ones are the others?

Karen: They subscribe to a collection, so it also contains *Story*, *Privé* and *Weekend*: juicy gossip, and *Panorama* and *Nieuwe Revu*. But those really are men's magazines, aren't they?

The second list of questions dealt with femininity, feminism and emancipation. Text fragments that answered them were again coded for each respondent in a uniform data matrix, in which each row represented a respondent. (For group or duo interviews a row was made for each informant.) The questions were: (1) What kind of woman am I (the informant)? (2) What do I have problems with? (3) What are my views about other women, women in general? (4) What do I have to take care of or for? (5) What do I dream of? (6) How do I feel about men? These questions were analytical instruments, which is to say that they were not posed as such during the interviews, but the interview transcripts were read as if answering such questions. The result was a giant data matrix that served the important goals of data reduction and focusing.

At face value the data thus organized suggested four 'interpretive positions': a traditionalist position (readers who value home-making and put their family first, who advocate part-time jobs and prefer domestic weeklies); a post-feminist position (career-minded readers with a preference for glossy magazines); a young woman's position (young readers who read mainly young women's magazines and regard them as little bibles on 'what to do if . . .'); and a feminist position (which displays a broad critical knowledge of women's magazines as a force of oppression and favours feminist magazines). However, it was very difficult to take this classification further theoretically. Was a position a 'way of reading' that inspires or strengthens a construction of femininity? Or did certain constructions of femininity lead to specific ways of reading and to a choice of particular magazines? Both mechanisms are probably at work at the same time, in which case it would be nearly impossible to separate them. Moreover, if both mechanisms work simultaneously, an analysis in terms of 'positions' would not help to clarify how women's magazines become meaningful.

A second conclusion, at the end of the first stage, was that the different positions appeared to share a particular way of using women's magazines, apart from escaping from daily obligations and obtaining practical advice and information. Women's magazines were often said to include case studies of the personal experiences of others that could be used as material to compare one's own situation or experiences with. I interpret that as meaning that reading can be a kind of inoculation: having some knowledge of the dangers that might befall one as a mother, a partner in a sexual relationship or a career woman may help to avert these dangers or help one to deal with them better. Thus, reading can strengthen one's sense of identity as well as provide specific knowledge that will give one a feeling of authority. This interpretation left me with a string of questions. If women's magazines empower (by strengthening a sense of identity and authority), then why are they also disappointing (a view that was often put forward)? And can women's magazines also be disempowering (by strengthening readers' dependency on roles and identities that make women powerless)? Are they a real help when readers' lives are indeed wrecked?

Evaluating the first stage, it became clear that although the interview method was basically well suited to eliciting as much information about women's magazines as possible, I needed more interviews to test whether a broad theory of women's magazine reading could be formulated, and I needed a more open framework for the interpretation of the interviews. To assign readers to positions was not very helpful because there were too many inconsistencies in the interviews, and readers tended to read widely different magazines, which accorded with very different positions. Moreover, if readers occupy 'positions', it is difficult to build a historical dimension into the research: readers change. Another drawback to a 'positions' approach is the fact that class, occupation and feminist sympathies were not very good predictors of reading positions or preferences. Housewives may read glossy magazines. Career women may read both glossies and domestic weeklies. In fact, I interviewed very few long-time faithful readers of any kind of magazine. Most of my informants occasionally grew bored with the magazines they were reading. Some were in the process of changing from one subgenre to another in the period I interviewed them. Return interviews with six of the women interviewed during this stage confirmed that change and disappointment are as important in women's magazines use as empowerment. Karen de Wit, quoted above, stopped going to the coffee-shop where she used to read magazines. Linda Zijlstra, another informant, had ended her subscription of the magazine she had been very enthusiastic about, and two more informants remarked that they were quite fed up with the same subjects always coming up. One of them had stopped buying *Cosmopolitan*; the other seemed to be suffering from a severe hangover during the interview and I would guess she had fallen out with women's magazines only temporarily.[3]

The second stage

The second stage mainly involved finding different kinds of readers, to see whether their accounts of women's magazine reading tallied with the accounts I had been given during the first stage and to substantiate my hunch that a broad theory of women's magazine reading could be formulated. At this point it had also become clear that I needed to do far more interviews than I had originally envisaged, to secure being funded for the research. Because I was now looking for readers of specific women's magazine subgenres, and readers defined by such characteristics as their gender, class background, ethnic origin and where they lived, acquiring interviewees was far more difficult than it had been.[4] I still used friendship pyramiding as an approach, but also sought other ways of finding informants, for example, through a respondent agency and a list compiled by a research firm.

To make this account at all readable, I have chosen to describe the second stage of the research in terms of the groups that were interviewed and to discuss the different acquisition methods that were used for each group. Since different themes are discussed for different groups, no attempt has been made to adhere to chronology. The interview strategy remained largely the same. If anything, the interviews became slightly more informal and conversational when I began to realize that it was not a specific question or questions that encourage informants to talk about reading women's magazines, but that it is of prime importance that they feel respected and listened to. After a little prompting at the beginning of the interview, informants would usually bring different perspectives to bear on women's magazine reading of their own accord, or use their particular expertise. I always took care to bring the conversation around to women's magazines again when it drifted off. Since television programmes had proved a good conversional lubricant during the first-stage interviews, and since I was still planning, at that time, to describe women's magazines as part of what Bausinger (1984) calls the 'media ensemble' (see chapter 1), I also took care to pose questions about informants' favourite television shows.

Cosmopolitan *readers*

The pilot interviews had given me quite a detailed impression of how traditional women's magazine are read. Interviews with two professional workers who appreciate glossy magazines (May Han and Lidy Rijkaard, a friend who has not been quoted in the book) suggested that a different set of arguments and legitimations might be brought forward by readers of glossy magazines. Even though I had become critical of identifying readers with a position or a single magazine, there seemed no other relatively easy and practicable way of finding a number of younger and older 'career women'. Also, additional funding was made available since it was thought to be important that informants were not recruited only through personal networks. Through a specialized agency ten *Cosmopolitan* readers were 'hired' for two group interviews (for which one paid a minimal fee to the respondents themselves; the agency was paid a fixed fee per respondent).

The respondents, used to marketing focus group interviews for product testing, were very enthusiastic about the interviews, which were more personal and asked more of their own interpretive skills than they were used to. For me, however, compared with the individual in-depth interviews of the first stage, the group interview was not a very productive method. Although it confirmed the view that reading *Cosmopolitan* is not very different from reading other women's magazine subgenres, the interview did not inspire new ideas. It was virtually impossible to understand how individual respondents organized their ideas about women's magazines and feminity. It was also quite obvious that five individual women who did not know one another before the interview became a group in quite a short period of time. I have a feeling they refrained from giving views they thought would be radically different from the views of the others and that they sometimes overemphasized statements they thought would make a favourable impression.

The transcript of the *Cosmopolitan* interview suggests that there was not much of a difference between these readers and the domestic weekly readers I had predominantly talked to in the first set of interviews. They appeared to have slightly higher incomes; they were more expensively dressed and wore more make-up than other informants; more of them had jobs. Their chief reasons for reading, however, were also entertainment and practical advice. Not surprisingly, it turned out that a sizeable number of them also read other kinds of women's magazines.

Gossip magazines: melodrama and tragedy

As it was set up at the same time as the *Cosmopolitan* interview and could not be cancelled, I also did a group interview with gossip magazine readers. To my delight, a policewoman who had been scheduled for the interview had to work an evening shift and was unable to come, but it was agreed between the agency and this respondent that I could interview her at a later date in her own home for the same rate. Since only four women had been scheduled for this interview, it was easier to do. Like the *Cosmo* readers, and like most of the other readers I spoke to before and after, these readers also read other magazines. Similarly, at the end of the interview they were uneasy about being paid 45 guilders (£15) and travel expenses, and worried whether I had to pay it myself. (I explained I did not, and that the money came from my research budget, allotted by the university.) I think they were uneasy because they had enjoyed the interview and felt that they had just 'chatted' for an hour and a half, which could hardly count as work.

The gossip magazine readers differed not only from other readers with regard to class (they all came from working-class backgrounds), but also in that they explained reading gossip magazines in terms that were not used for other subgenres of women's magazines. There was much more (melo)drama and talk of hardships and sorrow. Generally, in the phrase of Ien Ang (1985), in this group interview a shared 'tragic structure of feeling' surfaced. Recognizing like-minded souls, the women did not mind talking about all the problems they had faced in their lives or saying things like, 'It may sound strange, but you read these magazines to enjoy the misery of others.' Although they were hardly representative of the sizeable number of gossip magazine readers, it seemed to me they enjoyed reading these magazines more than they or others would ordinarily enjoy reading other women's magazines. They did not speak of 'disappointment' and 'value for money', but debated the issue of how much is true in these magazines in a way that suggested that knowledge of genre rules resulted in the ability to recognize which of the announced marriages or affairs a couple of weeks later would be 'off' or would turn out never to have been 'on'. Gossip readers, in short, seemed to have more fun.

Later interviews did not straightforwardly corroborate this finding. A possible reason for that might be that to enjoy talking about gossip magazines by definition presupposes a receptive audience, preferably a small group that shares the codes of gossiping or, as the case may be, the codes of making fun of gossip magazines. A situation in which one is interviewed by a single person who is from another background and not a gossip magazine reader herself may lead one to play down one's involvement with the genre, as was certainly the case with one of the women who participated in the group interview when I interviewed her again, on her own. This particular interpretation is also strengthened by my experiences with involved male readers of gossip magazines, who used 'camp' codes (in which I share more easily) to explain why it was such fun.

One of my last interviews about gossip magazines was not a success for yet another reason. It had been brought to my attention by friends who have ties with the Surinam and Antilles community in Amsterdam (which is concentrated in the Bijlmer, a south-eastern district of Amsterdam) that in this community gossip magazines are exceedingly popular. I managed to set up an interview with a woman who, according to her son-in-law, enjoyed reading gossip magazines and watching quiz shows on television as a kind of vicarious participation in another, richer world. Since his estimation was very close to my own perception of reading gossip magazines, it is quite possible I expected far too much from the interview. The first time I arrived for the interview, the door was opened to me just a crack; the curtains of the flat had been pulled tightly shut. The woman I wanted to interview was not there, the person who opened the door while eyeing me suspiciously told me. It took some time to find my informant and set up a new interview.

Since none of my previous interview appointments had gone wrong or had been misunderstood, I was a bit wary. And so was my interviewee. We had quite a friendly talk when we finally met at her daughter's house, where she was babysitting, but it was quite clear that she was not going to confide in me or spontaneously tell me more about her enjoyment of gossip magazines and related genres. The barriers of colour and my official status were too much to even out in one interview. I was too much a representative of official institutions (which are not much appreciated in the Bijlmer, where there are more social workers, more administrative staff and fieldwork officers in the unemployment bureau than anywhere else in the city; this part of town has the highest unemployement rates). Clearly she felt embarrassed by my visit. Why did I want to ask her about reading magazines? What knowledge did she have that she herself did not even know about? During the interview she relaxed a bit. The interview was saved mainly by the fact that she liked to chat, as she said. But it was one of my shortest interviews and the only one in which I was offered no refreshment at all. Neither of us was very sure what the other one was thinking.

Approaching coloured women

In general it also held true that the most difficult to find and interview were coloured women who read women's magazines. More potential respondents were hesitant; more refused. There was no point in trying the agency and a market research firm that was called in to find male readers. Women from ethnic minority groups are not (yet) of interest for market research. Nor are there all that many coloured people in the Netherlands, which means that a computer-directed survey, geared for aselective sampling, will not come up with a sizeable number in a timespan that will not cost a fortune (unless one were to limit the search to Amsterdam, for example, which has a fairly large migrant population). This meant I had to go back to snowballing. It also meant I had to crank up my nerve quite a bit.

It felt absolutely wrong and almost insulting to ask someone for an interview simply because she happened to be a member of an ethnic minority group. However, given the fact that coloured women are very much under-represented in women's magazines, it was imperative to go to some lengths to ask them about it. I managed interviews with an older Chinese-Indonesian woman (whose daughter and son I also interviewed) and with two black women who had come to the Netherlands from Surinam and from the Antilles. Three of the eleven English women I had interviews with were also coloured; among them too were a mother and daughter. All of these women were aware of the fact that black women and Asian women are hardly ever models for women's magazines. None of them felt that women's magazines (their preferences ranged from young women's and glossy magazines to the domestic weeklies and gossip magazines) were therefore not for them.

As a critical intellectual I am used to thinking about gender and ethnicity in terms of unequal power relations. My informants differed enormously as to their involvement and interest in politics. All of them were less angry than I had expected and little inclined to talk about racism. They shared a liberal, equal rights political vocabulary: colour is of no importance to the kind of person you are or the rights you have and everybody ought to be treated equally. Mrs Han, a very friendly and affable woman, came very near anger when I asked her if she felt different, or an outsider, when reading women's magazines, since they never feature ethnic women. She said, 'When I read *Margriet*, I am an ordinary Dutch woman, no different from anybody else.' No further discussion was possible. She did not deny it had been difficult for them as a family to settle in a small provincial town, but it was clearly more important to stress that eventually they did settle in and become part of the community: 'In the beginning people watched me in the supermarket. But that got better . . . It also made a difference when a Korean family came to live nearby.'

Evelyn Cauleta Reid (1988), in a report on the television habits of young black women in London, simply listed statements. A majority of the statements are very critical, in a heavy-handed manner, of the fact that there are hardly any black people on British television, in whatever capacity. Likewise, Philomena Essed's study on everyday racism (1991) reports on black women's criticism and awareness of unequal power relations. The political vocabulary used, especially by Reid's informants, recognizes racial discrimination as an issue for all coloured people all the time. My informants acknowledged that there are not many coloured people in magazines or on television, but they also said that they were not totally absent. It seemed more important for them to stress their equal status as citizens and offer examples that made clear that coloured women are to be seen on the pages of women's magazines and in other media, rather than to stress racial discrimination or lament their unequal status in terms of cultural representation.

To interview coloured women requires extra cultural capital since one has to enter close-knit communities held together by a common ethnic origin. I have recounted my adventures in the Bijlmer, where I did an interview about gossip magazines and met with suspicion and uneasiness. Keya Ganguly (1992) did ethnographic research among the immigrant Indian community in the United States from which she orginates and in which she occupies the strange intermediate status of a daughter and an outsider because she belongs more to the academic world than to the Indian community. Ganguly's article shows how her expert knowledge of the community's way of living helps immensely in making sense of migrant identity and experience. She knows which topics will get an enthusiastic response and which are sensitive.

Reflecting on Ganguly's work, it seems to me that gaining entrance to a close-knit community is a more important problem for a researcher than colour. The colour of one's skin, like one's gender, becomes meaningful in specific contexts. Black readers, like white readers, may well define themselves in terms that are to do not with colour, but, for example, with a professional career, even if racist discourse tends to emphasize ethnicity when one is not white. Nevertheless, a black reader may experience herself as white or as an ordinary Dutch women – 'colourless' – just as I, a white middle-class woman, can identify with black characters in novels. In relation to how women's magazines become meaningful histories of migration and colonialism seem more important than colour, in so far as the two issues can be separated from one another. Colonialism, an important part of Dutch and British history, constructed the idea of 'homeland' versus 'overseas territories', in which women's magazines played a role, simply because they were easily transported images that circulated among the colonial community as well as among the subordinated (see Spivak, 1990). Moreover, for my informants it was easier to talk about colonialist history than to discuss everyday racism or how one's ethnic status relates to what one reads. It could well be the case that many women felt they would lose face if they talked about everyday racism with a white interviewer, who might regard that as affectation, or, alternatively, who might then see them as a victim. Working on the assumption that discussing everyday racism could be a matter of pride, I chose not to pursue the subject if my informants did not want to discuss it.

Interviewing British readers

Devised as a check on the Dutch interviews and inspired by the fact that most of the literature on women's magazines is Anglo-American, I also interviewed seven British women in Birmingham and London. A pilot interview had taken place earlier with three British students who were in Amsterdam as part of a student exchange. It convinced me that interviewing in English would not be a major problem, and that there was not much difference between this interview and the interviews with Dutch young women, which betokened enough cultural similarity to make a comparison fruitful. Of course, there are important differences between Britain and the Netherlands. To name a few: race and ethnicity have become political issues, partly because of race riots, which the Netherlands did not experience on the same scale; class difference is far more important in Britain than it is in the Netherlands, which means, for one thing, that the women's magazine market is more segregated; it is more common and more accepted for women from whatever class to work outside the home in Britain that it is in the Netherlands.

To give another more extensive (and for me unexpected) example of the differences in points of reference between British and Dutch respondents: older women in Britain referred to the Second World War relatively often and in a totally different, far more romantic vein than would be the case in the Netherlands. The popular memory of the occupied, not surprisingly, is vastly different from that of the victorious. Even for someone of my generation the Second World War means the 'Winter of Hunger', the question of whether one's parents were 'fout' (in favour of the Nazi regime) and camps and atrocities, not only in Europe, but in Indonesia and Indo-China as well. I come from a typical Dutch-Indonesian colonial family in which the Japanese were seen as the crueller occupiers. Accounts of camp survivors, in Europe and in Asia, have been published and are often discussed in television chat shows. In the Netherlands, as in Britain romanticized war novels are available. However, the Second World War is a quite different reference point for older Dutch respondents compared with the British women whom I interviewed.

All the British informants were approached through friends in Birmingham and London, who also helped me interpret the odd expression I was not familiar with. For instance, one of my informants told me she thought *Woman* and *Woman's Own* 'too mushy', which, I was told later, meant 'sentimental'. Contextually it meant 'too many short stories about love affairs.' Not surprisingly perhaps, this particular respondent preferred the very pragmatic *Prima* and *Bella*. Three of my British informants were coloured, while eight had working-class backgrounds.

Interviewing men

Since I wanted to interview men (arguably a group of readers that would come up with absolutely new uses for and ways of reading women's magazines) and since I had to spread my sample away from Amsterdam, I asked a market research firm to compose a list of twenty readers of women's magazines, ten of whom were to be readers of gossip magazines. At least eight of these readers had to be male and all readers had to come from different parts of the country.

These readers were not going to be paid. It was costly all the same, but it seemed the only way of finding a sizeable number of men to interview and it would also ensure that the first-stage interviews could be checked for possible effects of the fact that I had used my own friendship and collegiate networks to get names and addresses. Comparing the earlier with the later methods, snowballing is the friendlier, though more labour-intensive, and it yields more results because one can, in a way, 'bargain' with go-betweens who would ask questions like, 'Do you mean you want a women's magazine addict or someone who occasionally reads them? It is OK if they read other magazines? Have a high level of education? Are young?' And so on. A personal introduction also makes the start of the interview much smoother and easier.

The interviews set up as a result of the telephone survey varied widely, but were, on the whole, more difficult. Respondents expected a questionnaire or would categorically refuse to talk about themselves. To visit one of the men I interviewed (who lived on the Dutch–German border) I travelled two and a half hours by train from Amsterdam and half an hour by bus, and then spent three quarters of an hour hitchhiking and walking. He turned out to have been too shy to tell the person doing the telephone survey that he did not read women's magazines. The telephone researchers had been instructed to be firm with men, since men tend to deny out of hand that they read women's magazines, while they often read their partners' magazines. In this case the instruction had been ill-advised. I heard a good deal about a new car magazine, but nothing about women's magazines. Fortunately, I was given a lift back to the train station, for which I was very grateful.

A total of sixteen men were interviewed. Nine were interviewed by me (names and addresses came from the market research firm and from friends, and three of the men had answered an advertisement asking for male and female readers of a Dutch feminist magazine). Two (brothers of friends) were interviewed together with a male co-researcher, who then interviewed five men on his own. Of the eight men recruited by the market research firm, five were interviewed (the young man who eagerly read the new car magazine was one of them). The other three refused. Despite the fact that they had explicitly been asked by the researcher whether they agreed to being approached for an interview that would take approximately an hour to an hour and a half, they did not want to give an interview. Two of them said they were too busy, with their children, with an orchestra, with sports – to which one of them added (reinforcing my impression that excuses were sought to avoid talking about women's magazines), 'I have better things to do than to chat about that for an hour.' Upon being prompted by me, he said he occasionally leafed through the magazines, but he 'didn't read them thoroughly'. I never even talked to the third man. His wife answered when I telephoned. She was very suspicious about my call and after my careful explanation said, 'My husband doesn't read those magazines and we are away from home a lot because I have had an operation. There's no point in trying to come to see us.'

I have lingered over these rejections to underline how difficult it is to find men to interview, despite that fact that, according to readership statistics, a good number of men say they read women's magazines (see appendix 2). The three men who were not interviewed had all told the research firm over the telephone that they occasionally read women's magazines. Simply trying to find men for interviews made it clear that women's magazines are not a topic men are supposed to have knowledge of or talk about. An added problem with a two-step method (first the research firm collects names and addresses, then a researcher makes the appointments for interview) was that many of those I rang thought they had already been interviewed. 'Interview' for many is synonymous with a telephone poll. Some of these men, quite probably, felt they had already 'done their bit' by not hanging up on the interviewer and patiently answering questions about which magazines they read or were familiar with. Against this argument, it must be pointed out that all these men gave their addresses and telephone numbers to the interviewers.

Apart from the reluctance of many men to be interviewed, there was another problem. Although I encountered nothing but hospitality and kindness from the men I interviewed, I did not feel at ease. With almost all the women I interviewed I established some form of rapport; with the men this was much more difficult. Following the argument of Carol Warren (1985), I suppose that my unease stemmed from the fact that it was difficult to maintain a boundary between 'establishing rapport' and 'flirting'. With women, establishing such a boundary had not been an issue, not because sexual attraction between women could not occur in an interview situation, but because the 'social rules' in such a case would give me more leeway. In some of the interviews with women I quite enjoyed the grey zone between attention and flirting, while in other interviews I enjoyed playing the role of the ideal daughter-in-law (kind, attentive, slightly deferential). With the men neither situation was fitting. With women

I could derive relative power from either role. With men the same roles would automatically have placed me at a disadvantage, given the nature of sexual relations between men and women and relations between fathers and daughters. It seemed the only thing I could do was to be very calm and professional, which does not lead to any form of rapport. The interviews were much easier when there were wives or mothers or partners around. I did not get the impression that my unease communicated itself all that obviously to my male informants. Since I could not be sure that was the case – the transcripts were too different from the transcripts of the interviews with women to make things clear one way or another – I was very happy to find a male student (Joppe Boodt) who wanted to do a 'research apprenticeship' and did not mind interviewing men about women's magazines.

We decided to do two interviews together, after which he would find a small number of respondents on his own, transcribe the interviews and write a report. By mutual agreement the findings were to be his to write an article about and I could use his material for my research. By snowballing he found three men. It was difficult to find older men who read women's magazines and men with little education. His oldest respondent was forty-seven (in 1990). He did manage to find someone who did not have higher or university education. In search of more informants he ran a personal advertisement in a free Sunday newspaper, which was answered by five men. One older man thought it was to be a telephone questionnaire and declined when he heard it was to be a face-to-face interview. Two youngsters played a prank. Two times Joppe travelled to the Bijlmer (where I too had had my most difficult interview) in the early morning to discover no one was there. The other two were genuine responses and with both men interviews were set up and carried out. Joppe interviewed five men on his own; we interviewed two men together and I had already interviewed nine men. Ten of the sixteen men had middle-class rather than working-class backgrounds and one was Chinese-Indonesian. Their ages ranged form twenty-three to forty-eight.

In general, it can be concluded that although men are familiar with women's magazines and frequently read them (according to many of the women I have spoken to and according to available statistical data: see appendix 2), many of them feel it is not *comme il faut* to talk about this. Possibly they sincerely believe that they do not know much about women's magazines, which weighed more heavily with them than the women, though they also frequently voiced the concern that they 'really didn't know all that much about women's magazines'. The exceptions to this general rule are men who have a professional interest in graphic design, art or health care and men who participate in camp-influenced student or gay subculture, in which enjoying and ridiculing popular culture are dialectic twins that reinforce one another. A third group of male readers of women's magazines consists of men who either do not care about conventions that assign interests and activities to men or to women or live in unconcerned ignorance of these conventions and men who take an active interest in the subjects women's magazines write about, such as how to maintain healthy relationships or child care. Their reading of women's magazines was not different from that of the women interviewed before them. Similarly, there are also women who express professional or camp interest in women's magazines.

Opzij: *out of the way*

Three of the men who were interviewed answered a personal advertisement in the national newspapers that asked male and female readers of the Dutch feminist magazine *Opzij* if they were willing to be interviewed. Although in retrospect the gossip magazines seem to be the women's magazine subgenre that has, more than the others, a character of its own because it elicits a qualitatively different response, beforehand this role was ascribed to *Opzij*, as a representative of the subgenre of feminist magazines. In the case of *Opzij*, as in the case of the men, I was lucky to find a co-researcher. Véronique Schutgens had just finished a content analysis of recent volumes of *Opzij* and was as curious as I about the readers of this magazine. Since *Opzij* is well known but not overly popular in our (academic) circle of friends, we decided an advertisement in the national newspapers would be our best guarantee of finding as mixed a sample as possible. This raises the problem of self-selection. Informal validation among friends and acquaintances after we completed the interviews and our analysis assured us that our findings were not far off the mark (some of them enjoyed the magazine, an aspect that we had not found in our interviews; others immediately recognized the moral pressure of subscribing to *Opzij*) and also led, among other things, to lively discussions of the magazine at the birthday parties I attended at that time.

The advertisement was answered by thirty-nine *Opzij* readers. We sent round a short open-answer questionnaire to enable us to decide who we should interview. There were a couple of demographic questions (asking for their name, date of birth, sex, profession, where they lived) and questions about how they used and evaluated *Opzij*. When do you read *Opzij*? With which articles do you start? Do you feel you learn from *Opzij*? And there were questions about other genres: do you read other women's magazines? Do you have a favourite television show? Do you read popular psychological self-help books? The last question asked them to name and describe someone they admired.

Thirty-five of the questionnaires were returned. For the interviews we selected according to the following criteria. We included all the men who responded (three). Among the women we looked for as much variety as possible. Respondents from different age groups and living in different kinds of urban and rural areas were chosen. Some of them lived on their own, others with a partner, with a partner and children, without a partner and children, in a commune. We included some who read traditional women's magazines or read self-help literature and some who did not.

Véronique and I agreed to work with the list of questions I had been using all along. We did the first interview together and split up the remaining thirteen interviews. When the interviews had been transcribed, we read them and questioned the other about her interviews. We were both taken aback at how little the women and men we interviewed were involved in feminism, which has become the leitmotif in our interpretation of the interviews. An important difference with the earlier interviews was that not only were the *Opzij* women better educated, they also talked more. All of these respondents were sent the Dutch text of an article we published about these interviews. Since informant feedback is considered an important technique for establishing validity, this seemed a good opportunity. Four out of fourteen respondents answered. One was critical (as revealed in chapter 4); one sent a change of address and, upon some prompting, an invitation to come to dinner rather than an evaluation; two agreed and felt it was a sharp analysis. All in all a rather meagre response.

Four other *Opzij* readers need to be mentioned separately. They answered an advertisement in the magazine itself that asked readers of self-help literature for interviews. Fifteen women responded. I placed the advertisement in *Opzij* for two reasons. I had become interested in self-help literature as a genre that seemed related to a central characteristic of women's magazines and I wanted to use it as an 'outlier' genre for a comparison with how 'central' women's magazine genres are read. Self-help literature deals at book length with issues that all women's magazines also deal with, such as how to keep your marriage (or relationship) young, how to live without stress, how to raise an adopted child and so on. A fair amount of the self-help literature that is published in the Netherlands[5] is more or less feminist in orientation. *Opzij* was thus an obvious avenue to self-help readers.

Approaching readers of self-help literature via *Opzij* was also an indirect way of making contact with women's magazine readers. I had hoped to engender 'spontaneous' talk about *Opzij* (in that the interview would officially be about self-help books) with higher so-called ecological validity (Hammersley and Atkinson, 1983: 10–1) as regards the concepts that were used to talk about *Opzij*, because they would have been introduced not by the researcher, but by informants themselves. My second intention was to compare the two genres. There was not much spontaneous talk about *Opzij* or about women's magazines in general. But what was said put the interviews with the *Opzij* readers who had answered the advertisement in the news-papers into perspective. The first group of *Opzij* readers felt far less comfortable about *Opzij* and about traditional women's magazines than the self-help and *Opzij* readers. This was possibly because the self-help readers were asked for an interview about a genre (self-help) that they were very knowledgeable about and that they cherished, while the *Opzij* readers had to negotiate a position that would not be interpreted as (radical) feminism. I hope chapter 4 has made this clear. Comparing reading *Opzij* and self-help literature showed that self-help literature is slighly more closely related to traditional women's magazines than to the feminist magazine. The more striking difference was that self-help readers are more knowledgeable about the genre and more enthusiastic when discussing it. They can give examples, name titles and spontaneously reproduce arguments from the books. The genre of self-help literature, while serving the same kinds of goals that women's magazines may serve, inspires a deeper commitment in its readers.

The knowledge of non-readers

Again to check on the material gathered previously, I also looked for a group I have called 'non-readers'. By non-readers I mean those who have not read women's magazines in their adult lives in their own homes. A characteristic of this group would be that they feel indifferent towards women's magazines. Yet, in waiting-rooms, at the hairdressers, or in trains they, like everybody, might pick up a magazine left behind or put there on purpose. I especially wanted to find older women who defined themselves as non-readers because I have often been told that taking care of small children and women's magazines go together exceptionally well, as long as you have the means to buy them, or a good friend or family member to pass them on to you. Women's magazines not only provide the right level of intellectual challenge (not much) and text that is built up in short blocks, easy to read and just as easily put down, they also provide practical advice that may strengthen your general feeling of being in charge and knowing what to do in all sorts of unforeseeable circumstances.

Not many women have never read women's magazines and it is even more difficult to ask them for an interview. 'I would like to talk to you about women's magazines and why you don't read them' was exactly the kind of question I did not want to pose. What I wanted to know about was how they remembered the years when their children were young; how they solved problems; what they generally did with the time not spent on the children. Eventually I found two women with grown-up children to interview. They both came from reasonably well-off professional middle-class backgrounds and had considerable cultural capital. Both discussed advice on child-rearing with their husbands and with Dr Spock, so to speak; they preferred reading novels to reading magazines.

A late find was the group interview I had asked my mother to organize (during the first stage), which, at the time it was held, seemed a total waste of time because two of the four women present had not read women's magazines for years and were critical of them in a standoffish way. I had already interviewed my mother on her own before the group interview and she held back her opinions a bit. The fourth woman present bought women's magazines, but only to browse through and put on her coffee-table. She could not define what she liked about them and tended to agree with the first two that women's magazines are not all that interesting to read and do not have much cultural value. At the end of the second stage I had the tape transcribed, only to discover it was a valuable interview after all because it validated the two other interviews with non-readers. It also showed a kind of critical bias against women's magazines and their readers that seems to stem partly from an intellectual perspective and partly from an uneasy relationship to popular culture. From the failed interview with the young man who read car magazines I learned that there is a group of people who simply have neither the money to buy women's magazines nor the cultural capital to want to read things. I interviewed no women who represent this category.

Summarizing the first and second stages

In the first and second stage, taken together, eighty people were interviewed: eleven were British, sixteen were male. Appendix 1 lists their names and relevant details. I classified various groups of informants by age and class background (see tables 3–9). Since I did

Table 3   Age and class background of British women (including coloured women)

Background	Age		
	18–29	30–45	Over 45
Working class	2[a]	3[b]	3[c]
Middle class	2[d]	1[e]	0

[a] Brooks, 19; Cuellar, 25.
[b] Brooks, 44; Priest, 34; nurse, not quoted.
[c] Carson, 74; Croston, 62; Parry, 62.
[d] Smart, 18; cultural studies student, not quoted.
[e] Atkinson, 39.

Table 4   Age and class background of Dutch women (including coloured women)

Background	Age		
	18–29	30–45	Over 45
Working class	1[a]	11[b]	5[c]
Middle class	8[d]	9[e]	8[f]

[a] Groeniers, 26.
[b] Becker, 30; Dobbel, 41; Duindam, 39; Fransman, 33; Gerards, 43; Gradanus, 30; Hansen, 32; Landman, 35; Poorter, 40; Veenstra, 35; Willems, 31.
[c] Dammers, 48; Jansen, 51; Klein, 70; Stemerdink, 50; Tillie, 50.
[d] Bank, 26; Kenter, 24; Koster, 28; Lemhuis, 27; Meertens, 29; Olders, 28; de Wit, 24; Zijlstra, 24.
[e] de Bruin, 42; Groothuis, 30; Han, 35; Janssen, 35; Rousset, 42; Sluiter, 44; Spoor, 34; Terberg, 32; van de Voort, 44.
[f] de Bouvry, 48; van Eijck, 57; van Essen, 48; Han, 64; Klein, 57; Machielse, 63; Redding, 52; Spanier, 55.

Table 5 Age and class background of men (all Dutch)

Background	Age		
	18–29	30–45	Over 45
Working class	3[a]	2[b]	1[c]
Middle class	5[d]	3[e]	2[f]

[a] van Straten, 26; Vlaming, 26; non-reader, not quoted.
[b] Messing, 31; Mortier, 32.
[c] Wiarda, 62.
[d] Bottenburg, 26; de Groot, 24; Paulsen, 28; Pennings, 23; Spaans, 27.
[e] Han, 30; de Jong, 37; Smit, 33.
[f] Stevens, 47; Vonk, 48.

Table 6 Age and class background of coloured women (British and Dutch)

Background	Age		
	18–29	30–45	Over 45
Working class	1[a]	2[b]	1[c]
Middle class	0	2[d]	1[e]

[a] Brooks, 19.
[b] Brooks, 44; Landman, 35.
[c] Tillie, 50.
[d] Atkinson, 39; Han, 35.
[e] Han, 64.

Table 7 Age and class background of Dutch readers of *Cosmopolitan* quoted in the text

Background	Age		
	18–29	30–45	Over 45
Working class	0	2[a]	0
Middle class	1[b]	2[c]	0

[a] Duindam, 39; Willems, 31.
[b] Kenter, 24.
[c] Spoor, 34; van de Voort, 44.

Table 8   Age and class background of *Opzij* readers (15 women and 3 men)

Background	Age		
	18–29	30–45	Over 45
Working class	0	2[a]	2[b]
Middle class	6[c]	4[d]	4[e]

[a] Fransman, 33; Hansen, 32.
[b] Jansen, 51; Wiarda, 62.
[c] Bank, 26; de Groot, 24; Koster, 28; Lemhuis, 27; Meertens, 29; Paulsen, 28.
[d] de Bruin, 42; Groothuis, 30; Janssen, 35; Sluiter, 44.
[e] de Bouvry, 48; van Essen, 48; Redding, 52; Spanier, 55.

Table 9   Age and class background of gossip magazine readers (7 women and 3 men)

Background	Age		
	18–29	30–45	Over 45
Working class	2[a]	4[b]	2[c]
Middle class	1[d]	0	1[e]

[a] Groeniers, 26; Vlaming, 26.
[b] Dobbel, 41; Gerards, 43; Gradanus, 30; Poorter, 40.
[c] Dammers, 48; Klein, 70.
[d] Spaans, 27.
[e] Stevens, 47.

not ask for self-definitions of class, it was difficult, especially with the Dutch respondents, to categorize them. Occasionally they spontaneously defined themselves in terms of class, but in most cases I combined my knowledge of their parents' occupation and family background with their own occupations, how they lived and dressed, and, in some cases, with their accent.

The amount of interview material gathered in the second stage necessitated using a simpler analytical procedure than that followed for the first-stage interviews. All the interviews were summarized for what was said about or in relation to women's magazines. An exception was made for the interviews about the feminist magazine *Opzij*, for which we also made summaries with regard to what was said about 'being a woman' and 'being a feminist'. This decision was made when we noticed that feminism was an uneasy topic for most of our informants, an unexpected result in interviews about a magazine that proclaims to be feminist on its cover. Striking, out of the ordinary, quotations were noted for all interviews, some of which were used.

The third stage

The third and last stage consisted of two parts. An analytical framework (described below) was developed as a basis for interpreting the interview fragments about women's magazines and to see whether they indeed provided evidence for my budding theory. The second part of this section deals with the quality of the analytical framework and of the data collection and analysis.

Analysing the interviews: the uses of repertoire analysis

Chapter 1 evaluated popular media research and theories of meaning production. Its central recognition consists of seeing women's magazines as very much part of everyday routines – so much so, in fact, that they are hardly reflected upon. In retrospect, this explained why very little was said in the interviews about women's magazines as such. Moreover, respondents would repeat what they had said before or simply not finish arguments and change to others. It would be difficult to cull a fully-fledged lay analysis of women's magazine reading from a single interview. On the other hand it was quite clear that readers referred to knowledge about women's magazines they supposed I shared with them. Since all readers referred to common or shared knowledge, it is safe to assume there are a limited number of shared sources of cultural knowledge from which different arguments (or parts of arguments) can be drawn. To reconstruct the various dimensions of knowledge about women's magazines I decided, as was outlined in chapter 1, to use the 'interpretive repertoire' concept developed by social psychologists Jonathan Potter and Margaret Wetherell, which they define as 'recurrently used systems of terms used for characterizing and evaluating actions, events and other phenomena' (1987: 149). Potter and Wetherell are functionalists in that they assume people feel a need to communicate adequately: if one kind of explanation or way of telling a story does not work, other repertoires or other styles of speech will be used. Such a perspective suited my interviews particularly well since they had all the characteristics of everyday conversation. Speakers switched from one series of arguments (leaving them unfinished) to another, and so on, in fact using them to perform different sorts of accounting tasks (Potter and Wetherell, 1987: 156).

Theoretically, there could be an infinite number of repertoires. However, the character of everyday reasoning (as has been pointed out by social phenomenology – see chapter 1 – and as is apparent in the interviews) is such that people will make do with available repertoires as much as they can. I see repertoires as a storehouse of possible understandings, legitimations and evaluations that can be brought to bear on any number of subjects. In practice, some repertoires will be specific to a subgenre of women's magazines, while other repertoires are more general and applicable to popular culture in general. Repertoires are 'practical ideologies' that according to Wetherell, Stiven and Potter (1876: 60), make up the systems of making sense available in a society. In the text I have made the repertoires I distinguished much more explicit than they would ever be in everyday conversation. Since, according to Michael Billig (1989), answering questions and articulating a point of view is complex and essentially argumentative in character. I am fairly sure that – given people's need to communicate adequately – virtually all repertoires that touch on or deal with women's magazines were drawn upon by informants. Billig (1989) has also argued that holders of strong views too may produce a variable discourse, contrary to what traditional study of attitudes would lead one to expect, which again strengthens my view that even in a small amount of interviews all relevant repertoires will be used. Eighty interviews with readers who vary in age, class background, ethnicity and sex and who read different kinds of women's magazines suffice to ensure that there are no repertoires that are relevant according to readers other than the ones that were found. Wetherell, Stiven and Potter, moreover, have noted that respondents are rarely aware of the contradiction in their discourse, which, in turn, allows the discourse analyst to reconstruct the different and contradictory views people hold in everyday life (1987: 65).

As was described in chapter 1, a repertoire analysis does not proceed from pre-set rules. The material – in this case all the statments about women's magazines (and, for good measure, the whole interviews were also checked and rechecked) – is worked through as often as it takes to recognize how recurrent themes related to underlying structures in the material. When a discursive structure is found, and checked for, by going through the material again from that particular perspective, it is used as a departure for a theoretical evaluation. This eventually leads to the development of a theory and to a selection of some fragments rather than others for this text, or for publications about the material in general. Appendix 3 includes a lengthy fragment (eight pages) from one of the British interviews and shows which parts of the text were summarized and which were eventually edited into readable quotations.

Not all statements could be related to recurrent themes and thus to interpretive repertoires, usually because they were too vague, and sometimes because they had absolutely unquestioned descriptive status, which defied an evaluative dimension.

Highly negative fragments were also difficult to place. In general they were short ('X is a stupid magazine') and not very informative. Another category of fragments that I did not use when reconstructing the repertoires were matter-of-fact statements, which were highly normative but upon which respondents felt it was silly to enlarge, such as, '*Margriet* and *Libelle* are magazines for housewives with two children who live in suburbs.' Karen de Wit and Linda Zijlstra, for example, thought they might come to be such women, but since they were not at that moment, that was it. This kind of statement does not say much about how, for the speaker, women's magazines become meaningful. It simply replicates a rather stereotypical prejudice about women's magazines that does not seem to be related to reading practices at all.

Although strongly focused on talk, or rather on interview transcripts, discourse analysis is very much compatible with a grounded theory approach. I used the theoretical notions that slowly developed during the first and second stages as an entrance into the transcripts, but from there on used the transcripts alone (and in particular the fragments that dealt directly with women's magazines or women's magazine use) as a basis on which to reach an understanding of how women's magazines become meaningful.

Controlling for quality

'Ethnography' means simply 'writing about a way of life'. Quite often ethnographies are written by lone fieldworkers. Not surprisingly, therefore, critics stress the unreliability of ethnographics. Phenomenology and discourse analysis, my other major theoretical and methodological sources, are similarly criticized. All three approaches study social life in its natural setting and describe it as seen and experienced by those involved (McNeil, 1990: 120–1.) Validity (or the extent to which the data present a true picture of that which is described) is supposedly high, reliability (or the replicability of the research) and representativeness (the generalizability) are said to be negligible. The question is whether ethnographic approaches are to be measured in the same terms used by, for example, surveys and experiments. I would like to argue that one ought partly to forgo the guarantees that have become part of other methods and concentrate on the specific strengths and qualities of fieldwork-related methods. Which is not to say that procedures of finding informants, doing interviews and processing data ought not to be explicitly described. Four strategies of quality control were used in this research.

Obviously reliability, or replicability – doing the same case study (use the same data collection procedure) and getting the same results (Yin, 1989: 40–1) – is not a norm tailored to qualitative research, since social processes tend to be subject to change. Kirk and Miller therefore advise the explicit description of observational procedures (1986: 41). Marshall and Rossman go further and propose 'dependability' as a quality check instead of reliability. Dependability is defined as the researcher's attempt to account for changing conditions in the phenomenon chosen for study as well as changes in the design created by increasingly understanding the setting (1989: 146–7). Such a stance seems closer to the view taken by grounded theory and it led to my first quality control strategy: the explicit elaboration of methods of data collection and description of changes in the research design.

The second strategy used was informant feedback, but it was not easy to realize and the results were rather meagre. Six of the first set of 10 interviewees were interviewed again, and I sent informants a summary of my results and thoughts beforehand. Only two of them had read the summary. They appreciated being consulted and were happy to recognize themselves in my text. The others, upon explanation, were interested in my ideas, though they were also amused and mystified in equal measure that someone would take so much trouble over women's magazines and an afternoon of talk. During the second stage, as was reported above, the *Opzij* readers were sent an article by myself and Véronique Schutgens, to which four out of fourteen replied. One woman was very critical because she felt that we did not do the feminist cause much good by publishing the article and did not take her views seriously (which we thought we did). Generally, when evaluating at the end of (later) interviews, informants recognized concepts and descriptions. Fairly often this suprised them, probably because they had never before given serious thought to women's magazines at all. My mother read and had helpful comments on an earlier version of chapter 3; she found it a disturbing portrait in parts, but recognized herself in it.

The third strategy was checking whether the repertoires could be generalized, or 'transferred', as Marshall and Rossman (1989: 145) sugggest using to avoid discussion about the representativeness of qualitative findings, from one particular woman's magazine subgenre to another. The question of generalization, or transferability, is most important for qualitative studies working with small samples or a limited number of case studies or settings. Since highly different subgenres coexist under the umbrella category 'women's magazines', it is important to test whether sets of reportoires found when analysing interviews that dealt predominantly with one genre also apply to other genres. Perhaps repertoires are specific not so much for magazine subgenres as for readers with particular cultural capital. In so doing one tests for transferability. Chapters 2–5 have shown that repertoires are on the whole particular to subgenres, though there are quite a few cases in which repertoires are used for other genres. It would seem to be that the repertoire structure as such can be transferred to other forms of everyday media use (even if the individual repertoires would probably be different) and that individual repertoires will also be used for other (women's) genres in combination with repertoires that would not be used for women's magazines.

The fourth strategy is called triangulation. Among methodologists there appears to be consensus that triangulation especially is of paramount importance to ensure that all conditions are favourable when attempting to transfer theory generated on the basis of a particular set of data to other settings or other (but related) problems (Jick, 1989; Miles and Huberman, 1984; Wester, 1987). Triangulation means using either different sources or different methods, and occasionally it means using different researchers to collect and interpret data. Ideally, a combination of complimentary methodologies is used by different researchers in the study of the same phenomenon through different case studies (Jick, 1989: 135) or in what Glaser and Strauss have called 'comparison groups'. Given the structure of the research and the checks made for differences in women's magazine readers who differed in various socio-demographic respects, the theoretical findings of this project are transferable. Checking for differences between groups of readers and between magazine subgenres is one form of triangulation. The checks for differences between groups made clear that it would theoretically be more opportune to concentrate on repertoires and magazine subgenres rather than groups of readers. Although class background, for example, will probably mean that a person does not have access to certain repertoires, and would not read certain titles, this is not always the case. For the readers I interviewed ethnicity did not appear to make a difference with regard to using particular repertoires to make women's magazines meaningful or to reading particular titles and not others. Gender does make difference, though not as much of a difference as I had expected (see chapter 2 for an extended discussion). Lastly, I worked with two other researchers and discussed findings with them to rule out the possibility that I was following an idiosyncratic trail.

It will have become clear that I set out to do an ethnography and ended up doing what might be called a genre study (even though it is based not on text conventions but on readers' shared references to structures of meaning in relation to different kinds of women's magazines). Some of the elements that I feel ought to be part of research that deals with everyone media use have, however, been salvaged. I took care to include quotations in which informants compare reading women's magazines with other forms of media use, or in which they give descriptions of other forms of media use. Other material that could have provided a better view of everyday media use as a whole or of how informants felt about 'being a woman' had to be left out, regrettably, because that would have taken up more space than was available. Chapter 3, the portrait of two readers, comes closest to the ethnographic ideal of 'thick description' (Geertz, 1973). This appendix should provide an answer to the amazed informant who asked, upon being told that I had four years to do the research and write up the results, 'But what do you do all day?'

Notes

Introduction

1. Of course, not all of the studies of women's magazines are inspired by feminism. Exceptions include the study by Braithwaite and Barrell (1988), which takes an enthusiastic view of 'the business of women's magazines'.
2. This definition is culled from John Corner's discussion of the concept of meaning and what he terms the 'New Audience Research'. See Corner, 1991: 271–6.
3. Based on Neale's shorter definition. See Neale, 1980: 7.

Chapter 1   Everyday Media Use

1. 'Fan' can be defined as someone who has expert knowledge of a low-valued or non-valued form of culture: for example, someone who knows every line of Barry Manilow's songs by heart (Jensen, 1992: 19).
2. Fiske (1992) draws on Radway's work with romance readers (1984) mentioned at the beginning of this section and Hobson's work with soap opera viewers and on how soap opera is used at work (1982, 1989). I believe these are generally seen as examples of studies that work with 'average' audience members rather than with 'fans', which points to the confusion regarding whether or not a difference is made between fan culture and everyday media use in media and cultural studies.
3. Watching is accompanied by a good deal of shouting; participants make a spectacle of themselves and of consumption. All sin against norms of 'proper' feminine behaviour.
4. I should like to thank Kirsten Drotner for recommending Jørgensen's work to me.

Chapter 2   Easily Put Down: How Women and Men Read Women's Magazines

1. See Potter and Wetherell, 1987, especially ch. 2 and pp. 163–5. Michael Billig (1989) has argued that every respondent's discourse is variable and contains contradictions. Contrary to what, according to him, attitude research would presume, he found that holders of strong views also produce variable discourse; thus, they adapt their opinions to specific contexts and defend views that are more different from one another than fits with a notion of attitude as a fairly stable or even rigid stance.
2. Cf. Ang (1985) on the ideology of populism.

Chapter 3   Portrait of Two Readers

I wish to thank my mother for allowing me to use the interviews with her in combination with my recollections of my childhood, and, especially, for reading this chapter, for her thoughtful comments and her encouragement and support. I should also like to thank Richard Johnson for encouraging me to use the interviews with my mother and his suggestion that I read Carolyn Steedman's *Landscape for a Good Woman* (1986).

1. This particular use of the term 'life cycle' was inspired by Carolyn Heilbrun, writing as Amanda Cross. See Cross, 1984.

Chapter 4   Reading a Feminist Magazine: Fantasizing the Female *homo universalis*

1. Fifteen women responded. I asked the self-help readers to write to me about their favourite self-help texts and to fill out a short questionnaire. From these letters four respondents were selected. The criteria were: the openness of their letters, whether they mentioned self-help texts that were also mentioned in the other letters and whether they lived outside Amsterdam (where a relatively large number of the *Opzij* respondents lived). Two readers who read *Opzij*, self-help literature and traditional magazines were selected deliberately.
2. In the interview Geraldine calls it by name: *Wordt Vervolgd* (a wry pun on 'to be continued' and 'is being persecuted').
3. As with all the titles mentioned by the self-help readers, when I was familiar with the book mentioned, I have given the English title. In some cases I have simply translated titles. I have included them to show the literacy of readers where self-help literature is concerned.
4. The original French title is *Les mots pour le dire*.

Chapter 5   Reading Gossip Magazines: the Imagined Communities of 'Gossip' and 'Camp'

1. The plural is used by the speaker to rob the singer of all individuality, the implication being that as an artist she is exchangeable.

2. The pleasures American readers take in supermarket tabloids are remarkably similar to those my interviewees took in European gossip magazines. For a highly interesting discussion and analysis of this gossip magazine related genre see Bird, 1992.
3. Schiff (1984) describes the same phenomenon for the New York gay community, in which D&D – Dinner and *Dynasty* – was at that time also a fixture of social life. *Dynasty*'s creator, Esther Shapiro, allegedly knew of 'a coven of BBD&O executives who re-enact *Dynasty* scripts every week, over champagne and caviar' (in Schiff, 1984: 64). I should like to thank Kim Schrøder for sending me this article.

Conclusion

1. I have stressed in chapter 1 and in this conclusion that readers did not have much to say. This is not as uncommon a situation as it would seem to be (and as I thought it was, for quite a long time). Andrea Press emphasized in a recent publication that many of the interviews she held yielded little information. 'However,' she stated, 'I am convinced that I would not have gathered the valuable information I did had I created a more closed, structured interview situation' (1990: 63).

Appendix 4   The Research (as) Process: a Methodological Account

1. To gather far more material than can ever be used is, of course, a common problem in ethnography. In this case, however, as will be described later in this appendix, I decided not to use the 'ethnographically interesting' material, such as descriptions of interiors, or clothing, or the drink and food I was offered, apart from only a few incidental examples.
2. Miraculously, with the first series of interviews there were no mechanical problems with the tape recorder. Some of the interviews in the second stage were ruined because the equipment I borrowed was faulty. Occasionally I did not manage to put the small cassette recorder I later bought close enough to an interviewee. Appendix 1, the list of informants, gives more detailed information.
3. Upon reflection, I do not think that these changes in reading patterns were an effect of the interviews. The first and second interviews took place a little less than a year apart; other readers whom I interviewed only once, also reported that they had periods in which they did not read women's magazines, and that their preferences changed.
4. Class, for example, in the Netherlands is difficult to define. This is partly because historically its society was divided along the lines of religion rather than class, and partly because since the Second World War affluence has created a sizeable 'in-between' class of those who have working-class roots but whose children have had access to higher education and thus to what used to be typical middle-class cultural capital.

There is no strong upper class, there are no 'public schools', there is no Ivy League. The Netherlands, in short, is a predominantly middle-class country.

5. A majority of the self-help texts published in the Netherlands are translated, while a few are originally Dutch.

References

Anderson, Benedict 1983: *Imagined communities*. London: Verso.

Ang, Ien 1985: *Watching 'Dallas': soap opera and the melodramatic imagination*. London and New York: Methuen.

Ang, Ien 1988: Feminist desire and female pleasure. *Camera Obscura*, 16, 179–91.

Ang, Ien and Joke Hermes 1988: Gender and/in media consumption. In James Curran and Michael Gurevitch (eds), *Mass media and society*, London: Edward Arnold, 307–28.

Ballaster, Ros, Margaret Beetham, Elizabeth Frazer and Sandra Hebron 1991: *Women's worlds: ideology, femininity and the women's magazine*. Basingstoke: Macmillan.

Bardoel, Jo and Peter Vasterman 1977: 'Sterren worden mensen, mensen worden sterren': de nieuwe aanval op het 'gat' in de markt ('Stars become ordinary people, ordinary people become stars': the new assault on the 'gap' in the market). *Groene Amsterdammer* (23 March).

Bausinger, Hermann 1984: Media, technology and daily life. Translated by Liliane Jaddou and Jon Williams. *Media Culture Society*, 6, 343–51.

Billig, Michael 1989: The argumentative nature of holding strong views: a case study. *European Journal of Social Psychology*, 19, 203–23.

Bird, S. Elizabeth 1992: *For enquiring minds: a cultural study of supermarket tabloids*. Knoxville: University of Tennessee Press.

Blix, Jacqueline 1992: A place to resist: reevaluating women's magazines. *Journal of Communication Inquiry*, 16 (1), 56–71.

Boodt, Joppe 1992: Mannen over vrouwenbladen (Men on women's magazines). *Inscriptie*, 1 (2), 4–15.

Bourdieu, Pierre 1980: The aristocracy of culture. Translated by Richard Nice. *Media Culture Society*, (2), 225–54.

Braithwaite, Brian and Joan Barrell 1988: *The business of women's magazines*. 2nd edn. London: Kogan Page.

Brinkgreve, C. and M. Korzec 1978: *'Margriet weet raad': gevoel, gedrag, moraal in Nederland 1938–1978* (*'Margriet* advises': emotions, behaviour, morality in the Netherlands 1938–1978). Utrecht and Antwerp: Het Spectrum.

Canaan, Joyce 1991: Is 'doing nothing' just boys' play? Integrating feminist and cultural studies perspectives on working class young men's masculinity. In Celia Lury, Sarah Franklin and Jackie Stacey (eds), *Off-centre: feminism and cultural studies*, London: HarperCollins Academic, 109–25.

Certeau, Michel de 1988: *The practice of everyday life*. Translated by Steven Randall. Berkeley: University of California Press.

Corner, John 1991: Meaning, genre and context: the problematics of 'public knowledge' in the New Audience Studies. In James Curran and Michael Gurevitch (eds), *Mass media and society*, London: Edward Arnold, 267–84.

Coward, Rosalind 1983: *Patriarchal precedents: sexuality and social relations*. London: Routledge and Kegan Paul.

Coward, Rosalind 1984: *Female desire: women's sexuality today*. London: Paladin.

Cross, Amanda 1984: *Sweet death, kind death*. London: Victor Gollancz.

Curran, James 1990: The new revisionism in mass communication research: a reappraisal. *European Journal of Communication*, 5 (2/3), 135–64.

d'Ancona, Hedy and Wim Hora Adema 1977: Vijf jaar *Opzij*: het gaat goed! (Five years of *Opzij*: we are doing great!) *Opzij* (November), 3–5.

Dardigna, Anne-Marie 1978: *La presse féminine: fonction idéologique*. Paris: François Maspero.

Driehuis, Gerard and Tom-Jan Meeus 1986: Het verschijnsel huisvrouw: de emancipatie is theorie gebleven (The phenomenon housewife: emancipation has remained theory). *De Tijd* (21 February), 9–13.

Essed, Philomena 1991: *Understanding everyday racism*. Newbury Park and London: Sage.

Ferguson, Marjorie 1983: *Forever feminine: women's magazines and the cult of femininity*. London: Heinemann.

Field Belenky, Mary, Blythe McVicker, Nancy Rule Goldberger and Jill Mattuck Tarule 1986: *Women's ways of knowing: the development of self, voice and mind*. New York: Basic Books.

Fiske, John 1990: Women and quiz shows: consumerism, patriarchy and resisting pleasures. In Mary Ellen Brown (ed.), *Television and women's culture: the politics of the popular*, London and Newbury Park: Sage, 134–43.

Fiske, John 1992: The cultural economy of fandom. In Lisa A. Lewis (ed.), *The adoring audience: fan culture and popular media*, London and New York: Routledge 30–49.

Flax, Jane 1990: Postmodernism and gender relations in feminist theory. In Linda J. Nicholson (ed.), *Feminism/postmodernism*, New York and London: Routledge, 39–62.

Fraser, Nancy and Linda Nicholson 1988: Social criticism without philosophy. In Andrew Ross (ed.), *Universal abandon? The politics of postmodernism*, Minneapolis: University of Minnesota Press, 83–104.

Frazer, Elizabeth 1987: Teenage girls reading *Jackie*. *Media Culture Society*, 9, 407–25.

Friedan, Betty [1963] 1974: *The feminine mystique*. New York: Dell.

Frow, John 1991: Michel de Certeau and the practice of representation. *Cultural Studies*, 5 (1), 52–60.

Gadamer, Hans-Georg [1960]: 1986: *Wahrheit und Methode: Grundzüge einer philosophischen Hermeneutik*. Tübingen: J. C. B. Mohr.

Gagnier, Regenia 1991: Review essay: feminist autobiography in the 1980s. *Feminist Review*, 17 (1), 135–48.

Ganguly, Keya 1992: Migrant identities: personal memory and the construction of selfhood. *Cultural Studies*, 6 (1), 27–50.

Geertz, Clifford 1973: *The interpretation of cultures*. New York: Basic Books.

Geertz, Clifford 1983: *Local knowledge: further essays in interpretive anthropology*. New York: Basic Books.

Glaser, Barney G. and Anselm L. Strauss 1967: *The discovery of grounded theory: strategies for qualitative research*. Chicago: Aldine Publishing.

Gramsci, Antonio 1971: *Selections from the prison notebooks*. Edited and translated by Quintin Hoare and Geoffrey Nowell Smith. New York: International Publishers.

Gray, Ann 1987: Behind closed doors: videorecorders in the home. In Helen Baehr and Gillian Dyer (eds), *Boxed in: women and television*, New York and London: Pandora Press, 38–54.

Gray, Ann 1992: *Video playtime: the gendering of a leisure technology*. London and New York: Comedia/Routledge.

Greer, Germaine 1990: *The change: women, ageing and the menopause*. London: Hamish Hamilton.

Gross, Larry 1989: Out of the mainstream: sexual minorities and the mass media. In Ellen Seiter, Hans Borchers, Gabrielle Kreutzner and Eva-Maria Warth (eds), *Remote control: television, audiences and cultural power*, London and New York: Routledge, 130–49.

Hall, Stuart 1980: Encoding/decoding. in Stuart Hall, Dorothy Hobson, Andrew Lowe and Paul Willis (eds), *Culture, media, lanuage*, London: Hutchinson, 128–38.

Hammersley, Martyn and Paul Atkinson 1983: *Ethnography: principles in practice*. London and New York: Tavistock Publications.

Heilbrun, Carolyn G. 1989 *Writing a woman's life*. London: Women's Press.

Henriques, Julian, Wendy Hollway, Cathy Urwin, Couze Venn and Valerie Walkerdine 1984: *Changing the subject*. London and New York: Methuen.

Hermes, Joke and Véronique Schutgens 1991: Voor slimme, linkse, boekenlezende poezengekken: een receptie-en tekstanalyse van het feministisch maandblad *Opzij*. *Tijdschrift voor Vrouwenstudies*, 12 (4), 453–69. An English version was published in 1992: A case of the emperor's new clothes? Reception and text analysis of the Dutch feminist magazine *Opzij*, *European Journal of Communication*, 7 (3), 307–34.

Hobson, Dorothy 1978: Housewives: isolation as òppression. In Women Studies Group CCCS (eds), *Women take issues*, London: Hutchinson, 79–95.

Hobson, Dorothy 1980: Housewives and the mass media. In Stuart Hall, Dorothy Hobson, Andrew Lowe and Paul Willis (eds), *Culture, media, language*, London: Hutchinson, 105–14.

Hobson, Dorothy 1982: *'Crossroads': the drama of a soap opera*. London: Methuen.

Hobson, Dorothy 1989: Soap opera at work. in Ellen Seiter, Hans Borchers, Gabrielle Kreutzner and Eva-Maria Warth (eds), *Remote control: television, audiences and cultural power*, London and New York: Routledge, 150–67.

Hochschild, Arlie 1989: *The second shift: working parents and the revolution at home*. New York: Viking Penguin.

Illouz, Eva 1991: Reason within passion: love in women's magazines. *Critical Studies in Mass Communication* 8 (3), 231–48.

Jensen, Joli 1990: *Redeeming modernity: contradictions in media criticism.* Newbury Park and London: Sage.

Jensen, Joli 1992: Fandom as pathology: the consequences of characterization. In Lisa A. Lewis (ed.), *The adoring audience: fan culture and popular media,* London and New York: Routledge, 9–29.

Jick, Todd D. 1989: Mixing qualitative and quantitative methods: triangulation in action. In John van Maanen (ed.), *Qualitative methodology.* Newbury Park and London: Sage, 135–48.

Jørgensen, Birte Bech 1990: The impossibility of everyday life. In Flemming Røgilds (ed.), *Every cloud has a silver lining: lectures on everyday life, cultural production and race,* Copenhagen: Akademisk Forlag, 20–8.

Jungschleger, Ineke 1987: Het hoofdbureau van het feminisme (Feminism's national headquarters). *De Volkskrant* (19 December).

Kaplan, Cora 1986: Sea changes: culture and feminism. London: Verso.

Kauffman, Bette J. 1992: Feminist facts: interview strategies and political subjects in ethnography. *Communication Theory,* 2 (3), 187–206.

Kirk, Jerome and Marc L. Miller 1986: *Reliability and validity in qualitative research.* Qualitative Research Methods Series, 1, Beverly Hills and London: Sage.

Kitzinger, Celia 1989: *The social construction lesbianism.* London and Newbury Park: Sage.

Knorr-Cetina, Karin D. 1981: The micro-sociological challenge of macro-sociology: toward a reconstruction of social theory and methodology. In K. Knorr-Cetina and A. V. Cicourel (eds), *Advances in social theory and methodology: toward an integration of micro- and macro-sociologies,* Boston and London: Routledge and Kegan Paul, 1–47.

Kobre, Sidney 1964: *The yellow press and gilded age journalism.* Tallahassee: Florida State University.

Leman, Joy 1987: Programmes for women in 1950s British television. In Helen Baehr and Gillian Dyer (eds), *Boxed in: women and television,* New York and London: Pandora Press, 73–95.

Lewis, Lisa A. 1987: Female address in music video. *Journal of Communication Inquiry,* 11 (1),73–84.

Lewis, Lisa A. 1992: Introduction. In Lisa A. Lewis (ed.), *The adoring audience: fan culture and popular media,* London and New York: Routledge, 1–6.

Lindlof, Thomas R. and Timothy P. Meyer 1987: Mediated communication as ways of seeing, acting and constructing culture: the tools and foundations of qualitative research. In Thomas R. Lindlof (ed.) *Natural audiences: qualitative research of media uses and effects,* Norwood, NJ: Ablex, 1–30.

Livingstone, Sonia 1990: *Making sense of television: the psycholology of audience interpretation.* Oxford: Pergamon.

Lyotard, Jean-François 1979: *La condition post-moderne: rapport sur le savoir.* Paris: Editions de Minuit.

Marcus, George E. and Michael M. J. Fischer 1986: *Anthropology as cultural critique: an experimental moment in the human sciences.* Chicago and London: University of Chicago Press.

Marshall, Catherine and Gretchen B. Rossman 1989: *Designing qualitative research.* Newbury Park and London: Sage.

McNeil, Patrick 1990: *Research methods*. London and New York: Routledge.

McRobbie, Angela 1978: Working class girls and the culture of femininity. In Women Studies Group CCCS (eds), *Women take issue*, London: Hutchinson, 96–108.

McRobbie, Angela 1991: *Feminism and youth culture: from 'Jackie' to 'Just Seventeen'*. Basingstoke: Macmillan.

Meyer Spacks, Patricia 1986: *Gossip*. Chicago and London: University of Chicago Press.

Miles, Matthew and Michael Huberman 1984: *Qualitative data analysis: a source book of new methods*. Beverly Hills and London: Sage.

Modleski, Tania 1984: *Loving with a vengeance: mass-produced fantasies for women*. New York and London: Methuen.

Morley, David 1980: *The 'Nationwide' audience: structure and decoding*. London: British Film Institute.

Morley, David 1981: The 'Nationwide' audience: a critical postscript. *Screen Education*, 39, 3–14.

Morley, David 1986: *Family television: cultural power and domestic leisure*. London: Comedia.

Morley, David 1989: Changing paradigms in audience studies. In Ellen Seiter, Hans Borchers, Gabrielle Kreutzner and Eva-Maria Warth (eds), *Remote control: television, audiences and cultural power*, London and New York: Routledge, 16–43.

Morris, Meaghan 1988: Banality in cultural studies. *Block*, 14, 15–26.

Muyen, Annet 1985: 'De opmars van *Opzij* (The advance of *Opzij*). *Haagse Post*, 23 (28 June).

Natanson, Maurice 1986: *Anonymity: a study in the philosophy of Alfred Schutz*. Bloomington: Indiana University Press.

Neale, Stephen 1980: *Genre*. London: British Film Institute.

NOTUschrift 1983: Een blad voor vrouwen die verandering willen: interview met Cisca Dresselhuys (A magazine for women who want change: interview with Cisca Dresselhuys). *NOTUschrift* (February).

Okely, Judith 1986: *Simone de Beauvoir*. London: Virago.

O'Neill, John 1974: *Making sense together: an introduction to wild sociology*. New York: Harper and Row.

Ong, Walter 1982: *Orality and literacy: the technologizing of the world*. London: Sage.

O'Sullivan, Tim, John Hartley, Danny Saunders and John Fiske 1983: *Key concepts in communication*. London and New York: Routledge.

Potter, Jonathan and Margaret Wetherell 1987: *Discourse and social psychology*. London: Sage.

Press, Andrea L. 1990: Class, gender and the female viewer: women's responses to *Dynasty*. In Mary Ellen Brown (ed.), *Television and women's culture: the politics of the popular*, London and Newbury Park: Sage, 158–80.

Rawday, Janice 1984: *Reading the romance: women, patriarchy, and popular literature*. Chapel Hill: University of North Carolina Press.

Radway, Janice 1988: Reception study: ethnography and the problems of dispersed audiences and nomadic subjects. *Cultural Studies*, 2 (3), 359–76.

Reesink, Maarten 1990: De waarheid, de hele waarheid en meer dan de waarheid: over de fascinerende *Privé*-grenzen tussen feiten en fictie, een verkenning van het leesplezier in het boulevardblad (The truth, the whole truth and more than the truth: on *Privé*'s fascinating borders between fact and fiction, an exploration of reading pleasure and the tabloid press). MA thesis, University of Amsterdam.

Reid, Evelyn Cauleta 1988: Viewdata: the television viewing habits of young black women in London. *Screen*, 30 (1/2), 101–14.

Rogers, Mary F. 1983: *Sociology, ethnomethodology, and experience: a phenomenological critique*. Cambridge: Cambridge University Press.

Röser, Jutta 1992: Nur Kinder, Küche und Konsum? Frauenzeitschriften im Zeichen von Differenzierungsprozessen. In Romy Fröhlich (ed.), *Der andere Blick: Aktuelles zur Massenkommunikation aus weiblicher Sicht*, Bochum: Universitätsverlag Brockmeyer, 183–206.

Ross, Andrew (ed). 1988: *Universal abandon? The politics of postmodernism*. Minneapolis: University of Minnesota Press.

Ross, Andrew 1989: *No respect: intellectuals and popular culture*. New York and London: Routledge.

Sawicki, Jana 1991: *Disciplining Foucault: feminism, power and the body*. New York and London: Routledge.

Schiff, Stephen 1984: What *Dynasty* says about America. *Vanity Fair* (December), 64–7.

Schrøder, Kim Christian 1988: The pleasure of *Dynasty*: the weekly reconstruction of self-confidence. In Philip Drummond and Richard Paterson (eds), *Television and its audience*, London: British Film Institute, 61–82.

Schutgens, Véronique (1989) Een stap *Opzij*, een stap vooruit: een onderzoek naar invullingen van feminisme in *Opzij* (A step sideways, a step forward: interpretations of feminism in *Opzij*). MA thesis, University of Amsterdam.

Schutz, Alfred 1962: On multiple realities. In *Collected papers I* edited by Maurice Natanson, The Hague: Martinus Nijhoff, 207–59.

Schutz, Alfred 1970: *On phenomenology and social relations*. Edited by Helmut R. Wagner. Chicago: University of Chicago Press.

Schutz, Alfred and Thomas Luckmann 1974: *The structures of the life-world*. London: Heinemann.

Segal, Lynne 1990: *Slow motion: changing masculinities, changing men*. London: Virago.

Seidler, Victor J. 1991: *Recreating sexual politics: men, feminism and politics*. London and New York: Routledge.

Seiter, Ellen, Hans Borchers, Gabrielle Kreutzner and Eva-Maria Warth 1989: 'Don't treat us like we're stupid and naïve': towards an ethnography of soap opera viewers. In Ellen Seiter, Hans Borchers, Gabrielle Kreutzner and Eva-Maria Warth (eds), *Remote control: television, audiences and cultural power*, London and New York: Routledge, 223–47.

Shevelow, Kathryn 1989: *Women and print culture: the construction of femininity in the early periodical*. London and New York: Routledge.

Shotter, John and Kenneth J. Gergen (eds) 1989: *Texts of identity*. London and Newbury Park: Sage.

Sontag, Susan [1964] 1982: Notes on camp. In *A Susan Sontag reader*, London: Penguin, 105–19.

Spivak, Gayatri Chakravorty 1990: *The post-colonial critic: interviews, strategies, dialogues*. Edited by Sarah Harasym. New York and London: Routledge.

Steedman,Carolyn 1986: *Landscape for a good woman: a story of two lives*. London: Virago.

Steiner, Linda 1991: Oppositional decoding as act of resistance. In Robert K. Avery and David Eason (eds), *Critical perspectives on media and society*, New York and London: The Guilford Press, 329–45.

Tolson, Andrew 1978: *The limits of masculinity*. London: Tavistock.

Tuchman, Gaye 1978: The symbolic annihilation of women by the mass media. In Gaye Tuchman, Kaplan Daniels and James Benét (eds), *Hearth and home: images of women in the mass media*, New York: Oxford University Press, 3–38.

Vance, Carole S. (ed.) 1984: *Pleasure and danger: exploring female sexuality*. Boston and London: Routledge and Kegan Paul.

Vries, Marlene de 1990: *Roddel nader beschouwd* (a closer look at gossip). Leiden: Centrum voor Onderzoek van Maatschappelijke Tegenstellingen.

Warnke, Georgia 1987: *Gadamer: hermeneutics, tradition and reason*. Cambridge: Polity Press.

Warren, Carol A. B. 1985: *Gender issues in field research* Qualitative Research Methods Series, 9. Newbury Park: Sage.

Wassenaar, Iris 1976: *Vrouwenbladen: spiegels van een mannenmaatschappij* (Women's magazines: mirrors of a male society). Amsterdam: Wetenschappelijke Uitgeverij.

Wester, Fred 1987: *Strategieën voor kwalitatief onderzoek* (Strategies for qualitative research). Muiderberg: Coutinho.

Wetherell, Margaret, Hilda Stiven and Jonathan Potter 1987: Unequal egalitarianism: a preliminary study of discourse concerning gender and employment opportunities. *British Journal of Social Psychology*, 26 (1), 57–71.

White, Cynthia L. 1970: *Women's magazines 1693–1968*. London: Michael Joseph.

Willis, Paul with Simon Jones, Joyce Canaan and Geoff Hurd 1990: *Common culture: symbolic work at play in everyday cultures of the young*. Milton Keynes: Open University Press.

Winship, Janice 1987: *Inside women's magazines*. London: Pandora Press.

Winship, Janice 1991: The impossibility of *Best*: enterprise meets domesticity in the practical women's magazines of the 1980s. *Cultural Studies*, 5 (2), 131–56.

Yin, Robert K. 1989: *Case study research: design and methods*. Newbury Park and London: Sage.

Zoonen, Liesbet van 1991: Feminist perspectives on the media. In James Curran and Michael Gurevitch (eds), *Mass media and society*, London: Edward Arnold, 33–54.

Index

Spock, Benjamin, 108, 199
Steedman, Carolyn, 66, 72, 210
Steiner, Linda, 3
Stiven, Hilda, 204
Story, 6, 37, 79, 118–19, 183
Strauss, Anselm L., 177, 207
structure of feeling, tragic, 187
subculture, 138
superficiality, 133
supermarket tabloids, 150

taken-for-grantedness, 22
taste, bad, 139; good taste, 141,
   158; low taste, 141–2
television, *see* watching
   television
text analysis, 6, 10, 146–7
textual criticism, 143
theoretical sampling, 177
thick description, 208
thrillers, 157, 161
Times, The, 115
Tip, 91
Tolson, Andrew, 60
tragedy, 187
transcript, example of, 167–75
transcripts, 182
transferability, 207
triangulation, 207
Tuchman, Gaye, 2

underground feminist press,
   159
understanding, 44, 132

unserious reading of gossip
   magazines, 122, 132

validity, 197, 205; ecological
   validity, 198
van Zoonen, Liesbet, 150
Vasterman, Peter, 118
Viva, 6, 18, 30, 34, 37, 39, 42,
   49, 53, 56, 84–5
Vogue, 153
Vorsten, 79, 118, 139

Warnke, Georgia, 147–8
Warren, Carol, 194
Wassenaar, Iris, 2
watching television, 7, 15, 122,
   127; television and women's
   magazine reading, 35, 188
Weekend, 30, 122, 129, 183
Wetherell, Margaret, 26, 203,
   204, 210
White, Cynthia L., 7, 10, 76
Willis, Paul, 14
Winship, Janice, 3, 4, 5, 10, 49,
   88, 93
Woman, 6, 159, 169, 192
Woman's Own, 4, 6, 52, 88, 159,
   192
Woman's Realm, 169
Woman's Weekly, 172
women's magazine genres, 6–7
women's magazine research,
   1–5, 151

Yin, Robert K., 206